Rachel's Daughters

Rachel's Daughters

•

Newly Orthodox Jewish Women

Debra Renee Kaufman

RUTGERS UNIVERSITY PRESS
New Brunswick and London

Sections of this book appeared, in different form, as "Women Who Return to Orthodox Judaism: A Feminist Analysis," *Journal of Marriage and the Family* 47, 3 (1985), courtesy of the National Council on Family Relations; "Patriarchal Women: A Case Study of Newly Orthodox Jewish Women," *Symbolic Interaction* 12, 2 (1989), courtesy of JAI Press, Greenwich, Connecticut; and "Engendering Family Theory: Toward a Feminist-Interpretative Framework," in J. Sprey (ed.), *Fashioning Family Theory* (Newbury Park, Calif.: Sage Publications, Inc., 1990), courtesy of Sage Publications, Inc.

Library of Congress Cataloging-in-Publication Data

Kaufman, Debra R.
Rachel's daughters : newly Orthodox Jewish women / Debra Renee Kaufman.
p.   cm.
Includes bibliographical references and index.
ISBN 0-8135-1637-4 (cloth)   ISBN 0-8135-1638-2 (pbk.)
1. Women, Jewish—United States—Religious life.   2. Jews—United States—Return to Orthodox Judaism.   3. Orthodox Judaism—United States.   I. Title.
BM726.K38   1991
305.48'696—dc20   90-42040
                                                              CIP

British Cataloging-in-Publication information
available

For Michael,
a man of valor I have found

Contents

Contents

Preface

This book begins with the stories 150 newly Orthodox Jewish women told to me over a three-year period. These are stories of a search for one's roots, a quest for meaning and order, and, as one woman phrased it, of a "coming home." The term *home* is used in both the literal and figurative contexts; for as the stories unfolded through hours of interviewing, observing, and even living for some time within two communities, I realized that these stories were as much about a search and eventual discovery of female identity, family, and domesticity, as they were about religious "conversion" and a turn to the right.

During the late 1970s, three of my own family became—and still are—Orthodox Jews. But it was my female cousin who most interested me. A sensitive writer from early childhood, she seemed destined for a journalist's career. She was, as an adolescent, eclectic in her pursuits, liberal in her thinking, and open to the countercultural influences around her. She was a budding feminist when she first went to Israel on a fellowship to do preliminary research for her dissertation in English literature. On her first trip to Israel she was, as I have come to call it, "picked up at the Western Wall." It is here, in Jerusalem, that many young people, often on their way to India or traveling on a year off, find themselves touring. For the Western Wall, a holy site to Jews, is the most immediate and tangible link to the Judaic past. A link that even those most unfamiliar with their Jewish heritage know about. Here, Orthodox Jews often recruit young persons to study at the *yeshivot* (seminaries) in Jerusalem. Recruiting often begins by asking a young person to spend a Sabbath with an Orthodox family. Under these conditions my cousin's turn to Orthodox Judaism began.

This book is not about her nor about those who are "picked up" at the Western Wall. They will have to write their own stories. But it is because of her that I began this research. While there is a little data on newly Orthodox men, there is even less written specifically about women. I am not interested in tactics used to recruit new members or even the socialization processes necessary for retaining newcomers, but as a feminist, I was especially interested in women's attraction to a tradition where the laws and customs are developed, interpreted, and enforced within a patriarchal context—that is, by men. My interest was not in Orthodox Judaism, nor in those who had practiced Orthodox Judaism all their lives, but rather in those women who had consciously chosen to embrace Jewish orthodoxy. Why were we witnessing in the 1970s and 1980s a return to tradition among many who had entered their late adolescence and early adulthood during the nascent stages of different social rebellions, including the women's movement? Why had these women seemingly turned away from any number of the Western liberation movements—liberal, Marxist, psychoanalytic, and feminist—to religion? Why would youth exposed to alternative life-styles consciously choose such a traditional context as adults? As an "orthodox" feminist, I could not understand such a political "cop-out"; as an "orthodox" sociologist I knew this had potential for a good social science story.

This study has enabled me to rethink the meaning of family, gender roles, feminism, gender differences, and even sociology. It has allowed me to rethink the complexities and contradictions that mark the lives we lead and the political, sexual, social, moral, and religious directions we take. No dichotomous sets of abstractions that often pass as theory can explain the data presented here. No path models can explain the variance in the paths taken or not taken by these young women. For the study of newly Orthodox

Jewish women has prompted a conversion in me, not to Orthodox Judaism, but to new styles of sociological inquiry, to the recasting of theories, and to the rethinking of feminism. This study has inspired in me a dedication to feminist analysis and a renewed commitment to empirical research. From both I have become aware of practices which vary considerably from Orthodox preaching.

Acknowledgments

The idea for this book was formulated one Friday evening as my husband and I were engaged in one of our usual lively conversations with our dear friends Alfred and Joann Ivry. Alfred suggested that the return of members of my own family to orthodoxy would make a good research project. (My project was born of a Friday evening.) Thank you, Alfred Ivry. Initially, I spent much time browsing through materials at the Center for Modern Jewish Studies at Brandeis University. Marshall Sklare, the director at that time, was most generous with his personal files. Later in the project, Sylvia Fishman helped me to locate materials and shared with me her own work on feminism and the Jewish community. Other professionals in the Boston Jewish community, such as Sherry and Richard Israel and Jay Brodbar-Nemzer helped me to map and think through the initial stages of this study. Charles Liebman, visiting professor at Brown University, was generous as well with his time and thoughts in the early stages of this study. Janet Aviad responded immediately and with support to my written inquiries. Rebbetzin Horowitz, the wife of the Bostoner Rebbe, and Naftali Horowitz, his son, were also helpful at different stages. My cousin Yaffa Gottlieb, despite her strong doubts that any outsider could capture, let alone understand, the meaning of the *ba'al teshuvah* movement in the United States, nonetheless has always been supportive and generous with her time and thoughts, even providing food and housing in the Crown Heights community when I interviewed there. My nephew the Reverend Elazar

Grunberger has always been available to me for help in locating Jewish source materials and the names of people involved in aspects of the recruitment of newly Orthodox Jews. To Judith Wegner, Rachel Biale, Rabbi Posner of the local Chabad House, and Rabbi Sharfstein, I am indebted for long telephone conversations.

As with each book there are many people who have informed this work. The writing of this book, unlike, perhaps, that of others, has witnessed several major incidents that have delayed and ultimately destroyed much material. A serious car accident postponed the meeting of my first deadline for this book and a fire in my office destroyed many of my reference and footnote materials. Therefore, it is with special pleasure and some trepidation that I witness the finish of this manuscript. Marlie Wasserman, my editor, with what I have come to understand as her usual good humor and intelligence, suggested that I cite an old Jewish saying that giving anonymously is the highest form of generosity. And to those others whom I inadvertently have missed citing in this acknowledgment, I apologize. Because most of my West Coast names were lost in the fire, I must therefore thank all of you who served as my informants in each community there jointly for your time and efforts. I thank my friends and colleagues Leslie Brenner and Natalie and Jon Olson for their care of me and wise counsel on my West Coast stay, as well as my aunt Esther Pogoler and aunt and uncle Sylvia and James Solomon. I wish also to thank Marcia Cohen.

For the women of this study who gave unselfishly and generously of their time, it is hard to express my full gratitude. In that you may understand your "return" to orthodoxy in ways expressly different from the one I have presented, I thank you for your understanding. My very special gratitude goes to those colleagues who have read drafts and redrafts and who have generously given of their thoughts, suggestions, and criticisms at different stages of this project:Lyn Atwater, Jessie Bernard, Wini Breines, Cynthia Fuchs Epstein, Laura Frader, Christine Gailey, Helen Hacker, Susan Handelman, Suzanne Keller, Eileen McDonagh, Barbara Nathanson, Susan Setta, Carmen Siriani,

Acknowledgments

and Hannah Wartenberg. I owe a special debt to Judith Baskin, Barbara Katz Rothman, and Judith Stacey for their close readings of different manuscript chapters and for their invaluable suggestions. This book was completed while I was a visiting scholar at the Murray Research Center of Radcliffe College. I thank my colleagues there for their help and support. Knowledgeable readers in Semitic and Hebrew texts will note that, with some slight modifications in spelling to accommodate lay readers and some inconsistencies in transliteration to account for popular usage among my respondents, who, at times, mix Hebrew and Yiddish and Ashkenazic and Sephardic pronunciations, I am using the general scheme of transliteration rules for Hebrew and Semitic languages of the *Encyclopaedia Judaica* (popular, not scientific). I am most indebted to the copyeditor, Elisabeth Gleason Humez, who scrupulously noted each inconsistency in usage and whose wise counsel I tried to follow. For any errors remaining, I am responsible.

I have saved my immediate family for the end. My love and gratitude go to my children, Alana and Marc Kaufman, who have given up vacation time to discuss ideas and to help proofread this manuscript. And finally, my deepest respect and gratitude go to Michael Kaufman, whose wit and intelligence have sustained me throughout a sometimes most arduous period of time and whose thoughtful suggestions and editing skills are seen on each page of this book.

and of conflicts and contradictions within all orthodoxy: feminist, religious, or otherwise.

Toward the end of the 1960s, apostles of atheism had pronounced God dead. However, reminiscent of Mark Twain's remark, pronouncements of religious death proved to be greatly exaggerated.[1] Instead, the following decades reflected religious ferment through upsurges of "cults," quasi-religious therapeutic movements as well as evangelical and neo-Pentecostal revival.[2] The return to fundamentalist biblical religion and a surge of Christian evangelicalism in America has been accompanied, with less media attention, by a renewed interest in Jewish orthodoxy.[3] A "convert" to Jewish orthodoxy himself, Michael Medved (1984) writes of the irony of such renewal. He notes that Irving Howe's poignant stories of Yiddish-speaking, immigrant, working-class parents devastated when their children embraced gentile values and practices are now mirrored in vignettes of middle-class, well-assimilated children breaking their parents' hearts by returning to their grandparents' Old World habits, dietary laws, and rules of Sabbath observance. And, while this phenomenon of *teshuvah*,[4] or "return" as it is translated from the Hebrew, is of interest in general, the turn to orthodoxy, or, for that matter, the choice by women of any patriarchal religious tradition, in the closing decades of the twentieth century, is particularly intriguing.[5]

This book explores the attitudes, values, experiences, and concerns of newly Orthodox women who have voluntarily entered the patriarchal world of Jewish orthodoxy. The data reflect in-depth interviews conducted with 150 newly Orthodox Jewish women (called *ba'alot teshuvah* in Hebrew) in the mid-1980s, in five major urban areas across the United States.[6] Although it seems obvious why men might be drawn to religious communities steeped in patriarchal tradition and staunchly opposed to any changes in the clear sex-segregation of religious roles, it is much more difficult to explain women's attraction. And, once they are drawn to such religious communities, what maintains their commitment?[7] But what is most puzzling is that although many ba'alot teshuvah openly reject feminism or what they perceive feminism to represent and advocate, they simultaneously main-

2

•

Introduction

. . . Watchman, what of the night? The watchman said, The morning comes, and also the night: if you will inquire, inquire: return, come.

Isaiah 21:12–13

The big lie of male supremacy is that women are less than fully human; the basic task of feminism is to expose that lie and fight it on every level. Yet for all my feminist militance I was, it seemed, secretly afraid that the lie was true—that my humanity was hopelessly at odds with my ineluctably female sexuality—while the rebetsen [wife of the Rabbi], staunch apostle of traditional femininity, did not appear to doubt for a moment that she could be both a woman and a serious person. Which was only superficially paradoxical, for if you were absolutely convinced that the Jewish woman's role was ordained by God, and that it was every bit as important spiritually as the man's, how could you believe the lie? (Ellen Willis, *Rolling Stone Magazine*, April 21, 1977, p. 76)

To feel fully valued as a woman in patriarchal culture is one of the many paradoxes I encountered when I interviewed newly Orthodox Jewish women. Indeed, this book is full of paradoxes: of "returns" to places never known; of feminist potential in reactionary stances; of reactionary potential in "radical" feminist positions;

1

Rachel's Daughters

Introduction

tain a gender consciousness that resonates with some aspects of contemporary and past feminist ideology. Like some feminists, these newly Orthodox Jewish women are woman-identified, celebrating the female and her life-cycle experiences,[8] however, they eschew feminist politics by choosing to enhance the status of women and to protect them as a group within the boundaries of patriarchal religion.

To comprehend this seeming paradox, it is important to understand the significance of Jewish orthodoxy from these newly Orthodox women's perspectives and experiences. How do these women react to the world of Jewish orthodoxy, reflect upon the meanings of phenomena in that world, interpret and communicate about those symbols? What do they incorporate, discard, and choose to ignore in their practice of orthodoxy? The answers clarify the paradox of how they seem simultaneously to accommodate to and to contest patriarchy.

The world of the ba'alot teshuvah is a microcosm of the ambiguities inherent in family, gender-role, feminism, and religious orthodoxy during the closing decades of the twentieth century. These women represent a case study of non-Christian religious-Right women. While they do not consistently identify with right-wing American politics nor with others of the religious Right, these ba'alot teshuvah are clearly right of the religious center. This exploration has led me to rediscover that the neat categories into which social scientists often organize their concepts may be misleading. Human thought, behavior, and political direction often express contradictory and ambivalent impulses. And, in this contradictory spirit I shall conclude before I begin. In the last analysis, if we are to make sense of these women's motivations, choices, and "born-again" attitudes, we must suspend preconceived judgments and assessments. The first stage of sociological understanding requires *verstehen*. In this case, the secular women who "return" to Jewish orthodoxy must be seen from their perspectives and their points of view, not those of the observer. By getting inside their worlds of meaning, it is possible to bring the women in this study to life as subjects, not objects of analysis.

Loosely structured interviews (what I call structured "conversations") allowed these women to reveal their own significant issues and concerns, rather than those the male leaders of the community might consider important. Thus, the interviews began, not with specific questions and probes, but with the women themselves, their concerns, their perspectives. Such a technique enabled them to speak in their own voices. Almost all of them spoke not as those nurtured, secluded, and structurally dependent upon Orthodox communities or institutions all of their lives, but as individuals who had at some time in their young-adult lives made a choice to embrace the structural and theological conditions of patriarchal religious living. A number of topics were used in each structured "conversation" to enable women to recount the history of their "return" to orthodoxy, their beliefs, practices, knowledge, and feelings about orthodoxy, their current familial and communal life-style, and their views about gender-roles and feminism.[9]

To understand these women's ties to one another, their links to families, community, and the theology they embraced, I spent many weeks in each community. Although this is neither an ethnographic nor participant observation study, I borrowed many of the techniques both kinds of researchers use. I attended lectures, Sabbath services, classes, informal afternoon gatherings, Sisterhood meetings, and coffee get-togethers. I changed diapers, walked in parks, celebrated holidays, shared La Leche and Lamaze notes from the days when my own children were that young. I visited wig shops, went to a *mikveh* (ritual bathhouse), sat behind a *mechitzah* (partition between men and women in the synagogue), ate meals in strictly kosher restaurants, to put the experiences these women described into a concrete context.

WHO IS A BA'AL TESHUVAH?

Ba'alei teshuvah (masculine plural), which in English means masters of return, are those who have consciously chosen to live an orthodox Jewish life. They are persons who have usually grown up or lived outside Orthodox beliefs and practices but who have found their way to Orthodox Judaism. My study defines the *ba'alat teshuvah* (feminine singular) either as a woman who currently practices and believes in Orthodox Judaism and who is more traditional than her parents in her practice and belief (this obviously includes "converts"); or, a woman who currently practices and believes in orthodoxy who had lapsed in that belief/practice for some period of time.[10] Orthodoxy was measured in two ways; strict observance of all the Sabbath laws and strict observance of all the laws of *kashruth* (Jewish dietary laws).

My interest is not in the many forms of traditional renewal among contemporary Jews, but specifically, in those who have "returned" to orthodoxy, the most fundamental and sex-segregated branch of Judaism. Although from five to ten thousand Jews have organized scores of *havurot* (religious fellowship groups) around the country (Riesman, 1977), and while the Young Leadership Cabinet of the United Jewish Appeal claims that many of the annual two to three thousand new members eventually gain significant knowledge in Judaism and begin to observe more of the ritual practices (Cohen, 1983), orthodoxy represents a more traditional renewal in Judaism. Havurot, for instance, often challenge women's subordinate position and practice in public religious rituals and roles.[11] In Jewish orthodoxy there are no significant roles for women either in the synagogue or in the world of study. Most blatantly, women are not given the opportunity to study the very texts that give meaning and interpretation to the code of law that rules their everyday lives. Therefore although havurot represent a kind of traditional renewal, they constitute an overt challenge to established hierarchy and are clearly distinguishable from communities where strict adherence to the practice and interpretation of *halakhah* (authoritative Jewish religious law) as binding over Jewish practice, as central to Judaism, and as the basis for making decisions about Jewish teachings and for resolving conflicts is required.[12]

WHERE TO FIND BA'ALEI TESHUVAH

The literature on newly Orthodox Jews is spotty and inconsistent, ranging from popular-press articles, such as the one found in

5

the magazine *Rolling Stone*, to only two scholarly books on the topic, one by Janet Aviad (1983) and the other by M. Herbert Danzger (1989). Aviad's book is essential in defining some of the characteristics and properties of the ba'alei teshuvah, however, it is confined to the study of newly Orthodox Jews within *yeshivot* (live-in schools of higher education) and in Israel. Moreover, while the yeshivot make the "return" to Judaism plausible, they cannot account for the maintenance of commitment, particularly among women, beyond the *yeshiva* (singular) experience. What happens to commitment and ideology when ba'alot teshuvah are not in yeshivot (or, for that matter, not living in self-defined communities), but residing in geographically dispersed communities as traditional women? What sustains their commitment? Danzger's book reviews the history of the ba'al teshuvah movement in both Israel and the United States. Specific consideration of those with the most puzzling motivations for "return"—those newly Orthodox women who were either participants in or recipients of the achievements of the women's movement—is missing.[13]

At the time of my study, there were no parameters of the ba'al teshuvah population in America nor for their numbers.[14] Therefore, unlike studies of well-defined populations, this investigation demanded a flexible and multifaceted approach. Several methods were used to locate respondents. Interviews with leading rabbis, lay community leaders, and known ba'alot teshuvah in each of five major urban cities across the United States helped locate newly Orthodox women within three identifiable frameworks in contemporary orthodoxy—modern Orthodox (25), strictly Orthodox (40), and ultra-Orthodox (85).[15] Although all Orthodox Jews acknowledge that halakhah is basic and essential to Judaism, they vary in their style of dress, their relationship to the secular world, and their interpretation of some laws, with modern Orthodox being the most "liberal," and ultra-Orthodox the most "stringent."[16]

Who Is Most Likely to Become a Ba'alat Teshuvah?

Most of the women under study came from middle-class backgrounds, were well educated, and were well assimilated into the secular culture. Almost a full 80 percent of those under study had had some years of college or a college degree when they "returned" to Orthodox Judaism.[17] Seventy percent had had at least one parent working in a professional or manager-proprietor category of occupation while they were growing up; and a little over 50 percent had at least one parent with education beyond an undergraduate college degree.[18] Most of them had had only a rudimentary Hebraic or religious background during their formative years, with only one-fifth having had more than a Sunday school education. In this study, 64 percent of the women were between twenty and twenty-five years of age at the time of their "return."[19] On the whole, this group closely approximates the portrait of Jews in America and the profile of newly Orthodox Jews as it is currently emerging.[20] Most of the ba'alot teshuvah were not married at the time of their "return" to Jewish orthodoxy. Fifteen had been divorced and ten were engaged to be married.

Why Jewish Orthodoxy?

For all the women in this study the "return" to Orthodox Judaism constitutes a conscious rejection of secular culture and the relativism of modern living. Most ba'alot teshuvah describe themselves as trying to make moral sense of their lives. As they told their stories of return, women reported a common experience: that their lives had been spiritually empty and without purpose before their return. Regardless of age, virtually all women suggest that they were "searching." Some labeled that quest a "journey homeward." I was to find some irony in that designation, for although it initially implied that they were seeking their roots as Jews, it also served as a metaphor for what orthodoxy meant to them—home, family, and a moral community with clear dictates about how to live both one's public and private life. Their "return" to orthodoxy, in some fundamental way, constitutes a protest against secular society, which many characterized as masculine in orientation and organization.

All women interviewed expressed concern about the loss of boundaries in marital, familial, and sexual relationships before their "return." They spoke freely about their poor heterosexual relationships and especially of their relationships to men unwilling or incapable of making lasting commitments. As one respondent put it:

> There I was, twenty-five years of age. I had had my fill of casual sexual relationships, drugs, communal living. I looked at myself and said: What will I be like at forty years of age? An aging hippie with no roots and maybe just a history of bad relationships? I wanted something true and lasting.

For many of these women the "dark side" of individualism, that strain of thought stressing self over others and freedom over responsibility, had become a real, not an imagined or theoretical problem in their personal lives.

Interestingly, these women claim that their "return" to the patriarchal setting of orthodoxy put them in touch with their own bodies, in control of their own sexuality, and in a position to value the so-called feminine virtues of nurturance, mutuality, family, and motherhood. Indeed, they describe orthodoxy as "feminine in principle," correlating that which is associated with the female in orthodoxy with the spiritual and sacred meaning of life. It is in Orthodox Judaism, they assert, that they have found their identities as women. "You know," says one unmarried twenty-three-year-old, "I think this is the first time in my life I have felt really good about being a woman."

These women "returned" to orthodoxy primarily spurred by a search for meaning in their lives. When probed about what values they sought, a majority responded that in addition to the spirituality they craved, Orthodox Judaism provided a dignity to the lives they led as mothers and wives.[21] The specialness of woman and the importance of her sphere of activity were stressed throughout the interviews and often juxtaposed to a rather rigid

8

conception of what they described as feminism. The majority of these women define feminism as a movement that dismisses differences between men and women and focuses on the world of work, where equal pay is the most important issue. Most felt that the priorities set by feminists neglected the family and what they believed to be important feminine values. In general, these women believed they had gained a new dignity through their orthodoxy and especially through their roles in the family, a pride they felt most contemporary feminists either disregarded or devalued.

What was surprising was that while they minimized the importance of feminism in their lives, they used feminist rhetoric and emphases to describe their Orthodox lives. Contrary to the common assumption that nonfeminist women are unable to identify as women and to act in their own interests, these ba'alot teshuvah are quite conscious of their status as women and defend that status. Nowhere is this awareness more evident than in their discussions of the laws of *niddah*, which prescribe a two-week sexual separation between husband and wife during the woman's menstrual cycle. The laws of niddah, which many have viewed as patriarchal orthodoxy's derogation of the female, are interpreted by these newly Orthodox women as giving structure, regulation, and control to them over their sexuality.[22] One respondent's description captures the general attitude of these ba'alot teshuvah toward this most important dimension of their lives as Orthodox Jewish women:

> I am a child of the liberated generation. Since we are talking about niddah now I will refer to sexual liberation although I think what I am saying applies to many areas of liberation. . . . For all the sexual freedom I felt in my late adolescence and early adulthood, I can tell you that it was more like sexual exploitation. I felt there were no longer any rules; on what grounds did one decide to say no? If the rule was casual sex and if you engaged in it on what grounds did you say no. . . . What rules did you use? If you see what I'm saying, without overriding rules, or without protection of some sort, the sexual liberation meant that women were free to be exploited more by men . . . the laws of *taharat hamishpacha* [family purity

laws, regulating sexuality and requiring about a two-week abstinence each month during the woman's menstrual cycle] make so much sense. For instance, I am not a sex object to my husband; he respects me and respects my sexuality. Because he does not have access to me anytime he wishes, he cannot take me for granted. The separation restores our passion and places the control of it in my hands.

Perhaps even more significant is that these women claim that such laws provide them with a sense of dignity and more control over their bodies than they felt was possible in the secular world.

Adopting the stance that many values traditionally associated with women, such as mothering and the capacity for connectedness, are undervalued in society, these ba'alot teshuvah link the feminine and the female with the sacred and spiritual meaning of life, turning their devalued status in the secular world into a high-status aspect that the Orthodox community confers. In the religious world, these women claim, the female and the family, and that which is associated with them, are seen as a positive source of value, not only for the self but for the community at large. The ba'alot teshuvah claim that in Orthodox Judaism they are able to make demands upon men as husbands and fathers in ways they believe less possible in the secular world.

BA'ALOT TESHUVAH AS "POSTFEMINIST" WOMEN?

Why, over the last few decades during the ferment of different social rebellions, including the women's movement, are we witnessing a return to patriarchal religious tradition among some women? In a society where the number of divorces is slowly coming to equal the number of marriages, where one in three women can expect to be sexually assaulted by a man during her lifetime,[23] where women continue to earn unequal wages compared to men despite their talent, experience, and education, it is not surprising that since the mid-1970s many women have found their way to patriarchal religious communities where they can find, what Judith Stacey (1987) calls "patriarchal profamilialism." Aggression, self-indulgence, and an individualistic orientation (often equated by them in a secular context with masculinity) are replaced in the religious world, claim these religious-Right women, with humility, self-restraint, and a collective orientation and identification with the church or synagogue and the home.

Changes in family and work life and the seeming absence of viable alternatives for heterosexual men and women to the traditional sexual and familial structuring of society, have encouraged conservative groups, especially the religious Right, to mobilize under the banner of the profamily movement. Claiming that feminists have rejected the family, they expediently equate the feminist movement with those very qualities of a self-centered and hedonistic culture that many feminists themselves have attacked.[24]

Until recently our focus on religious-Right women has been almost exclusively on their participation in antifeminist activities.[25] More recently, however, ethnographic and other studies have given us a broader, if not more complex, picture of women who belong to fundamentalist, Evangelical, and charismatic Christian groups.[26] While generally it is true that women who turn to patriarchal religious traditions outrightly reject feminist politics, recent data also suggest that some of these same women also make claims for an enhanced status for women and for greater claims upon men as husbands and fathers within those patriarchal traditions. While these religious-Right women may attack feminism and feminists, often what belies this hostility is a wariness of men's morality and consequently of feminism when they believe it supports men's irresponsibility.[27] Therefore, despite many "born again" women's distrust of feminism, their focus on raising women's status, promoting female interests, and altering gender-role behavior of men as fathers and husbands, resonate with issues long of concern to feminists.

In fact, "postfeminist," rather than "antifeminist" or "sexist," is the term Rosenfelt and Stacey (1987) use to describe the gender consciousness and the family and work strategies of many contemporary women.[28] This "postfeminist" consciousness, argues Stacey (1987), can be found even among "born again" women as

11

they incorporate, revise, adapt, and, most important, Stacey reminds us, depoliticize many of feminism's central goals. Stacey argues that increasing numbers of women have developed this "postfeminist" consciousness in response to the new difficulties and opportunities of a postindustrial society.[29] Whether this process applies to the ba'alot teshuvah under study, as well, is left for the reader to determine at the conclusion of this book.

Irrespective of that conclusion, however, it would be too facile to describe the "return" of contemporary women to religious orthodoxy as simply reactionary, or merely as their search for order, stability, and security in a world bereft of overarchinig standards. Explanations must also include their perceptions of how familial and gender-role experiences have directed that search as well. Indeed, the burgeoning literature on wife abuse, child abuse, and rape within marriage reveals some of the stresses in the modern nuclear family. Furthermore, for the majority of American women, work and family demands are incompatible. Despite their increases in the labor force and some positive legislative reforms, women still earn less than men in every occupation, irrespective of their training, skills, and qualifications (Kaufman, 1989). Moreover, even for those who are well trained and educated, women's career lines may be limited by informal barriers to success, barriers that are hard to reform legislatively or even address publicly. And while the structural conditions in the labor force have been difficult to change, the normative expectations surrounding the sexual division of labor within households have proved resistant to change, too. Irrespective of paid employment, women maintain the major responsibility for domestic and childcare activities (Pleck, 1977; Berheide, 1984; Fox and Hesse-Biber, 1984). Women are still held primarily responsible for the "expressive" functions of a society grown less connected to others and to public life in general.[30]

If inequalities in the labor market put women at a disadvantage, the contemporary "corporate climate" that focuses on acquisitive individualism and "fast-track" options (Stacey, 1987) further erodes stable work and family relations. There is the growing recognition that feminism (at least as a popular movement) may have failed a significant number of women[31] because it has been unable to develop a "politics of the personal,"[32] particularly for heterosexual women amid the destabilized family and work conditions of the past few decades. For instance, vigorous legislative reforms aimed at promoting gender equality often fail to bring about real changes in the private arena of life, most particularly in the role behavior of men. Both evangelicalism and Jewish orthodoxy have strict codes of behavior for men as well as women. Organized religion's effective use of "patriarchal profamilianism" is what many "born again" women seem to find so appealing.

The ba'alot teshuvah argue their choice of life-style within a contemporary familial context. They regard orthodoxy—from the family purity laws to the value and dignity accorded them as wives and mothers—as institutional protection. Consequently, they believe they are no longer dependent upon individual males, but upon a theology they believe is "feminine in principle." Moreover, in communities as highly sex-segregated as Orthodox Jewish ones, these women claim they can participate daily in a community of women whose social and religious practices represent the ethic of care and commitment they value and had been seeking. Sex-segregated living reinforces a woman-centered identity and reasserts the importance of female-linked practices and symbols.[33] Stable intimate relationships, so critical to the survival of all organized religions, are clearly reflected in Orthodox Judaism. Historic writings about the need for women's sexual satisfaction and clear laws about her care within marriage suggest that early rabbinic authorities recognized that male authority alone would and could not ensure stable familial life.

In the remaining chapters I will amplify many of the issues touched upon in this introduction. I am indeed intrigued by the complexities, ambiguities, and richness of the stories told to me by these "born agains." Are these women simply religious fanatics? Reactionary antifeminists? Or is this too limited a portrayal? The human condition, like the feminist tradition, is varied. One analytic tool that the feminist perspective provides is the recognition that all categorical distinctions are abstractions about reality, not reality itself. Therefore, to separate women into pro or anti, on any issue (family, sexuality, gender differences, spirituality) succeeds in the hardening of categories, not necessarily in an exploration of the variety of forms gender politics has taken as we approach the twenty-first century.

•

Youth and Its Discontents

Ba'alot Teshuvah as Seekers

The 1960s marked a period of social turbulence in the United States—rapid technological advances, the full emergence of the civil rights movement, urban riots, the assassinations of the Kennedy brothers, Malcolm X, and Martin Luther King, antiwar protests, the beginnings of the women's movement, racial pride among Blacks, flower children, a drug culture, and strong antiestablishment feelings, particularly among young people. The countercultural upheavals of the 1960s witnessed an upsurge of cults, the increased popularity of oriental religions, quasi-religious therapeutic movements, neo-Pentecostal revival, as well as a steady growth in evangelical and conservative churches (Robbins, Anthony, and Richardson, 1978). Jewish orthodoxy, unfashionable and outmoded throughout the 1950s and into the 1960s, participated in this neo-Orthodox revival and "new" religious ferment.

The links between this heightened spirituality and the counterculture are many. The "hippie" movement, as the counterculture has often been referred to, was characterized by both its antirational thrust and its rejection of conventional values, particularly those that represented a technocratic, bureaucratic society dependent on science as the primary source of truth (Roszak, 1968; Glock, 1976; Wuthnow, 1976; Yinger, 1982). The countercultural rejection took many forms, expressed at times through drugs, politics, or music. At times the values were contradictory—"tuning in, turning on, and dropping out" versus political struggle against racism, sexism, poverty, and war. At times God was declared dead, at other times only moribund, and sometimes rediscovered.

Although there had been neo-Orthodox revivals before the counterculture, the hippies' attraction to such movements recast and popularized them. The ba'al teshuvah movement in America originated in this period of hippie religious sentiment. Writing about the history of the contemporary revival of Orthodox Judaism, Danzger (1989) notes that the late sixties and early seventies brought a new population of believers to Jewish orthodoxy.[1] In 1966, Rabbi Shlomo Carlebach, a Lubavitch Hasid[2] and folksinger, opened the House of Love and Prayer in San Francisco, partly as a commune and partly as a synagogue. Carlebach, writes Danzger (1989), created a brand of musical mysticism that mixed traditional liturgy with free-form song and dance. Young women and men raised in non-Orthodox families, many of whom espoused countercultural values, began turning to Orthodox Judaism. Danzger believes that hippies were initially attracted to Jewish orthodoxy because they found an affinity between their countercultural interests and their distorted understanding of Hasidism. According to Danzger, hippies were attracted to Hasidism because of its mystical philosophy, its gurulike rebbe,[3] its emotional expression of religiosity and its communal organization. Danzger also notes that, paralleling Eastern religions, Hasidism placed a "far heavier emphasis on ritual than was found in established American religions" (1989, p. 81).[4]

Danzger (1989) writes that despite orthodoxy's potential appeal to countercultural youth, most of the Orthodox communities were not prepared to accept these hippies. Even the Lubavitch (except for the charismatic Carlebach) were unprepared to deal with these countercultural youth. The first most successful educational outreach programs for American ba'alei teshuvah, therefore, began in Israel. Established and staffed by Americans for Americans, ba'al teshuvah yeshivot were designed to attract and accommodate the large concentrations of American ba'alei teshuvah who found their way to Israel. The first of such yeshivot, which still exists, is Har Tzion, established by Rabbi Mordechai

Goldstein after the Israeli Six-Day War. Goldstein was Carlebach's Israeli counterpart. Accepting hippies as they were, he was "ready to work with them with no preconditions, requiring nothing from them—not that they cut their hair nor give up their girlfriends (although they could not continue to live together without marriage—separate quarters were provided), and it was rumored, not even that they give up drugs immediately" (Danzger, 1989, p. 87).[5]

From 1967 to 1972, recruitment of ba'alei teshuvah, both in Israel and the United States, increased. In 1973, in his native Boston, Rabbi Levi Yitzhak Horowitz, known as the "Bostoner Rebbe," developed a program for ba'alei teshuvah in his synagogue, Beth Pinchas. In 1972, the Lincoln Square Synagogue on the Upper West Side of Manhattan started an educational program for ba'alei teshuvah, and in 1975 developed what was then called a beginners' service, specifically designed to support those just finding their religious roots.

Perhaps the knowledge that Jewish youth were deeply involved in countercultural groups provided the impetus for such "outreach" programs. Not only were Jews heavily represented in such radical political movements as Students for Democratic Society and the Free Speech Movement (Glazer, 1970), but it was estimated that they were overrepresented in such groups as the Reverend Sun Myung Moon's Unification Church, Zen Buddhists, and the Hare Krishna movement (Melton and Moore, 1982; Selengut, 1985). More than two-thirds (104) of the women under study were involved in one form or another of the countercultural turbulence of the sixties and seventies.

Sixty-six percent (99) of the women I interviewed were in their late teens and early to middle twenties in the decade between 1966 and 1976. Therefore, most of the women in this study began their journeys toward orthodoxy in their youth during the counterculture, or in its wake. Of these women, almost 71 percent (70) identified with the hippie counterculture of the sixties and early seventies.[6] That is, they either had ties to the seemingly apolitical life-styles associated with the counterculture (such as drugs, music, dress) or to radical political organizations and protests. Few characterized themselves as leaders in any of the groups of which they were a part. Although some came to their protest as teenagers in high school, most were involved during their college years. The most common radical politics among this group included civil rights demonstrations, university protests, marches, and/or anti–Vietnam War protests, and, for a few, farm protests.

Twenty-five women claimed to have identified with and/or participated in the women's movement. Ten had been actively involved in feminist consciousness-raising groups. Although only twelve were active in the prochoice campaigns of the early seventies, most of the women described themselves during their searching years as prochoice and claimed that certainly in appearance they were "liberated" women. Their embracing of orthodoxy, long before most even believed in it, demanded that they give up the freedom many of them had come to associate with jeans and pants and little underwear. Although the drastic change in their life-styles at first seems contradictory, on closer observation their change from radical left to radical right appears congruent with the most important issues these women faced at that stage of their lives.

Those women who had identified with the women's movement, for instance, eventually were disappointed by what they perceived to be the concerns of the early women's movement. For many, the focus on individual rights and personal independence left the larger issues of "how to" live one's life in a meaningful manner unformulated. One woman elaborates on this theme:

> I was in a feminist consciousness-raising group. We talked a good deal about our problems . . . about being women, students, lovers, and working women . . . we talked about whatever it was that was going on in our lives at that time, but we never really were able to formulate anything beyond or larger than ourselves. . . . We were good at defining the negatives.

Those attracted to other politically liberal causes found that, both as women and as whites, they felt marginalized. For instance, a woman who had been involved in "left politics" felt that "men ran the show . . . we ran off the leaflets and made the coffee." Others, by the end of the sixties, no longer felt "comfortable," as Whites and as Jews, in the civil rights movement.[7] Other studies of that same period corroborate some of these sentiments. For instance, in their study of the Jesus movement, Richardson, Stewart, and Simmonds (1978) note that former political activists felt that the Civil Rights Movement had excluded whites by the end of the sixties. Even when the women under study were actively involved, many felt disappointed and frustrated at how little they could achieve. One woman describes her Peace Corps days as ". . . an important learning time for me. It was a time when I thought I could really 'right' the world. It was one of the most frustrating experiences I had ever encountered. So much was needed and we could give so little."

Many of these ba'alot teshuvah describe the late sixties and early-to-mid-seventies as a time of growing disillusionment and frustration for them. They describe themselves as concerned about the draft, the war in Vietnam, and later, for some, the Watergate scandal and the Kent State University killings. As one woman put it: "You know, all the 'macho' issues." Disillusioned, feeling marginal, and perhaps as Richardson, Stewart, and Simmonds (1978) note, shocked at a state that was willing to kill its children, either abroad or at home, forty-nine of these self-identified countercultural women moved from secular, political, activist identities to Jewish orthodoxy. Twenty-one detoured on their way to Jewish orthodoxy by joining either one of the "new" religions or personal growth movements of the late sixties and early-to-mid-seventies.

Overall, over one-third of all the ba'alot teshuvah joined or participated in the "new" religious or quasi-religious therapy movements of the sixties and seventies, ranging from the Eastern mystical traditions (such as Zen, transcendental meditation, Buddhism, Hinduism, Taoism, Sufism, and yoga) to the personal growth movements (such as est or Scientology).[8] Three women briefly flirted with such neo-Christian groups as Jews for Jesus.[9] The research of this period suggests that these movements may have helped to reintegrate countercultural youth into the dominant culture.[10] Richardson, Stewart, and Simmonds (1978) suggest that fundamentalist-oriented social movements, such as the Jesus movement, might have provided a "cooling off" period for many young Americans who were searching for alternative lifestyles. Tipton believes many of the religious and quasi-religious therapy groups reintegrated sixties youth by helping them accommodate countercultural values into the bureaucratic and rationalized sociocultural milieu many had protested against. "[D]isoriented by drugs, embittered by politics, disillusioned by the apparent worthlessness of work and the transiency of love," these movements, writes Tipton, provided many such young people with "a way to get along with conventional American society and to cope with the demands of their own maturing lives" (Tipton, 1982, p. 30).

Yet despite the attraction, all fifty-four of those who had joined or participated in "new" religious, or quasi-religious, therapy or personal growth movements found them disappointing. Reflecting back on those years, the majority of those involved in Eastern mystical groups (30) felt that such groups were too focused on the self through "inner spiritual awakening" and "intrapsychic" consciousness, and too unfocused on fixed moral codes as a guide for their everyday behavior.[11] One woman referred to her early seventies experiences with transcendental meditation as if it were "a great big organized be-in." She remembers, "Something was missing. I didn't want to be; I wanted to do. I wanted to feel I could make decisions that would lead to 'right' actions. There were just 'rules of thumb' as to what was 'right' behavior, no real guidelines."

The focus on self and "inner consciousness" troubled many who had become involved in quasi-religious therapy, therapeutic and human potential movements as well.[12] The relativistic and subjective moral systems of monistic movements, and the predominant focus on inner consciousness in the quasi-religious therapy groups, forced many of these women to continue searching for a coherent system of beliefs and a stable moral community meaningful to them.[13] One woman recounted her early experiences through this narrative:

I had been active in the civil rights movement during my college years. In fact, you could say I participated in every kind of "in" you can imagine—at first, sit-ins, and then later be-ins and love-ins. I marched and I protested. I think I protested everything imaginable. My first husband was a Black man. In retrospect I think it was through him that I realized that I missed an identity—a sense of who I was beyond that which I had found . . . beyond just what was going on inside of me. We had a most unhappy breakup, but it is from him that I realized that I could do no good in this world until I knew more about who I was, what good really meant, and where I belonged in this world.

For the remainder of the ba'alot teshuvah—that is, even for those who were not politically aware during the sixties, or who had come into their young adult years in the late seventies, and/or who were not from upwardly mobile, middle-class families—similar themes emerged: their search for a moral community of both public and private virtue, and, above all, their need for a moral framework in which to make decisions. The need, as one woman put it, for "official values."

Frequently these women exhibited strong antipathy toward all forms of self-consuming and self-interested behavior. Many complained of the "superficiality," "phoniness," and self-centeredness of middle-class American culture.[14] As with many of their countercultural sisters, a crisis in meaning sent them in search of a pattern of personal and social relationships steeped in an ethical tradition of moral certitude. Jewish orthodoxy provided these women with clear ethical guidelines and both historic and transcendental ties. Moreover, it was a tradition with which many of them were familiar, if they were not knowledgeable about it.

The ba'alot teshuvah, refer to themselves as "Torah True" Jews: ones who believe that the Torah (the first five books of the Old Testament) is God's literally revealed word and that Jewish law derives, directly or indirectly, from that act of revelation. The data reveal that the inviolability of Jewish law is the key attraction to orthodoxy for the women under study. In orthodoxy, the basis of authority is unambiguous—the inviolability of halakhah.

These women articulate emphatically the dilemma we all face in making decisions at critical points in our lives. They claim that the beginning of adulthood came for them when they had to make independent decisions about the direction their lives would take. For most of them, the most anxiety-provoking decisions were those that affected the way in which they were to live their personal lives as women—lovers, mothers, wives, friends. The issues surrounding those choices and the search to discover upon what grounds to make those kinds of intimate and personal decisions dominated the discussions of their "returns" to orthodoxy.

Modern living heightened their anxieties about decision making. "On what basis do you make any decisions?" asked one respondent. "Is there any place out there," asked another woman, "where you can find answers to questions of how to live on a day-to-day basis, a 'good' life. I mean not just what feels good but what is a good life. Philosophy is too abstract. . . . I mean, how do you live good and bad on a day-to-day basis?"

In this context of a search for guidelines, the very admission that orthodoxy may not be the literally revealed word of God destroys the certainty about the moral, ethical, and meaningful decisions in life so many of those "returning" to orthodoxy were seeking. Therefore, accommodations to the law which are commonly found in the more "progressive" wings of Judaism (Reform, Reconstructionist, Conservative), while serving some contemporary needs, also serve to undermine the claim of each to absolute authority. Similarly, while feminism may emphasize the challenges modernity presents to theology, it may inadvertently also bring into relief the challenges theology presents to modernity. Orthodoxy's appeal for these women is in its claims to moral certitude and absolute truth.

But there is more to orthodoxy's appeal than moral certitude. The ultimate attraction of Jewish orthodoxy and what maintains the commitment of the ba'alot teshuvah were couched in a very specific language of women's personal needs. For most, one of the most troubling qualities of modern living was expressed as the culture's confusion and ambivalence toward women, women's sexuality, family and gender roles. Even those who had been part of the women's movement did not feel that there was a coherent set of social norms governing expectations about gender roles. On the contrary, they believed that the dismantling of many of the gender-related norms, spurred by the women's movement, often left women more vulnerable to men's manipulation than ever before. Most felt this was particularly true in the area of sexuality.[15]

One young woman noted:

> I needed something that spoke to me directly about being a woman . . . decisions about my sexuality, for instance. I had had enough of one-night stands . . . orgasm alone was just that, an orgasm—masturbation could and did fulfill the same function. I didn't want moralizing; I wanted to know how sexuality would fit into my life; you know, over the long haul. Orthodoxy had an answer to that . . . when I learned about the family purity laws . . . they immediately made sense to me. In fact, my boyfriend and I practiced taharat hamishpacha while we were living together. Neither of us could take our sexuality or me for granted.

A recently engaged woman expressed her search for familial values in a community which supports those values in these terms:

> Both my fiancé and I are on the job market together. Since we have become Orthodox we have made some very important decisions. We are looking for jobs which give both of us real flexibility. I mean, we want time for ourselves and time for family in our lives. An Orthodox life-style promotes that—family comes first. It is clear to both of us right from the beginning that our family life will have priority over everything else we do. Menachem [the fiancé's fictitious name] will be a part of a community that enforces that commitment and I will be part of a community that makes that commitment real.

"You know," volunteered one older, divorced woman,

> orthodoxy provides a game plan. At first you accept a whole system, letter-perfect, that has survived thousands of years. Yet, even

though it has such history, it speaks directly to you on a day-to-day, week-to-week, season-to-season basis. It speaks to you about the most personal things in your life—the way to go about dealing with others, your friends, your husband, your children, even how to go about having sex.

Another woman who had been a ba'alat teshuvah for over ten years stated:

You start with something true and tested, and then slowly this whole tradition becomes your own; you find yourself in it. You find your life in it as a woman, as a mother, as a wife. Even if you begin without belief, after a while just by practicing on a day-to-day basis, you develop an understanding. You need no convincing; the whole thing just makes such good sense.

MANY ROADS HOME

In the United States two Hasidic sects have been most influential in reaching out to attract ba'alei teshuvah: the Lubavitch Hasidim and the Bostoner Hasidim (the reference is not specifically to Boston, but rather to the American style characteristic of the founder and father of the current Bostoner Rebbe). Although in the past, most Hasidic groups did not proselytize in order to avoid contacts with the non-Hasidic world, the Lubavitch and Bostoner Hasidim have attempted to reach out to other Jews.

Rebbe Menachem Schneerson, who, in addition to his religious education, received a secular education at the Sorbonne, directs his worldwide staff from his Crown Heights office. The rebbe has launched a national campaign to reach Jewish youth through centers which now exist throughout the world. He created a Jewish Peace Corps to send students and young couples to communities throughout the country. He established the Lubavitch Women's organization and a youth organization that operates the so-called *mitzvah* (good deed)-mobiles. The Lubavitch have established residential houses (Chabad) where new recruits can study, eat, and learn. These houses are strategically located near college campuses. Sabbath and holiday services as well as adult education programs are also offered.

The Hasidim resocialize recruits by providing families or "new" parents or sponsors for new devotees. Since many of the new recruits are just coming into their young-adult years and often have rejected the values of their families, such techniques are quite successful. One young woman remembered how taken she was with Hasidic family life. Nothing "duplicitous" about that life-style, she said, and compared it to her own:

> My parents talked a good liberal game but when push came to shove they were always on the play-it-safe-what's-in-it-for-you side. My very liberal parents made sure we moved to the "whitest" suburb in the city, even while they supported civil rights organizations with money. I could not stand the hypocrisy.

Another noted, "Both my parents were lawyers, and while we often spoke of the miseries of life and injustices, we never talked of our own family injustices."

Sharot (1982) argues that Hasidim use no prolonged indoctrination period to process converts into the movement. Acceptance into the community depends upon conformity to a strict religious orthodoxy. One is considered recruited when a person places him- or herself completely under a tzaddik's direction and authority (Sharot, 1982, p. 197). The brightly colored "*mitzvah*-mobiles," coming through Jewish neighborhoods or appearing at rallies for Soviet Jewry or Israeli Day parades, have been particularly effective and are the distinctive identification of the Lubavitch. Yeshiva youths between fifteen and twenty years of age, confront individuals directly, and, if the questioned is Jewish, the students ask the individual to engage in some religious ritual: putting a *mezuzah* (a small case that contains a piece of parchment inscribed with verses 4–9 of Deuteronomy 6 and 13–21 of Deuteronomy 11, traditionally attached to one or more doorposts of the home) on their doorposts or keeping a charity coin box, or bringing a prayer book into their home. Other times they will offer candlesticks to women for Sabbath lights or offer to help men put on *tefillin* (phylacteries, box-and-leather-strap devices a man affixes to his head and left arm, while offering weekday morning prayers). If it is a holiday, the recruiters will ask the individual to make a blessing with the appropriate symbol. Dressed in their black suits and hats and with untrimmed beards, these recruiters offer no explanations for ritual behavior—potential recruits are just encouraged to act.[16]

The Bostoner Rebbe, writes Aviad (1982), is one of the two rabbis best known outside Israel for their outreach programs. Rabbi Levi Yitzhak Horowitz, the Bostoner Rebbe, has attracted large numbers of students in the Boston area, as well as from across the country.[17] Both he and the Lubavitcher Rebbe are known as charismatic figures.

Unlike other Hasidic rebbes, the Bostoner Rebbe gives his sermons in English, not Yiddish. But like the Lubavitcher, he offers twenty-four-hour retreats, or Shabbatons, from sundown Friday nights to sundown Saturday nights. There are communal meals, dancing, singing, study groups, and discussion. At the New England Hasidic Center there are the Lionel Goldman Seminary for women and the Talmudic Academy for men. Morning and evening classes in English are held throughout the school year, and crash courses are given in the summer. Both the Lubavitcher and Bostoner rebbes are considered particularly skilled in reaching and working with young people. Given the extensive outreach programs of these two Hasidic sects, it is not surprising that over half of the women in this sample claim a Hasidic identity within one of these two groups.

But Hasidism, despite its extensive outreach and particular attractiveness to countercultural youth, is not the only branch of orthodoxy to experience a revival. In a special feature on religious revival among the Orthodox, *New York* magazine (November 17, 1986, pp. 53–60) reports that about fifty years ago, the Upper West Side of Manhattan was home to several thousand Orthodox Jews, and that it is now experiencing a revival after a sharp decline in the 1950s. With over three thousand members and five Sabbath services, Lincoln Square Synagogue has been at the center of this revival. Its founding rabbi, Shlomo Riskin, like the two Hasidic rebbes, has been described as charismatic. Associated with the synagogue is the Joseph Shapiro Institute, an adult education program. Like the Lubavitch, Lincoln Square Synagogue undertook publicity campaigns and an active outreach program. Perhaps Lincoln Square Synagogue is best known for its specific strategy to reach young, single Jewish professionals who are independent of family but who seek new relationships. The synagogue offers a series of lectures, concerts, outings, parties, and the like for this young population. One of their most successful programs was a series on sex and the Jewish single person.

The Northeast does not have a monopoly on revival of traditional Judaism—Hasidic or non-Hasidic. A flourishing network of Chabad-Lubavitch schools and synagogues can be traced from San Francisco to San Diego. Los Angeles has witnessed a revival of modern Orthodox as well as Chabad schools. But, perhaps, Venice, California, is one of the best examples of the "Western" Orthodox revival. Its boardwalk houses the Bay Area Synagogue, located amid the roller skaters, rap music, joggers, and tarot card readers on a beachfront park. The rabbi there, Rabbi David Lapin, is unlike either the charismatic Riskin or the Hasidic rebbes. He is described as a rather reserved South African (Cowan, 1980). He differs, for instance, on theological issues from other Orthodox rabbis. While he insists on a mechitzah that separates men from women in the synagogue, he has no objection to the ordination of women rabbis (Cowan, 1980).

And just as orthodoxy varies somewhat from coast to coast, so does the sequence of events leading to orthodoxy. Discontent with current life events started most of these ba'alot teshuvah on a search. Many were no longer living at home, had had bad experiences with drugs, sex, and/or men, and were longing to live in a moral community. Often such discontent was framed in the context of personal crisis or decision making. In general, most found themselves at a transitional stage of life—entering college, graduating from college, entering a new job, or ending a job. Just under a third of them had experienced a death of a parent or close relative, loss of a romantic attachment, a divorce, or a major illness.[18]

One fifth of the women in my study found their way to orthodoxy while studying or living in Israel.[19] "I guess you would have called me a hippie in those days," recounts one woman.

> I had done a lot of experimenting in my first few years of college and had become part of the baba culture [followers of Meher Baba, an Indian spiritual master]. Then in my junior year off from school, I decided to go to India. I was in my "metaphysical mode"—I felt I would bring it all together in India—back to my roots or to my beginning—something like that. Well, on my way over I decided to make a stopover in Israel. That, too, after all, had roots for me. It was a last-minute decision and I had made no plans for where I'd go or what I'd do. So where do I go? I go to the "kotel," the Western Wall. I don't know why, but I was so moved. I knew very little about Judaism but I knew that this was a holy wall—the remaining wall from the Temple. So that's how it happened. You know, its a common story. I had made no plans, no where to go, not even a hostel arrangement. A young man with *peyes* [earlocks] asked me if I would like to spend Shabbos [the Sabbath] with an Orthodox Jewish family. Don't ask me why—maybe it was the sun, maybe it was the wall—I said yes. The long and the short of it is this: I stayed two years studying at a ba'al teshuvah yeshiva. It was a very ambivalent time for me. The people had such faith in me, even though I was so ambivalent—maybe that's why I kept holding on. My parents were beside themselves. At first they thought, well, this is better than India—then they saw that I was really hooked—they did everything to get me to come home. They visited twice. After the second time they decided maybe this wasn't so bad after all.

Others went to Israel as a junior year abroad or on a vacation. None intended to stay; none planned to study in a yeshiva. "I was picked up at the Wall," laughs one woman. "I was just searching; I wanted something spiritual in my life." Another speaks of her time in Israel as a time of "discovery." "I liked being with Orthodox people . . . and the rebbetzin, she was incredible . . . spiritual, learned, capable. I wanted to be like her . . . to be so sure of myself."

In the yeshivot, students learn complex systems of rules and regulations which guide all aspects of Orthodox Jewish life. They acquire the subtle nuances of speech, dress, and the mannerisms and behavior of Orthodox Jews. Almost all of the women who studied in Israel attended the most traditional (ultra-Orthodox) of the yeshivot, with the majority attending Neve Yerushalayim. In all yeshivot, women may study prophets, philosophy, Bible, and those practical laws that apply to them; however, in traditional yeshivot they do not gain the necessary training to study the law and never reach the requisite status and recognition for formulating halakhah.[20] As Biale notes:

Women have participated in the evolution of the halakhah only in the "prenatal" and "postpartum" stages of the process. They encountered problems and conflicts in daily life and raised questions that required halakhic decisions: from the minutiae of the laws of kashrut in their kitchens, to the momentous problems of marriage, divorce, procreation, abortion, and rape. At the end of the process women, like men, implemented the rulings of the halakhic authorities, who were exclusively male. (1984, pp. 3–4).

Five newly Orthodox women attended Shappell College of Jewish Studies for Women, a more "modern" yeshiva. Here women are trained through the use of classical texts, have the opportunity to study the Gemara, and are allowed more public expression of their religiosity. However, four out of the five who attended a "modern" yeshiva in Israel returned to strictly Orthodox or Hasidic communities in the United States.

Sixty women either attended extension courses offered through educational institutes or the seminary for women, Bais Chana, a Lubavitch boarding school in the United States, or both. Forty women attended Bais Chana either for a two-month summer program or for a one-month program in January. Some returned several times and others still go for refresher courses. Classes are scheduled from morning to night and vary in intensity and in topic. *Tanya*, an eighteenth-century text, written by Shneur

Zalman, the founder of Lubavitch Hasidism, anchors the school's curriculum.[21] There is a good deal of "*dvar* Torah," homilies on how Torah ideas or Hasidic lore connect with contemporary life issues. Young women who grew up in Lubavitch communities are sent to the institute to serve as counselors, role models, and teachers, offering classes in Jewish law, prayer, Bible, the prophets, Hebrew language, and the Jewish calendar. The rabbi and founder of the seminary, Manis Friedman, teaches Hasidic philosophy (Hebrew, *Hasidut*) and expounds upon Rebbe Schneerson's thoughts.

Newly Orthodox Jewish women who were not currently Hasidic found their way to orthodoxy in slightly different ways. Unlike Hasidic women, non-Hasidic women were less likely to have been identified with the counterculture, were more likely to have completed their secular studies at the time of their "return," and were more likely to have had more religious education. Seven of the eight "lapsed" Orthodox Jews in this study were either "modern" or "strictly Orthodox" in their religious identification. For them, the "return" to orthodoxy came generally through a close friend or a boyfriend. Non-Hasidic women's journeys to orthodoxy generally began by their taking a course in college or attending a class or beginners' service (such as those offered at Lincoln Square Synagogue). As with the Hasidic program for ba'alei teshuvah, there are a host of courses in Bible, basic Judaism, Jewish living, Hebrew, Jewish philosophy, history, texts, and ritual. And like the Hasidic methods of recruitment, there are encounter weekends. Here, too, selected members of the community invite individuals to their homes for a Sabbath meal. Lincoln Square, for instance, also has innovative recruitment techniques and support services for novices. There are rap sessions, a newsletter, programs for the various holidays, flyers, and treats for Purim. Sometimes recruiters have been known to go into singles bars to distribute those Purim treats.

Perhaps because they were better educated in Judaism than Hasidic women were, often non-Hasidic women reported having begun their "return" to orthodoxy by taking courses. Reminiscing about her "return," one woman notes:

I decided to enroll in a few Judaic studies courses and became interested in Middle Eastern philosophy. From there I became more interested in Judaism per se. The school was well known for its Judaic studies department and I found most of the professors well grounded in philosophy, and most were also "Conservadox" [very traditional but not Orthodox] in practice. Gradually, I became involved with other courses. I had always been very good in languages and began to study Hebrew again. I also began to learn Aramaic as well. There was a small group of us who banded together—we lived off-campus, kept kosher, and even began our own *minyan* [quorum for prayer]. We had a lot in common—most of us had been Bar or Bat Mitzvahed—and then we had ended our Hebrew education. We were rekindling our interest together.

Of the few who had not been born Jewish, conversion to orthodoxy usually took place after a long-term relationship with a man who wished to become a ba'al teshuvah.

WHEN ARE YOU A BA'AL TESHUVAH?

Irrespective of how they began, it was a long journey to orthodoxy for these women—adopting one Orthodox law after another, taking courses, attending Orthodox services, visiting and sometimes living with other Orthodox families. Rarely did any woman say she knew immediately she was to live a life of an Orthodox Jew. Many noted that the "conversion" to orthodoxy came slowly. Very few were immediately drawn into the community. One who was, reports:

There I was at this *farbrengen* [gathering for Lubavitch] and I saw the rebbe [referring to Rabbi Schneerson] and I knew this was a Divine messenger—I was intoxicated. It was an immediate and complete conversion for me. I moved to Crown Heights within three weeks and I have never left since then.

Another atypical, but interesting, story suggests that the embracing of orthodoxy is not an automatic response for women when their husbands do so. One Orthodox couple had been high-school sweethearts, had gone to college, married, and had three children when he became interested in a Lubavitch life-style:

> We lived together over ten years while my husband kept Orthodox, studied and identified with the Lubavitch, but lived outside the community with me and our children. He kept kosher and the Sabbath, while I did none of the latter. He had his own pots and pans and would frequently prepare meals for all of us—although I still had *tref* [unkosher] food and dishes around. At that same time, I did not even keep kosher, I kept my job and we struggled with this dilemma. The rebbe counseled my husband wisely—he said I was not ready, and I wasn't—and that my husband's commitment to me and the children should take precedence over his desire to live in the Lubavitch community. After ten years, I finally decided to try it—my husband had changed in good ways . . . and I slowly tried to follow the laws. I slowly made friends with some of the women. We sometimes spent a Shabbos in the community—I grew comfortable and I liked the focus on family life. . . . I grew more and more comfortable with orthodoxy. . . . I wanted to keep our marriage and spend the rest of my life with him.

Most claimed they knew they were truly on the journey home when they no longer felt the desire to live any other way. "I knew I had committed myself to orthodoxy," said one woman, "when I finally gave away my Bob Dylan records."

"CULTURE IN CRISIS" THEORIES AND THE SEARCH FOR MEANING

Predominantly middle-class, educated, and somewhat liberal, these women struck out in many directions. Like other counter-cultural youth who protested the Vietnam War, the amoral use of technology, the racial, ethnic, and gender injustices, or like those coming of age in the wake of the counterculture who moved in religious directions, these women found the quality and focus of contemporary living deeply troubling. All women, even those who were not part of the sixties countercultural turbulence or its successor movements, as Bellah (1976) refers to them, consciously reject some aspect of secular culture.

In telling their stories, they report a common experience: their lives had been morally vacuous before they came "home" to orthodoxy. Almost to a woman these ba'alot teshuvah describe their searches in terms of the need to anchor their everyday lives in a world that "counts" and one that is "moral." Perhaps one of the best quotations is from the young woman who needed "relief" from her "existential despair." For those seeking a meaning system in a world devoid of a coherent set of values, Orthodox Judaism became a haven in a "valueless" world. Because it did not assimilate by trying to integrate Judaism into the modern secular world, as did the Reform and Conservative denominations, orthodoxy retained a set of values not contingent on changing social conditions and thereby able to provide these discontented youth with an immutable value system and a "timeless" moral community.

The postcountercultural era has been described as a time of turning "inward." The stories these ba'alot teshuvah tell reveal that they were seeking self-enhancement, but not through the creation of self. They rejected "liberation" movements that had no institutional frameworks to define the parameters of that liberation. All their stories questioned the nature of such radical liberation. If one is freed from inhibition, to what is one responsible? What is worthwhile? What has meaning? In the absence of moral frameworks, individual freedom creates problems for these women. As Tipton notes: "Precisely because the individual is free to construct the order and meaning of her own private life she experiences its meanings as unreliable and even artificial" (1982, p. 25).[22]

Action and the shared sense of collective self, which were missing for some of these women in the monistic or therapeutic groups of the seventies, are possible only if there is a strong public life and where social roles demand more than individualism (Sennett, 1974). Tipton (1982) points out that the expressive individualism of the seventies may have contrasted with, but did not alleviate, the problems generated by the individualistic, economic pattern of the self-made man with which the parents of most of these ba'alot teshuvah identified. He suggests that the self-actualized goal of therapy transformed "looking out for number one" to "being your own best friend." For many newly Orthodox Jewish women the focus on individualism undermines community, social values, and social virtues.[23] Writing in the mid-seventies, Ellen Goodman astutely picks up on the problems of "self" pursuit:

> [T]he impulses that prod us to find the meaning of life, not in material goods but in experiences and pursuit of self, can also . . . lead to encapsulated private lives with fewer and fewer intimate connections between people, and a diminished sense of personal responsibility to others (*Boston Globe*, October 18, 1976).

All ba'alot teshuvah framed their discontent within a context of a personal value crisis. Bellah (1976) argues that civil religion, a complex of symbolic meanings that had united Americans in a moral community, has been slowly disappearing from the American scene since last century. Robbins and Anthony (1979) refer to Bellah's analysis when they write: "A number of writers have related the upsurge of deviant movements to a crisis in 'American Civil Religion.' . . . A weakening of the linkage between private and public value systems has created a disjuncture between personal expressivity and broader social concern, thus generating a proliferation of privatized and 'narcissistic' self-actualization movements" (p. 78). In the early seventies Eister (1972) wrote that we were in a cultural crisis because the structure for discussing values and meanings had broken down, resulting in confusion and a loss of coherence. Although stated in different ways, many scholars view the past few decades as a time of cultural confusion and a loss of value consensus.[24]

In some ways the return to orthodoxy appears to be for these women the sociological corrective to psychological reductionism—bringing the self back into social action and community. If, as Sennett suggests, the twentieth-century form of community takes shape as a collective personality (generated by a collective fantasy), then ultimately collective being is substituted for collective action (1974, p. 223). The next few chapters will reveal the ways in which these women equate religious values with a coherent set of symbols which, they claim, value the "feminine." In addition, they see these values as rooted in a stable social setting which, according to them, honors the social practices associated with the female. They equate their religious duties with their everyday activities as women, mothers, and wives. This congruence provides many of them with an ethical system that connects their public and private lives. They have, as Tipton (1982, 1983) might describe it, bridged the gap between the moral and the actual. As we shall see in the remaining chapters, the ba'alot teshuvah find not only a community in which moral issues are clear and known, but a setting in which values of the private sphere, and those associated with female and family, so they claim, are publicly shared, respected, and, most important, acted upon.

CHAPTER TWO

•

Four Portraits

Ba'alot Teshuvah as Finders

The following scenarios present composite portraits of ba'alot teshuvah according to two kinds of Hasidic and two kinds of non-Hasidic categories of orthodoxy.[1] I have introduced the women under study in this way to capture the feeling and tone of the interviews, the respondents, and, to some degree, the interviewer. All conversations are verbatim transcripts from field notes. The incidents are real, although the specific likes and dislikes, incidents, locations, and descriptions of houses, clothing, and conversations, while taken in detail from field notes, have been thoroughly mixed to maintain anonymity. So, too, the demographic profiles, history of events, names, and occupational titles have been varied so that similarities to particular families or individuals, if any, are purely coincidental.

The portraits have been carefully drawn, to reflect, on average, differences among the women by category of orthodoxy.[2] Hasidic women, for instance, were less likely to work, or to work part-time, more likely to have experienced divorce and to have a greater number of children than strictly Orthodox or Modern Orthodox women. Each portrait approximates the average woman in each category by such variables as age, number of children, life-course stage, and socioeconomic status. As a group, Hasidic women tend to be slightly older and are lower in socioeconomic status than are the non-Hasidic women. Since only 20 of the 150 women interviewed were not married at the time of the interview, the portraits are all of married women. Almost all women have been ba'alot teshuvah at least from the time of their marriages (on average, about five years).

Each composite portrait represents a typology of one of the four categories of women under study—two kinds of Hasidim (Bostoner and Lubavitch) and two kinds of non-Hasidic (strictly Orthodox and Modern). My main objective is to make evident through their own language and stories the central themes, issues, and concerns these women share as women. The portraits capture what these women have found in Orthodox theology and tradition.

CHANA: THE LUBAVITCH

Chana meets me at the door of her small crowded apartment. She smiles. "You are Professor Kaufman? Please come in and don't trip." She has spoken with me on the telephone several times and knows that her good friend Chava has recommended her as someone with whom I'd like to talk. Several children (some are neighbors' children) surround her as she makes way for me amid the creative playthings, Yiddish coloring books, pencils, crayons, paste, and jars that mark my way to the living room. A large trampoline sits in one corner of the room. She notices my attention to it. "Oh, that is for rainy days." After we have settled in, I with a cup of tea, she with an assortment of "treats" for when the children get restless, we begin the interview. She asks in a slightly singsong fashion (a hallmark of those trying to infuse Yiddish into their vernacular)[3] what it is I am doing. She is interested in the idea of someone writing about ba'alot teshuvah but suspects that an "outsider" is probably not the right person. She asks about my own background, my Jewish identification and current practices, my family, and what I teach at the university. I answer all her questions, ending with the final note that it is my professional curiosity, not my personal search, that has brought me to the community. She smiles and says knowingly, "Maybe so."

After I have given her as much information as she seems to want, her four-month-old baby awakens. We both go into the nursery shared with two of Chana's five children. She casually lifts the baby, propping her on one knee as she picks up the blanket and the diapers she will need. We return to another, smaller room, the study, and she begins to nurse the baby. In a far corner, I see an attractive bookcase. Again she notices my attention. She teasingly asks if I know what it is. A Victorian bookcase, I offer. She explains that they keep all of their most holy texts in that bookcase. She tells me that she loves antiques and that this one comes from an old brothel. She confides that this is something she wouldn't tell the rebbe.[4] Indeed, there are several photographs of Rabbi Menachem Schneerson throughout the house. I would come to see those same photographs in most Lubavitch households.

In this room there are photographs of her children, wonderful candid shots from many different seasons. "In my wild and wicked days, I was an avid photographer; you can see I still am an avid photographer." I like her sense of humor. She reminds me of many of my old college friends; a long denim skirt substitutes for jeans,[5] a frilly blouse (covering the elbows) and a denim vest in place of ponchos and Indian tops. Strands of long dark hair slip out from under her *tichel* (headcovering, a scarf in her case)[6] whenever she speaks animatedly. Her style and air are distinctly familiar. I know her from a few decades ago, although at almost thirty-seven she is five years my junior. The style of the times demanded a nonconformity that Chana still maintains. I am dressed in my most professional interviewing outfit.

"You probably want to know why, hmm? Why have I become this fat contented lady with five children? You know, I once was very radical, very discontented, and very thin, really. When I was in college I protested everything. I can remember how everything during that period of my life seemed so wrong. I don't mean wrong for me personally but wrong with the world. No one seemed able to live up to any ideals of any sort—the universities seemed morally bankrupt. I had friends who had been involved in protests who were thrown down flights of stairs by campus police."

Chana elaborates upon her feelings about the world at large and her role in it. "There is nothing spiritual out there, nothing holy, nothing moral in any consistent way. What can you appeal to out there? . . . I cannot, as I once did, become a part of that. You know they say you can't go home again once you have left. It is true I could not go back to my old way of living. I have come home to something bigger than me. Everything I do is spiritual, every act I do is guided by *Hashem* ("the Name," Yiddish word for God]. There is a sense of the rightness of what I am doing. Every physical act that I perform . . . what I feed my family, how I dress, how I make love to my husband.

"Now," Chana says, "my life is filled with the details of being a woman, a mother, and a wife." I ask her to elaborate and suggest how her answer might differ from other women, wives, and mothers. "Well, I gave up my work as a social worker within our own community with the birth of my fourth baby. You see, I married late [at thirty years of age], after I had had quite a checkered career, in and out of different agencies. It was too much for me to manage this large family and have much energy for other families as well. I was constantly juggling time and energy on the job and at home. I was doing a balancing act. How much time for my clients, how much time for me and mine. Now I have been truly productive for the last seven years. It just depends on where you want to put your energies. 'Baruch Hashem [God willing],' I want to have as many babies as God will allow. This is a choice women no longer believe they have . . . it is a real shame. Orthodoxy gives me this option."

Chana continues to talk about her choices. "Marriage, family, children—that's what it's all about. My husband, you must meet him. He's so sweet, so gentle, so loving, so good. To tell you the truth, when I was younger I wouldn't have even noticed him. He is so shy. But what a sweet man he is, and our children, Baruch Hashem, have his temperament."

We are interrupted by the sound of the horn of the car-pool driver for the day. Chana hands me the baby and runs to the door to greet her two school-age youngsters, Fivel and Yosele. She asks them many questions and introduces me to them. They are lively, questioning, and hungry. Chana has snacks for them but they must say the blessings before they are allowed to indulge. She watches them with pride and then returns to the interview. While she has been with the children, I have noticed how organized she is. There is a bulletin board full of five different children's schedules, music lessons, and even art lessons, all, she explains later, given by her other talented ba'alot teshuvah friends. "We bring many talents to Orthodox Judaism. We haven't given up our loves; we've just redirected them."

She allows the children to play records—Yiddish versions of *Sesame Street*. There are no signs of a television or a radio, but ample evidence of tape recorders and cassettes. Chana explains that they do not have any secular newspapers, magazines, or other media in the house. I notice, however, that she does subscribe to the weekly Jewish newspaper and that there are copies of the *Mosheach* (Messiah) *Times*, the official newspaper of the Lubavitcher children's group. She tells me that she and her husband do not allow the children to watch television or go to the movies, and that the whole family entertains themselves with tapes and recordings of music and lectures given by noted Hasidic entertainers and rabbis. She also notes that they do a lot of arts and crafts together as a family, especially around holidays.

We pick up our conversation about her feelings as a woman, wife and mother. "Mostly when it comes to decisions here at home Moishe [her husband] defers to me. You know, I'm the expert here. When we have religious questions, since we are both ba'alei teshuvah, we ask the rebbe."[7] I carefully inquire about what kinds of questions they might ask the rebbe. "I feel foolish bothering the rebbe because of our ignorance, but if we are really troubled or feel anxious about a decision we do seek advice from him—whether my husband should quit his job or whether we should move to Israel or where we should eventually send our son for schooling. Oh yes, we wrote to him before we were married to ask for his blessing also."

Chana continues discussing the rebbe, noting that she and some of her other ba'alot teshuvah friends have written to him for advice on one point or another of doctrine or on how to deal with members of their families who are not Orthodox. She admits that, although the rebbe initially encouraged her to attend her brother's wedding to a non-Jewish woman, she could not bring herself to do so. "I think," she says, "the rebbe knew that this has been a real source of pain for me. Although I love my brother, it is impossible for me to continue in a relationship with him. My parents are pained by this, but they have reluctantly come to accept my decision." She parenthetically remarks that her brother is now separated from his wife and, although she has tried to make contact with him, he refuses to answer her calls and letters. She admits to me that this has been one of the real "costs" of becoming Orthodox.

She returns to her discussion of the rebbe. She speaks of his charismatic presence, recounting the times she has seen or heard him. "To hear and see him is to know you are in the company of one of the great men of history. He is so wise, so impressive. He is the link for our community from one wise sage to another, from one generation to another. There is a quality of holiness in his company."

Interestingly, however, Chana's sense of spirituality and connection to orthodoxy comes not so much from public occasions with the rebbe, nor from personal communication with him, but rather in relationship to her religious obligations as a Jewish woman. Orthodoxy is so appealing to her because as a woman, she claims, she brings spirituality into the world: "You know, since the destruction of the Second Temple, the family is like the 'holy tabernacle' on earth. Each week I bring divine presence into this household by preparing for Shabbos, I *make* Shabbos. . . . When I separate and burn a portion of the *challah* [Sabbath bread], when I light the candles to welcome the Shabbos queen, I am like a high priestess.[8] When I went to Bais Chana we learned that women create the *middot* [character] formation of the Jewish people. You know in *Hasidus* [Yiddish form of Hasidut],[9] it is said that it is through women's work and efforts that the Mosheach will come. Through my actions, my understanding, my feminine sensibilities, light and understanding are brought into the world. We women take care of the goodness in the world; we nurture and protect it."

Chana eschews what she sees as secular views about money, success, and work. "I want my husband to make a *parnosoh* [living];

that's all. Enough for us to support ourselves. Moishe is giving up his job as a physicist in a very large firm, where he makes a nice living . . . but it demands too much of his time; there is no end to it. If he is going to be able to live fully in this community he has to make the change. He's going to be a computer analyst and work out of the house . . . we'll see. Success and money, what does that mean compared to living a life of mitzvot?"[10]

Chana is on her third nursing when we finally end the interview. She asks that I take some tapes and pamphlets with me. The tapes are lectures from a well-known Chabad rabbi and teacher. She notes that what she has told me is how she feels about her orthodoxy. She thinks the tapes will help explain things more. She claims that it is hard for her to explain to me the complicated theology, and even harder, she admits, for her to keep up with studying. She tells me that she still tries to pray at least once a day, but that she does not study *Tanya*[11] or read the psalms as often as she did when she was a young ba'alat teshuvah. Time has become more precious, but she says that she and her husband still discuss the portion of the Torah reading for that week on Friday nights, that she tries to meet with a woman friend once a week to read from the Psalms or sometimes to read from *Tanya*. She takes crash courses in the summer when she can. She admits that it is hard to keep up but that she still calls a friend once a day just to talk, even for ten minutes, about something other than the children, car pools for the little ones, recipes, and parent effectiveness training classes.

Miriam: Another Kind of Hasid

A well-known scholar in the community has recommended Miriam as a possible respondent; she knows the ba'al teshuvah community well. Before granting the interview, she has agreed to meet first in a small strictly kosher cafe in the neighborhood where she works. She is on a lunch break—a biomedical researcher in a nearby university. She is dressed as a modestly understated yuppie in a short-jacketed suit, sleeves covering the elbows, and an A-line skirt to the midcalf. She works part-time. We order lunch and she is direct and forthright: "I assume, since you are a sociologist, you must have a lot of ideas about who ba'alot teshuvah are . . . there has also been a lot in the Jewish and popular press about us." She hands me some clippings and then continues: "We're either presented as druggies, cultists, or dropouts, or as marginal women, desperate for structure in life, afraid to face the world on its own terms, and, maybe what's worse, that we are getting on in age, our biological clocks ticking, the marriage pool shrinking, and we are primarily searching for husbands." I am stunned and I wonder if she is planning to write a book about her life as a ba'alat teshuvah.

My immediate silence softens her a bit. "I'm only saying this because I want you to know that there are a variety of ba'alot teshuvah around—some were druggies, some were looking for a guru, some for a husband, and some were looking for both, but by no means all of us, and even then, that is just part of the picture. I have been a ba'alat teshuvah for over seven years and I'm older [age thirty-four] than most. The anxieties about life that may have led to becoming a ba'alat teshuvah are anxieties we have throughout our lives; they just change in the kind that they are. . . . It's a part of live having to balance our so-called options. Frankly, there are a lot easier paths to take than orthodoxy. You'd be better off, I think, finding out what holds us in rather than what got us here." I tell her that I am interested in her life-style as she experiences it now as a woman who has embraced orthodoxy. "Why don't we meet at my home this evening," she offers. "It will be more relaxed and we can talk a bit about this." I assume this means we have an interview.

The evening brings me to a small two-story wooden shingled house in a secluded neighborhood in the middle of a busy suburban community. She greets me at the door. She is no longer wearing a wig, but a tichel, a scarf, covering most, but not all, of her hair. I am introduced to her husband who serves us both tea and poppy-seed cookies he and the girls have just made (the kind of cookies my grandmother used to make) and asks if I would like to interview him after Miriam. "I am a ba'al teshuvah, too," he claims. I tell him that I am particularly interested in women, the concerns and issues they face as ba'alot teshuvah, but that I would enjoy talking with him after the interview if he is still interested. He smiles and excuses himself. "I'll put the girls to bed," he offers, and leaves. Miriam explains that he won't be back. "He has to prepare for tomorrow." She tells me that he used to be an executive for a large business firm and now has become an administrator for a school in the Orthodox community.

She begins by telling me that she has three daughters. Her eldest is from her husband's previous marriage and the two younger are from this marriage. She, too, was married before. They have been married five years. She is almost immediately interrupted by a telephone call. She takes it because it is an emergency call. While she is gone, I browse through the many books on the shelves in the living room. There are as many medical and educational texts as there are religious ones. There is as much Hasidic art as there are Impressionist reprints hanging on the walls. In the corner is a handsome stereo unit; opera seems to be the main focus, to judge from the jackets of the records that rest on top. There appears to be no television or radio. *The New York Times Magazine* sections are neatly piled in a corner, and the weekly Jewish newspaper is also there.

Miriam returns and apologizes for the interruption and then explains that she is active in the community's outreach program for the sick and terminally ill. She notes that while the sisterhood of the *shul* (Yiddish, synagogue) is not something that interests her, this is. She has been close to a family that has been dislocated and the youngest child is suffering from leukemia. "My medical background helps somewhat in keeping me as a liaison person for distraught families. Even for families of faith, this is a very hard ordeal."

Miriam then speaks to me about the belief system she now embraces: "The Torah is simply amazing. It understands the human psyche—what makes us tick. It has answers for all the key questions in life. At first, I simply did the mitzvot, because it was what you did as an Orthodox Jewish woman. I mean, I was tired of picking and choosing. I wanted something tried and true. I figured if I am going to be Orthodox, I'd have to buy the whole package. The night before I made the decision not to eat tref, I went to

Chinatown and literally, you should pardon the expression, pigged out. Foolishness, no. But that was who I was then. . . . Now I cannot understand how I could have done that.

"I have found meaning in all this ritual . . . meaning I have never really had at any other time in my life. Torah has so much to say to me as a woman. My feelings about myself as a sexual person . . . the family purity laws are so in line with me as a woman . . . it is commanded that I not be sexually taken for granted, that I have two weeks each month for myself. . . . It is mind-boggling to me to think that this wonderful Torah has known who I am as a woman for centuries."

In response to my follow-through question on what helps her to maintain this good feeling about herself as a woman, Miriam answers: "Every moment of my waking life is so full of the sense of my holiness as a woman. I have found a tradition that senses the positive in who I am . . . you know what the concept *tznius* means? . . . It's such a wonderful way of presenting oneself . . . it means modesty. It means you should present yourself as caring, soft-spoken, gentle, you know . . . in a feminine way. That's what orthodoxy is really all about. Tznius doesn't just apply to women; it's meant for all Jews. We are supposed to be separate, different, apart . . . different from a world that can do such things as a Holocaust."

Later in the interview she challenges me to think of one area of life where caring and nurturing are the key values. "Even in the academic profession, where you supposedly have intellectuals . . . thinking, intelligent human beings, there is so much of what I call 'corporate backbiting,' gossiping . . . moving upward is almost always on someone's back. Individuals 'making it,' isn't that what it is all about? Is my happiness, my fulfillment, my success the only important thing? Even family life has succumbed. How can we call ourselves a child-centered society when there is so much neglect and brutality? The world needs more of what we do as women naturally. We must teach and guide men. You know, in orthodoxy women are not required to do any of the time-bound commandments.[12] Men need the discipline; we don't. We are closer to God—we are the *Shekhinah* [indwelling of God, God's presence]. We provide understanding—knowledge alone means nothing. We have a natural understanding of things. We don't need to go to shul three times a day or study regularly to fulfill our bond with God. Our discipline is in the everyday actions of our lives in our intuitive understanding of what is right. In Judaism this is recognized.

"Look," Miriam says, "I don't mean that we should not take advantage of education and other opportunities. Chaim [her husband] agrees with me when I say that Dvorah [their daughter] should be afforded every opportunity to go to medical school. She is very good in science, like I was. This, of course, after she has had a good religious education and has her values straight. You know, there are Orthodox women doctors. There is nothing in orthodoxy that prevents women from receiving advanced training or education."[13]

Miriam is tired as am I. It has been a long day. We make plans to meet again, for she would like to tell me more about her specific life as an Orthodox Jewish woman and she realizes that she may have "gone on a bit much." We agree to meet the following week at the small café where we had met earlier in the day.

ALISA: THE STRICTLY ORTHODOX

Alisa opens the door to her small four-room apartment. She lets me admire her, as she must all those who first meet her. Her beauty is almost overwhelming. She is tall, blond, blue-eyed, and slender. Despite the comb[14] that holds it back, the bulk and flow of her beautiful hair is evident. She is dressed as if she has just walked out of a Laura Ashley shop—a high-necked, long-sleeved, midcalf-length dress in a soft paisley print. She asks if I have had any difficulty finding the apartment, for she is the first in that community that I am to interview. Moreover, there are two last names on the nameplate, hers and her husband's. She has been married for only one year. Her husband is a psychologist and she is working toward a law degree. She looks older than her twenty-five years. She was a psychology major prior to her entrance into law school, but found that after a year of graduate work she wanted more of a career. Law had always attracted her. "I studied Talmud for a while," she tells me, "and I really like the challenge of rigorous and logical thinking." She had attended Brovender's school in Israel for a short while. "You know, I really think that my law career will profit from not only the rigor of studying Talmud but from the ethical teachings of Judaism. It's a good *shidduch* [Hebrew for "match"], isn't it?" She asks very few questions of me as she brews herbal tea. When she returns, she takes her shoes off, tucks her feet beneath her dress on the comfortable sofa, and smiles. We begin.

Alisa confesses that she has been a ba'alat teshuvah from the age of sixteen. "My family was Reform but I had a close friend who attended an Orthodox day-school. I convinced my parents to send me to a very Conservative temple afternoon school.[15] I bought my own dishes, cooked some of my meals, and off and on kept the Shabbat, and tried as best I could under those conditions to be an Orthodox Jew. I studied as much as I could and, in college, I took courses in Judaic studies. But in college I slipped away from orthodoxy. I just didn't find the same desire I had had as a teenager to pursue it. But I loved to study Jewish sources, so I continued to take Hebrew and a little Aramaic as well. I really got involved with Hasidut, too. In fact, I loved it, although I could never live a Hasidic life-style."

I ask her to tell me why she loved Hasidut. "There is no doubt that what I love about it is the way in which women are understood. The intensity of women's relationship to God is overwhelming. I think women are the collective unconscious way of safeguarding prayer in Judaism. Women in the Bible are known for their prayers—Sarah, Rachel, and Chana [Hannah]. They have such an intense relationship to God. . . . It reminds men that what goes on in shul is not important, but that the relationship to God is. We are the holders of the key for the most important aspect of inner life. The experience of being a woman in Judaism I would say is like Jungian 'anima'—a profound introspection and inner intensity."

The telephone rings and it is Alisa's husband. She smiles and says, yes, she loves him too and that, yes, she is still in the middle of the interview. She smiles at me. "We are still newlyweds, although I just learned this week that I am pregnant. We look forward to the baby and to my degree; they should both arrive at the same time." She continues to talk about what it is like to be a ba'alat teshuvah. "I am very involved in my work, and that takes up a good deal of my time. I really look forward to the Shabbat—sometimes it's a time to socialize with friends whom we haven't had time to see all week and sometimes it's a time for my husband and me to be alone. We go to shul together and *daven* (Yiddish for pray). We often study together and talk about the Torah portion of the week. My husband is not a ba'al teshuvah; he has been Orthodox all his life and is yeshiva trained, a black-hatter [one of the men who wear hats, not just yarmulkas]. We argue a lot over interpretation . . . mostly because I feel he is too studied in his approach. I tell him to let go a little . . . feel it a little more. I don't think it is in men's natures.

"You know, when I go to shul I love to pray behind a mechitzah, not because I feel I will distract men, but because I do not wish to be distracted from prayer. I just like to feel my spiritual self—alone with God. To me shul is for davening. I like to be alone in prayer. I am glad that women do not have to obey the time-bound commandments. It is so much more meaningful for me to be spontaneous in my prayers. You see, there is a holiness to Judaism that I love. I like the fact that the men and the women are expected to reach holiness through different means. I think it suits our personalities. Before I was married I tried davening in an all-women's prayer service, but I always felt something was missing. I like being with men and being separated. It makes two statements simultaneously—that we are separate, different, yet together."

Alisa leaves the room to refill the teapot. I notice several cinema and theater schedules tacked to her bulletin board, along with a schedule of the Jewish community center's activities and a sisterhood list from the synagogue. The house is tastefully decorated in a traditional decor with several framed Renaissance reproductions mounted beneath recessed lights. When she returns, she continues her thoughts.

"I mean, I feel strongly about many things. . . . I contribute to

a few environmental groups and I really feel strongly about equal
rights for women. I may even specialize in that area of law. I'm
fascinated by the comparable-worth issue. But I am not a feminist.
See, I think feminism has missed the boat. We should be equal,
but not lose our differences. Frankly, I like what women do, the
way we approach the world, and I wouldn't want to lose that. I
don't think what women do is really valued. I think, outside of the
Orthodox community, women get rewarded for doing things the
way men do it.

"In a *frum* [Yiddish for observant] life there is a focus on the
beauty and spiritual quality of our everyday lives in the family and
as women. I love the feeling that I am simultaneously physical and
spiritual. It all fits so well. It is a wonderfully meshed system of
belief and practice. I cannot find that same intensity in any other
endeavor that has ever been a part of my life. I am part of a community of timeless truths beyond the here and now and beyond
you and me. I am part of a community that practices what it
believes."

After several hours Alisa asks if she has given me what I wanted
in the interview. "You've asked so few questions," she says. I tell
her that I am interested in what she believes to be important about
herself and her life as a ba'alat teshuvah. I tell her that, in general,
I have to ask very few questions; the interviews just flow. She asks
to see anything that I might write on the topic. I promise to keep in
touch with her, but until interviewing is complete I cannot share
any of my findings or feelings.

Debra: The Modern

We are sitting on the boardwalk looking into the ocean. The colors
are muted and it is a hot day. Debra is lightly made-up, smartly
dressed, with a brightly colored turban matching her long skirt,
high socks, and heeled shoes.[16] I wonder throughout the interview
why she does not perspire and never seems to be uncomfortable
despite the heat. One of the members of her synagogue (Young
Israel) waves to her as he lunges forward on his surfboard into the
ocean.

We have left her spacious ten-room house, furnished in modern lines and vibrant colors, to drive to the ocean together. Other than the mezuzot on the entry posts to the doors of the rooms in her home, there are few signs that this is an Orthodox Jewish home. The *Saturday Evening Post*, two daily newspapers, including the *Wall Street Journal*, and the local Jewish Community Center's most recent brochure are all on the den table. The house is spotless. Debra has two small children and a live-in mother's helper. Her husband is a lawyer. They were married six years ago when she was twenty years of age. Debra is a journalist. She can do most of her work at home, and on her own hours since she does free-lance work.

I have come to the part of the interview where Debra is describing her life as a ba'alat teshuvah. "I think living a Torah life has given me inner peace and serenity. . . . I know who I am, what I'm supposed to do, and how to do it. If this sounds unthinking to you, it really is not. That is, on a day-to-day level, I can integrate my need for something spiritual in my life with who I really am— a woman. My writing is always better for it. I see things I have never seen before, my imagery is so much cleaner and sharper. I see the spiritual in everything. I also paint a bit and I realize now that the colors I had always been searching for, the shapes I had tried to understand, are inherent in the new view I have of the world from a new perspective.

"I know this is going to sound strange to you," Debra says, responding to my question about her life as a ba'alat teshuvah, "but I feel like a spiritual feminist. Often when I awaken in the morning and I am saying my prayers I feel this profound spirituality; it's actually liberating. I go to this wonderful workshop once a week. It is offered by a frum woman who is a psychologist. There is music, meditation, group exercise, and, since most of us are vegetarians, some veggie snacks.

"We study the role of the feminine in Jewish thought. I feel so in touch with myself and the rhythms of my body. We've learned a lot about Jewish mystical thought.[17] In the past I have taken a lot of courses—mostly having to do with ethics—you know,[18] and one where we read a synopsis of the Hafez Hayyim's[19] work on *lashon hara* [Hebrew for "gossip and slander"]. There is no doubt, however, my workshop for women is the most important one. The others just make me know what good sense the Torah makes for personal living and mental hygiene, but my course on feminine spirituality relates the most to me as a woman. You know, I don't just feel good but I feel connected to a past and to a future. As a woman I connect one person to another."

The day is very hot, and I am growing more and more uncomfortable. I wonder if Debra engages in mixed swimming,[20] and as if she can read my thoughts about Orthodox practice, she says almost out of the blue: "I know one thing . . . even if I were to stop practicing orthodoxy, I wouldn't ever lose the sense of who I am as a woman. That will be something I carry with me all my life. I love being a woman in this tradition. The Jewish people, the Torah, and the Shekhinah are all feminine in the way I see Judaism. All the most important things that can happen to you in life—loving, birthing, working—are put into a feminine framework. It sort of makes a qualitative existence possible on a day-to-day basis." She stops abruptly. "You know, I think I'm beginning to sound like a brochure. . . . I don't believe in proselytizing. Let me start again . . . what I mean is this; forget the romanticization. Ritual behavior is a consciousness-raising of sorts—it's hard work—but it also reminds you daily just who you are. Everytime I buy food, dress myself, prepare for almost anything, I'm reminded that there is a different way for me to do things than there is for others. Not only because I'm a Jew but because I'm a woman. There is no romanticizing, there is no idealizing—it's hard work. Ritual behavior helps you find that divine inner core that is a part of all of us.

"I think in a world that isn't frum, most women are male-identified. I think before I became Orthodox, I was male-identified. You know: what's male is better. Not in Judaism. If anything, it is a bit reversed. Difference doesn't mean inferiority. In fact, only in Judaism have I found out who I really am. I am different, not just because I am Jewish but also because I am a woman. I have taken part in antinuclear demonstrations because I truly believe that women, more than men, understand those things which are civilization-threatening. Those insights about women are all there in the Torah. I like being with other women a good part of the time; I like studying about myself and other women, with other women; I like being separate with other women. It is a real sense of strength for me."

A resplendent sunset interrupts our conversation. We are both silent for the moment. "Look, I don't want to leave you with the impression that I don't like men . . . I do. But in Judaism what's male is not idealized—the most important religious symbols . . . the people of Israel, the Shabbat, are all feminine. I love men when they are a part of this community. Can I tell you that a yarmulka really turns me on . . . even black-hatters. I know that if they accept the principles of orthodoxy they are good people. Do you have some time? I'd like you to meet my teacher." I agree to meet her and we leave the ocean and the sunset behind.

HASIDIC AND NON-HASIDIC WOMEN: THEOLOGICAL DIFFERENCES AND SIMILARITIES

Despite their disparate life-styles, socioeconomic standing, and individual differences in style and taste, the structured conversations with the women under study reveal distinct and common themes. Their return to orthodoxy contains no world-escaping visions, no models for alternative realities, but rather a tradition with a moral ordering in which they, as women, play a major role. For them, the Orthodox religious and social community is more than synagogue and study. The women in this study seem to celebrate their difference as both women and Jews. Women, they claim, in their roles as mothers and wives, are central in maintaining those rituals which separate Orthodox Jews from other Jews and from the larger gentile world. From their perspective, the female in her everyday life as wife and mother, and the feminine qualities she represents, are central to Orthodox living.

These women use the feminine and the family to relate to the world in a spiritual and moral way that they claim is personally satisfying. They find purpose and meaning in their female activities and positive self-definition in feminine attributes. The familial and the feminine provide a counterbalance for them to a world "run amok" with masculine notions of success, achievement, and status acted out through competitive individualism and self-aggrandizement. They view themselves not merely as passive reflections of male imagery, but rather as moral agents for positive action. They not only believe in gender difference, they celebrate it.

While these women do not directly challenge male authority in the Orthodox community (thereby limiting whatever effect they can have on the community as a whole), they focus on the most powerful and sacred images of themselves and their functions in the religious tradition. Some women emphasize classical theological sources in describing their roles as Orthodox Jewish women. For instance, the family, "their" domain, is described as "the sanctuary on earth." They often refer to the Sabbath as "feminine" or as "a taste of the world to come." Among many of the Hasidic women, there is an implicit belief that they "will prepare the world for the coming of the Messiah." Still others refer to the "indwelling" of God as female. These powerful images embody a sense of the sacred community of which they are a principle part as "feminine," in direct contrast to the male, secular culture which they have rejected. In this study, even the non-Hasidic women, who were more involved than Hasidic women in the secular world, were quick to point out that the most valued part of their lives had to do with their lives as women within Jewish orthodoxy.

These women claim that a great part of what attracts and holds them in a traditional life-style is the nature and description of the "feminine" and the female in orthodoxy. Both Hasidic and non-Hasidic women invoked classical Jewish sources to express their positive identification and participation in orthodoxy and, consequently, in the world at large. The selected bits and pieces of tradition and theology they chose to relate strongly suggest that they consciously reformulate that orthodoxy in their own image. They associate the sacred and themselves with positive purpose and positive self-definition. This ideology is held in place through the structure of their everyday lives.

Marriage and the family are key components. One woman suggests that marriage is at once a personal and a sacred act. Through her familial practices as wife and mother she is able to make a "dwelling place for God below." Another woman stated that marriage is the symbol of the highest relationship possible: "The day God gave the Jewish people the Torah is called the 'day of his wedding.'" These ba'alot teshuvah assert an unambiguous "profamily" stance based on strong assertions that the family is essentially their realm. Images of light pervade their descriptions of themselves as religious women—symbolized most explicitly by the lighting of the Sabbath candles. A working mother of three children captures this sentiment when she says:

> All the mitzvot that women must do surround their relationship to the family; the lighting of the Sabbath candles brings light to the family; the baking of the challah is related to women's nurturing roles; and obeying taharat hamishpacha give our most natural lives a spiritual and holy quality.

Not one woman doubted that she came from a divine source. One woman, non-Hasidic but intrigued by Kabbalah, claimed: "You know the Shekhinah is not only female, but as I remember was called Sarah in the time of Abraham, Rebecca in the time of Isaac, and Rachel in the time of Jacob."[21] "We were the first to be told the Torah," claims one woman. "We did not participate in the making of the golden calf and for our reward we were given Rosh Hodesh [the celebration of the New Moon, a time when some of the women under study do no housework and read from the psalms and/or congregate with other women]." "We did not believe the lies of the spies sent into Israel," claims another. Most of these women believe in "natural" and "eternal" differences between the sexes. Their discussions make clear that despite gender differences or, perhaps even more important, because of gender differences, women in orthodoxy are fully spiritual beings, derived from and clearly reflecting a divine source. "We," as one woman stated it, "actualize the divine plan."

Hasidic women were more likely than non-Hasidic women not only to affirm their honored place in the theology, but to assert that their sensibilities might even be superior to those of men. Indeed, some invert the gender hierarchy by claiming that the highest levels of spirituality are reached through female life-cycle experiences. While all of the Hasidic women, and most of the non-Hasidic women, accept that the Torah was given in entirety at Mount Sinai, many of the Hasidic women also believe that God told Moses to teach the Torah first to the women and afterward to the men. For them, this is yet another indicator of women's superior sensibilities compared to men's. Indeed, Hasidic, rather than non-Hasidic, women were more likely to claim that the reason why they are not obligated to perform most time-bound positive commandments, as are men, is because they are not in need of such spiritual reminders. As women, they claim, they are considered to be innately more self-disciplined and by nature more in touch with their spiritual potential.[22]

Since over half of the women interviewed were Hasidic, differences between them and non-Hasidic women create important distinctions. Some of the differences between Hasidic and non-Hasidic women have to do with the way in which Hasidism incorporates mystical and kabbalistic thought. According to Sharot (1982), Hasidism borrows from kabbalistic ideas and terms and then attaches different meanings and emphases to them. In Sharot's discussion, every object and activity in this world contains a spark of divinity. Borrowing from the idea proposed by Isaac ben Solomon Luria that many divine sparks had fallen into the sphere of evil, Hasidism represents a monistic system where absolute evil has no independent existence. The key task of the Hasid is to uncover or penetrate the appearance of evil in order to see and have contact with the real. This places great emphasis on contact with and transformation of the material world. It is women's greater association with the physical and material world (and their life-sustaining functions) that seemingly support the Hasidic women's claim to an ability equal to, if not greater than, that of men to uncover the appearances of evil.

In her thought-provoking paper on the feminine and Jewish mysticism, Susan Handelman presents an interesting argument for the "feminine principle" in Jewish mysticism and specifically in Hasidut.[23] According to Hasidut, argues Handelman, the "higher an idea . . . the more concealed and 'lower' the form of its expression" (1984, p. 10). She concludes:

> Now if the more concealment, the more essence, it follows then that in this lowest crude, physical world where God is so concealed there must be found an aspect of the highest essence, and indeed Chassidus [Hasidut] proposes that the truly new and remarkable thing in the universe is the physical (p. 10).

Handelman argues that in Hasidut the feminine is associated with the body, the physical, concealment and ultimately essence. She writes:

> [T]he body potentially has the capacity to express or relate to essence more than the "spiritual" levels of man. The body is a more appropriate vehicle in which and by which to reveal essence. In the world to come, and at the time of the Messiah, the purified body will be the vehicle of the highest revelations of the essence of God, not the soul . . . the same holds true for the feminine principle which is associated with the body, the physical, concealment, essence . . . (1984, p. 10).

For some women under study, familiarity with Chabad interpretations of classical sources (this includes non-Hasidic women) has led to their own belief that the female and the feminine are indeed central to orthodoxy.

The hidden, subtle, and, therefore, seemingly deeper spiritual quality of the female is given some credence in other areas of Hasidut as well. According to Handelman, in Hasidic thought, one of the three intellectual powers of a person is called the Mother. On a physical level, writes Handelman, "the feminine power of Binah corresponds to the ability to take the male seed, and develop it into a totally new human being, who contains the essence of its parents" (1979, p. 12). In addition, these women's frequent references to the Shekhinah provide a good example of the way in which they see themselves: the female symbolized as mysterious, and even as the inner essence of God.[24]

Hasidic women were more likely than non-Hasidic women to affirm their honored place in the theology and to assert that orthodoxy itself is associated with the feminine—with godliness. Among the many books, tapes, brochures, and pamphlets I received from women anxious that I read the sources for many of their views, was a magazine, *B'Or Ha'Torah*. The following quotation from Manis Friedman, the somewhat charismatic head of Bais Chana, reinforces these Hasidic women's view of orthodoxy and the "feminine." Speaking of the "feminine" aspect of every Jew, he asserts that this part of being Jewish is not "concerned with evil, it doesn't want to change the world. It wants G-dliness. It absorbs G-dliness" (1981, p. 12). The argument Friedman is building culminates in the following:

> We're all out there fighting the dragons. We're all out there trying to overcome the darkness, but what about the light? Who's taking care of it? Who's taking care of G-dliness and holiness in the world? Who has a sensitivity for right? We're all very sensitive about what's wrong, but who still knows what's right? Who still has a feeling for the G-dliness that you can't always explain? Generally, women (1981, p. 14).

In general, however, despite some familiarity with and knowledge of Hasidic interpretations, non-Hasidic women, while valuing the feminine and the female in orthodoxy, were less likely to claim women's superiority and more likely to refer to the complementarity between men's and women's roles. One woman put it this way: "The beauty of orthodoxy is that it recognizes men and women's strengths . . . it is our complementarity that will bring the peace and justice and the truth to the world." "In Judaism," states another, "there is nothing that values brute force or power for its own sake. The Jewish men I have met, particularly the ba'alei teshuvah, are men who reject those notions of masculinity. I believe that our different Orthodox roles suit our dispositions as men and women. The sacred is the complementarity of the masculine and the feminine . . . the virtues of male and female coming together to create the world." Another woman noted: "Orthodoxy stresses that men's activities are incomplete without the work of women, and vice versa."

Perhaps Hasidic women are not so concerned with unequal gender status because they have a mystical tradition to call upon that strongly supports their view of themselves as spiritually and morally equal to men. If there were any discussion of gender inequality it was to come from non-Hasidic women. Some even saw potential changes in the structure of gender-related roles: "Oh it will probably take another three hundred years," stated one philosophy Ph.D., "but it will happen even in orthodoxy . . . the mechitzah will come down, women will be called to the Torah. We will, if we want, even be rabbis. . . . It's just time, the unfolding of the word takes a long time. . . . I'm in no hurry. These things don't interest me now . . . for now it is enough to be who we are." Therefore, while non-Hasidic women may not pose female activities or sensibilities as superior to those of men, neither do they claim them to be less important or less spiritual.

Whether Hasidic or not, no woman doubts her theological equality in Orthodox Judaism. Women believe they are as capable and worthy of achieving full spiritual bonding with God as men are. In addition, the different relationship between men and women to Torah learning and the synagogue is often characterized in a positive manner. Since their religious obligations are not generally timebound, as are men's, many women experience their female and familial roles as inextricably linked to their religious roles. Women's general exemption from time-bound commandments connotes to many, especially Hasidic women, a greater self-discipline than that of men and an innate spiritual sensibility. Non-Hasidic women, while valuing the feminine symbols and female-related functions, see their gender differences, in role and disposition, as complementary to men's.

Irrespective of their Orthodox stance, it is clear that these ba'alot teshuvah do not see themselves as second-class citizens in orthodoxy. The women under study tend to reflect the apologetic perspective when citing sources or discussing Orthodox Jewish law. Are these women reworking Jewish law and symbols to make a virtue out of necessity? Or, as Biale (1984) suggests, is the "monolithic" and reactionary presentation of Orthodox Jewish law more characteristic of the response of modern Jewish orthodoxy to secularism than a central feature of the law? There is no easy answer to either of those questions. Wegner (1991) perceptively points out that both apologetic and polemic work is flawed by a neglect of primary texts that are, respectively, unfavorable and favorable to women.

The texts that form the basis for Jewish law are voluminous and complex. The style of argumentation is nuanced and intricate. Narrative and law are intermingled in complicated ways. Hauptman claims that the Talmud "defies literary classification" (1974, p. 184). "The Talmud is not," she notes:

> exclusively a law code, a biblical commentary, or a collection of courtroom decisions. It does include commentaries on the verses of the Bible, development of legal concepts and their application to contemporary living, anecdotes from the lives of the rabbis, dialogues with non-Jews, scientific theory, medical advice, and individual opinions on a variety of subjects . . . (1974, p. 184).

Hauptman writes that the Mishnah (a six-volume code of law) forms the superstructure of the Talmud and includes all the legal developments from the time of the Torah. She writes:

> In succeeding generations Jewish scholars, rabbis, began studying this code intensively, explaining the underlying legal principles and applying these laws to new situations as they arose. In the many academies in Babylonia and Israel, notes and questions and answers were appended to the individual laws, and in time this material—the Mishnah together with the explanatory matter, relevant anecdotes, and abstracts of philosophical and theological discussions—coalesced into a work called the Talmud . . . (1974, pp. 184–185).

Chapter Two

The development of and the change in the laws, as well as the transmission of a wide range of opinions (minority as well as majority rulings), attest to the claim that Jewish law is as much a system of argumentation and process as it is dogma.[25] In fact, Biale believes that the law has been characterized "more by disagreement than by consensus . . . more by mechanisms of change than by forces of rigid conservatism" (1984, p. 5). The scholarly material on Jewish law makes it clear that the image and status of women, even in classical rabbinic texts,[26] while reflecting cultural attitudes toward women, are more complex than polemic or apologetic arguments would suggest.[27] Indeed, a selective review of halakhah from biblical to contemporary times finds support for both kinds of arguments and often within the same text.

Another critical issue is that the social reality reflected in the Mishnah and Talmud "is unavoidably distorted by the perspective of the framers and interpreters" (Wegner, 1991, p. 102) and, therefore, represents a highly selective interpretation. Since rabbinic law represents men's social reality (Neusner, 1979; Greenberg, 1981; Nathanson, 1987; Baskin, 1985), it is difficult to know how women may actually have carried on their lives. In fact, some scholars have suggested that the whole corpus of rabbinic law and interpretation is focused on women primarily in relation to men: that is, as daughters, wives, mothers, widows, divorcées, or, as Adler succinctly states it, "as peripheral Jews" (1983, p. 13).[28] Jacob Neusner, scholar of ancient Judaism, writes that the Talmud is a "man's document and imagines a man's world" (1979, p. 94). Furthermore, he notes that in such a worldview, men are the norm and women the aberration. Therefore, versions of social reality gleaned from androcentric interpretations and commentaries on legal ordinances may tell us very little about actual social practices in a specific time and place.[29]

While Wegner contends that the "legal-cultural-social system, now called rabbinic Judaism,[30] which developed in Palestine and Babylonia during the first six centuries C.E., was destined to become normative for virtually all Jewish communities for the next twelve hundred years" (1991, p. 103), other scholars remind us that the halakhah also represents development, change, and controversy (Greenberg, 1981; Biale, 1984). For instance, in following the development of only a few of the laws affecting women, we can see that individual rabbinic authority and specific historic conditions temper the interpretations of what is considered normative Orthodox law for any sociohistoric moment.

Wegner's analysis of the mishnaic rules of women's status reveals two important facts: "First, the system does not treat all women alike; some women are independent of male control and hence can never be treated as chattels. Second, even those women who fall under the authority of specified men are treated as persons in all contexts but one" (Wegner, 1991, p. 104). The most severe restrictions for women, claims Wegner, surround their sexual and reproductive rights. Dependent women, writes Wegner, such as minor daughters, wives,[31] and levirate widows[32] are in stark contrast to autonomous women, such as emancipated (adult, unmarried) daughters, divorcées, and regular widows. For instance, a minor daughter's marriage is arranged by her father, while an adult daughter negotiates her own. Penalties for the rape of a minor accrue to her father, but if she is of age they are given to the woman herself. Wegner explains that the rules follow ownership of sexuality:

> As for wife and divorcée . . . because he owns the sole right to benefit from her sexuality, a husband can revoke his wife's vows that may impair conjugal relations . . . but no one can countermand the vows of a divorcée, since no one owns her sexual function. . . . A husband who divorces his wife for adultery . . . can place no limits on her sexual freedom once released (1991, p. 105).

Wegner continues her analysis of women's low status by noting that a husband divorces his wife by unilaterally renouncing his sexual rights over her body. The wife has no corresponding power. Likewise, the levirate widow is released from marriage only if her husband's brother chooses to do so. On the other hand, Wegner highlights the striking contrast between "the low status of woman as sexual chattel and her far higher status in all other aspects of mishnaic private law" (1991, p. 107).[33] Generally, "In private transactions," writes Wegner,

> the law treats women unequivocally as persons. Thus a wife participates in a reciprocal arrangement of matrimonial entitlements and obligations, performing specified household chores and producing a requisite amount of cloth in return for maintenance at a prescribed standard that befits her social class. . . . Another interesting rule preserves the wife's title to property she brings to the marriage . . . and even her power of sale (though this requires her husband's consent, because of his legal right to the earnings of her property). Likewise, a husband cannot sell his wife's property without her consent. . . .
>
> A wife can appoint agents to transact her business . . . and can act as her husband's agent to sell his goods. . . . She even possesses a right of action against him, for she can petition the court to compel a divorce for specified infringements of her rights . . . at the same time, the court expects the wife, as a person, to honor her obligations (which, in all legal systems, are as much a mark of personhood as is the possession of rights) . . . (1991, pp. 107–108).

In contrast, the autonomous daughter and widow, as long as they remain unattached, are virtually always treated as persons under mishnaic rules. Writes Wegner,

> In a special exception to the rule that women are incompetent as witnesses . . . the autonomous woman can even testify to her right to the bride-price of virgins, when arranging her marriage or when recovering her marriage settlement on termination of the marriage. . . . A woman is deemed as competent as a man to answer certain business-related oaths (1991, p. 110).

In summary, except for the dependent woman's control of her sexuality, the primary source for the status of women in Jewish law, the Mishnah, supports the view that women are persons in their own right for virtually all areas in the private domain of life. In contrast, rules governing women in the public domain virtually exclude women from all the "intellectual and spiritual forms and forums of mishnaic culture" (Wegner, 1991, p. 111).[34]

While Biale (1984) agrees that there is consensus in the halakhah on many issues and that there is a general resistance to change, she also notes a trend toward increasing woman's rights and protection in many areas of halakhah.[35] For instance, postbiblical changes made it increasingly difficult for husbands to divorce their wives and provided opportunities for wives to petition the courts to compel their husbands to give them a divorce. The *ketubah*, a marriage contract, outlines the general obligations of husbands toward their wives and lists their financial commitments both within and at the dissolution of the marriage. Although women were generally still passive in the creation and dissolution of a marriage, the circumstances under which a woman could compel a man to divorce her included "offensive physical conditions, violation of marital obligations, and for some authorities sexual incompatibility, and wife-beating" (Biale, 1984, p. 96).[36] Over time, other changes aimed at protecting and expanding women's rights, particularly in marriage, were forthcoming.[37] By the Middle Ages, Rabbenu Gershom of Mainz, Germany, banned "forcible divorce (issuing a get without the wife's consent)" (Greenberg, 1981, p. 64). He also "temporarily banned polygamy upon pain of excommunication. [A]lthough its time limit expired in the Hebrew year 5000, polygamy never again was practiced by Jews in Ashkenzic Europe. In oriental countries, where multiple wives were common, Jews continued to practice polygamy right through the modern period" (Greenberg, 1981, p. 64).

Biale (1984) writes: "The laws of *onah*, the sexual relations between husband and wife . . . require a man to satisfy his wife's sexual needs, and at the same time forbid him to rape his wife" (1984, p. 6).[38] Unlike the laws in forty-three American states in which a husband cannot be charged with the rape of his wife if they are living together (Russell, 1982, p. 23), the Talmud makes it clear that rape in marriage is possible. Biale cites several sources, including Maimonides, which define rape in marriage as the husband's coercion of his wife to have sexual relations.[39] She writes of the basic trend in the evolution of the halakhah concerning rape as representing "a conscious effort to protect women from the charge that they were willing participants in a prohibited sexual act, that they 'brought it on themselves,' or that their hidden wish is to be coerced into intercourse" (1984, p. 255). She notes that the talmudic text makes clear that even if a woman "refuses to be rescued from her rapist," if the sexual act began under "duress and intimidation," it is still rape (1984, p. 255).

However, all extensions of women's rights are set within a patriarchal mind-set.[40] Biale writes:

Much as the rabbis and later legal authorities at times impress and even surprise us with their comprehension of the condition of women in their society, and their efforts to better it, whatever could be done to increase women's legal rights and protect them remained within a legal system which women could never penetrate. The authority to make halakhic decisions has always been the province of men. . . . While women could and did gain more halakhic rights in the course of generations, they never gained halakhic power. They have been silent recipients, outsiders to the process (1984, pp. 7–8).

Moreover, although women are taught some of the laws, they are not taught to trace the developments and extensions of the laws to new situations, even when such situations directly affect activities for which they are responsible (Danzger, 1989).[41]

Saul Berman, former head of Stern College, the leading Orthodox college for women in the United States, gives further credence to this view when he notes (1976) that the talmudic sages made no attempt to formulate a general principle governing the status of women. The closest they came, he claims, was in the attempt to define, under a single heading, the affirmative precepts from which women are exempt. However, although women are bound like men to all commandments not limited by time, they are not, in fact, exempt from all time-bound commandments. Berman readily points out the inconsistency of this. For instance, some affirmative principles limited to time such as eating matzah, rejoicing on festivals, and *hakhel* (assembling) are required of women, and others, not limited to time, such as the study of Torah, procreation, and redemption of the first born, are proscribed. Berman cites serious debates among noted talmudic scholars as to whether women are indeed exempt from individual, positive, time-bound precepts.

In response to apologists for orthodoxy who argue that women are exempt from such time-bound activities as daily prayer and study, but are not forbidden to do them, Berman notes that such distinctions undermine the reality that women's exclusion from the public world of synagogue and study results in their inability to represent the community at large. He writes:

> While not self-evident, it is clear in rabbinic literature that the exemption of women from obligations of participation in communal worship results in their disqualification from being counted in the quorum necessary to engage in such worship. For each member of the *minyan* must stand equal in obligation and capable of fulfilling the obligation on behalf of the entire *minyan* (1976, p. 122).

He makes clear that the same insidious process operates in civil law:

> Similarly, in civil matters, the fact that women are relieved of the obligation to testify, results in their inability to be part of pair of witnesses who bind the fact-finding process of the court. The law begins with the desire to exempt women from mandatory public appearances and therefore deprives the courts, in effect, of subpoena power over women. But, in turn, the inability of the court to compel her presence results in the correlative loss on the part of women of the power to compel the court to find the facts to be in accord with their testimony (1976, p. 122).

Yet, despite the patriarchal rules and processes, the women under study maintain strong woman-centered identities and values and make claims upon men for nurturance, commitment, and communication. The next chapters will trace how they do so, as we look at them in relationship to their bodies, to their families, and to one another.

CHAPTER THREE

•

Sex-segregated Living

Celebrating the Female

Two Jewish feminists underscore the problems Orthodox Jewish women face in recreating women's experiences in patriarchal living. In describing women's ritual responsibilities within orthodoxy, Rachel Adler stresses that while the Orthodox woman's commandments reinforce family and community, they do not "cultivate the relationship between the individual and God" (1983, p.13). She describes the Orthodox woman's ritual responsibilities in the following way:

> A woman keeps kosher because both she and her family must have kosher food. She lights the Shabbat candles so that there will be light, and, hence, peace, in the household. She goes to the *mikvah* so that her husband can have intercourse with her and she bears children so that, through her, he can fulfill the exclusively male *mitzvah* of increasing and multiplying (1983, p.14).

Susannah Heschel argues that the older biblical, rabbinic, and medieval images and attitudes toward women inherited from a male-dominated perspective "affect the personal lives of men and woman" (1983, p. xxxi). She claims that "if woman is Other in the synagogue, . . . liturgy, and theology, she is bound to be treated as Other in the home, family, and community" (1983, p. xxxi–xxxii). Theology's role in transforming women within Judaism is paramount to Heschel: "Questions of role and identity cannot be raised outside the larger context of the images which give rise to them and the theological positions which legitimate them. Clearly there is a need for theological reinterpretations to transform women in Judaism from object to subject" (1983, p. xxxii).

There is no doubt that the theological foci in rabbinic Judaism are male-oriented. The synagogue and yeshivot do play important roles in structuring the public and corporate community that calls itself Orthodox. The sociological and theological portrait of orthodoxy presented at this public level is indeed a male universe. Leadership, both sacred and secular, is male-dominated.

There is also ample evidence, both sociological and theological, that attests to women's second-class status within orthodoxy. Feminists have emphasized the most blatant, and, the not-so-obvious areas of discrimination and oppression. They have asked for changes in divorce law, inclusion in the secular leadership of Jewish communal agencies, and for concrete changes in the structure of the community (from day-care centers to the acceptance of single mothers and homosexuals within the Jewish community). The inviolability of the Jewish code of law mitigates against the possibility of women challenging a legal system developed, defined, and continuously refined by males. Moreover, if women are not encouraged or given the opportunities to study the very texts (Gemara, for instance) from which the interpretations of those laws derive, there is no opportunity for them to challenge those laws in a manner that the community will perceive as authentic or legitimate; or to develop female leadership.

What, then, maintains these women's commitment to a past not of their own making? How is it possible to conclude that these women's lives are anything but oppressive and "alienated"? To account for women's commitment to patriarchal settings, some feminists have relied upon arguments that stress "false consciousness," or a powerlessness to change the conditions of their existence. What is missing in these portraits, however, is the understanding that women are often simultaneously victims and agents, subjects and objects. Theoretical categories cannot distinguish between an "authentic" and an "alienated" woman's experience. Vital human experiences cannot be reduced to abstract orthodoxies—feminist or religious. When we describe lives according to a series of purely abstract claims we form what Eleanor Leacock (1977) would call an unwarranted teleology. Jean Elshtain (1984) calls for analytic categories as rich and robust as the lives people really live. Rigid analytic categories, she notes, will not capture the complexities and tensions that make up everyday behavior. We seldom, she writes, see the world through such complicated self-understandings.

Some Jewish feminists base their analyses on abstractions, which of necessity ignore the historical effect ongoing dynamics have on the production and social influence of ideas. The portraits of these ba'alot teshuvah come from their own language and self-understandings. In this study I have not relied on historical abstractions to explain a woman's "place" in Jewish orthodoxy, but rather upon immediate and concrete experiences (Foucault, 1976).

The feminist theologian Elizabeth Schussler-Fiorenza notes that formal patriarchal law is generally more restrictive than actual interactions and relationships among men and women; and, more important, are projections of male reality (in Setta, 1984, p. 96). Anthropologists have long understood that women often use their differences from men as a way of manipulating their position in society. Writes Rosaldo: "By accepting and elaborating upon the symbols and expectations associated with their cultural definition, they may goad men into compliance, or establish a society unto themselves" (1974, p. 37). Therefore, reasons Rosaldo, "the symbolic and social conceptions that appear to set women apart and to circumscribe their activities may be used by women as a basis for female solidarity and worth" (1974, p. 37).

Jewish feminists' theological conclusions pose the beginnings of important sociological questions. Do women experience orthodoxy in the way in which they are theologically described? Schussler-Fiorenza (in Setta, 1984) asserts that texts and historical sources must be read as androcentric and warns that prescriptive statements do not capture women's actual "social religious status." How do we avoid an analytical framework that reduces women to "robots," "fools," or "victims"? asks Judith Stacey (1983). Is there a greater range of relationships to the practices of orthodoxy than that which Adler describes? Do women experience themselves as Other, as Heschel believes?

The norms and behavioral patterns associated with the family purity laws perhaps best exemplify how the ba'alot teshuvah observe patriarchal law, while recasting its social meaning. Their interpretation of one of the most important laws pertaining to their lives as Orthodox women illustrates simultaneously how they accommodate and recast Orthodox ritual. The rituals surrounding niddah and mikveh have deep historic and biblical ties. In the way they observe and interpret these rituals, many ba'alot teshuvah place their sexuality in a timeless, spiritual, and sometimes quite erotic context, rather than in a merely physical or personal realm. They describe their sexuality within marriage not as a biological need or self-expression, but rather as a holy ritual. Initially, many began their "journeys" toward orthodoxy as a response to their frustration with contemporary living. These ba'alot teshuvah rejects the idea that the self is the only "authentic" core of reality. They wanted something that transcended the self; they wanted moral certitude, and they wanted it most especially in the reconstruction of their personal lives.

In Jewish orthodoxy, sexuality is not self-expression alone, but a communal and spiritual act. Noting the two-week separation between husbands and wives required during her menstruation, one woman noted: "One half of the month I belong to my husband; the other half to God." Intimacy is placed in a sacred and communal context. Moreover, intimacy is not dependent solely upon individual needs or wants, but upon Orthodox role-playing with all of its rules and limitations.[1] For these women, sexuality is not reduced to an idiosyncratic self or to a core identity, but rather to Orthodox role-playing incumbent upon both men and women. These women claim they have reconstructed their personal lives by reconnecting the self (through expressive actions in their most private lives) to the public Orthodox community of timeless truths.[2] They describe a world in which both the private and the public are sacred and morally ordered.

THE LAWS OF NIDDAH: MENSTRUAL IMPURITY AND SEXUAL PROHIBITION

In Jewish law the menstruant woman has a defined status, she is a *niddah* (excluded person). The laws which define this status are complex. They rest on the foundation of two different contexts: the laws surrounding purity and impurity and those surrounding sexual prohibitions. The niddah appears in Leviticus in two contexts: laws intent on excluding an impure person or object from entering the Temple (Biale, 1984, p. 147), together with other forms of defilement, impurity, and death (Leviticus 11:24–15:33)[3] and laws regulating forbidden sexual relations (Leviticus 18 and 20). Adler (1976) writes that the cycle of *tumah* (impurity) and *taharah* (purity) is the way in which the Jew acts out her or his death and resurrection:

> *Tumah* is the result of our confrontation with the face of our own mortality. It is the going down into darkness. *Taharah* is the result of our reaffirmation of our own immortality. It is the reentry into light. *Tumah* is evil or frightening only when there is no further life. Otherwise, *tumah* is simply part of the human cycle. To be *tameh* [ritually impure] is not wrong or bad, often it is necessary and sometimes it is mandatory (1976, p. 64).

In the ancient religious worldview, she reasons, tumah was not perceived as causing physical consequences, nor was it viewed as dangerous in any way. Since some of the basic human functions and behaviors cause tumah, every member of society regularly underwent the cycle from tumah to taharah (an accepted component of the human condition). Biale underscores Adler's point, when she notes that there is no particular gravity attached to impurity, let alone indication that it is considered an offense or sin. Again, the state of impurity in and of itself is not a transgression; it meant only that an individual could not enter or partake of food in the Temple precincts in Jerusalem until purified. In Leviticus 15, writes Biale, impurity is an objective, if not undesirable, state which one should seek to avoid and remove by following proper

71

ritual (1984, p. 154). Similarly, Biale argues, in Leviticus 15, intercourse with a niddah causes a state of impurity, but "there is no hint that it is considered a sin" (1984, p. 155).[4]

To counteract the state of impurity (the length of time one remained impure varied according to type of tumah contracted),[5] immersion in a ritual bath (mikveh),[6] a natural gathering of freely flowing water or its equivalent, was necessary. Symbolically, the contact with death could then be reversed and a person returned to a state of ritual purity. Adler describes the mikveh as a "primal sea from which all life comes, the womb of the world, the amniotic tide in which the unborn child is rocked" (1983, p. 68). To be reborn, she writes, "one must reenter this womb and drown in living water" (1983, p. 68). In this way, she notes, we confront and experience our own death and resurrection.[7] It is a renewal, a recreation, a regeneration of the life forces. In the ancient cultic world, the tangible communal reward was access to the sanctuary (Greenberg, 1981).

Postbiblical sources, sources following the destruction of the Second Temple in Jerusalem in 70 C.E., reveal a fundamental transformation in the laws of niddah from the realm of ritual impurity to marital and sexual relations. The emphasis shifted to the second context and meaning of the laws of niddah in the Bible: the sexual prohibitions.[8] In fact, Biale notes that this shift from purity laws to sexual taboos is even evident after the First Temple was destroyed.[9] However, the transformation became more pronounced after the Second Temple was destroyed and as Judaism changed from a sacrificial cult to a community or family-centered religion. Rabbi Emanuel Feldman explains that "cultic purity was extended to the home, and later on, study of Torah was substituted for cultic sacrifice and deeds of loving kindness for sin-offering, so it was now natural to take over the purity-rules and to endow them with ethical, therefore with everyday, communal significance" (Feldman, 1977, p. 89).[10]

Blu Greenberg (1981) suggests that the postbiblical treatment of the laws of niddah, despite the shifting emphasis to sexual prohibitions after the destruction of the Second Temple, never completely lost an association with impurity and defilement.

Sometimes the two themes, she writes, are "intertwined, sometimes overshadowed, sometimes parallel" (p. 112). Specifically, she notes that when the Mishnah was codified, approximately two hundred years after the destruction of the Second Temple, it is significant that the tractate *Niddah* fell not under the section head "Women," but under "Purification." Adler makes clear, however, that the newly created legal category, "Purity of the Family," changes the interpretation of the purity ritual from an individual spiritual experience to an enabling activity. She continues her analysis:

> The *mitzvah* itself was reinterpreted, not as an individual spiritual experience born out of the metaphor of one's own bodily cycle, but as an enabling activity through which women safeguarded the purity of husbands and children: the purity of the *family*.
>
> Yet all this evidence, damning as it is, does not invalidate the original *mitzvah*. *Tumah/taharah* remains one of the few major Jewish symbolisms in which women had a place. Having so few authentic traditional experiences on which to build, is it worthwhile to reject *niddah*, because later generations of men have projected their repugnance for women upon it? (1976, p. 71).

Other writers have pointed to the often negative attitudes toward menstruation and the menstruant woman found in both talmudic and post-talmudic sources (Greenberg, 1981; Hauptman, 1982; Biale, 1984; Baskin, 1985).[11] Biale (1984) suggests that sometimes extremely negative interpretations found their way into mainstream opinions and, in some instances, were in direct contradiction to the halakhah. In postbiblical halakhah, the exclusion of a menstruating woman from cultic life in order to prevent her from approaching the Temple shifts to restrictions on the niddah in the private realm of husband-wife relations. However, the laws of niddah proper do not exclude a woman from contact with others or even from attending synagogue, since without the Temple, impurities do not pertain, and, as Biale writes, "since it is of no consequence if others come in contact with her and become impure, and since the Torah scroll, the 'holy object' in a synagogue, is immune to impurity" (1984, p. 167). Yet customs and actual practice appear to have limited the menstruating woman considerably. Biale writes that while "the Halakhah restricts the *niddah* in her relationship with her husband but not in her interaction with other family members, friends, and society at large, the custom of many Jewish communities did curtail the activities of the *niddah* in the public sphere" (1984, p. 167). Biale conjectures that the custom may have prevailed because the synagogue "is symbolic of the Temple where in biblical times the presence of an impure person was indeed prohibited. Perhaps it is also because the degree of isolation of the *niddah* from public affairs in general was greater in practice than was mandated by the Halakhah" (1984, p. 167).

It is clear that the laws concerning a woman in niddah could be viewed in oppositional ways. Using Washbourn's (1979) "demonic" and "graceful" categories, Ginsburg elaborates:

> The graceful is that which integrates a woman's physiology into a wider social and symbolic framework. The demonic reduces female identity to its biological aspects. In the initial context of purification rites for the temple [sic], the Jewish laws concerning the *nidda* reflect a graceful development that includes women in sexual sanctions applied to all members of the community. In the second Levitical reference, the menstruant woman is selected out from the rest of the community as offensive in terms of her reproductive physiology. These two interpretive options have been differentially stressed as women's social roles have changed according to historical and material circumstances (1981, p. 4).

Feminists have pointed to the insidious dimensions of the belief in menstrual impurity and that such beliefs continue to exist in a more diluted form in our contemporary culture (Douglas, 1966; Culpepper, 1974; Dinnerstein, 1976; Delaney, Lupton, and Toth, 1976; Weideger, 1977). The rituals concerning the menstruating woman can be interpreted as either "graceful" or "demonic," to use Washbourn's terms. How do these contemporary ba'alot teshuvah experience niddah and mikveh?

PRACTICING FAMILY PURITY LAWS

According to talmudic law, separation between husband and wife should be maintained for at least twelve days, five for the actual period of flow and seven additional days during which no bleeding is visible (called "clean" or "white" days). On the evening of her seventh "white" day, or any day thereafter upon her choosing, a woman goes to the mikveh.

On that day she handles no sticky substances that might adhere to her skin. Before the ritual immersion she removes all foreign things from her body, such as wigs, jewelry, Bandaids, nail polish, and makeup. She cuts her nails, takes an ordinary bath, washes and combs her hair, and brushes her teeth. In fact, food is prohibited after her bath and before her immersion in the mikveh.[12] Usually a woman makes an appointment with the attendant to use the mikveh after sunset. Once in the ritual pool, with her legs slightly apart, arms outstretched and fingers spread, she immerses herself completely until every strand of hair is covered. This act performed in the presence of an attendant, is repeated twice after she recites a prayer blessing the act of immersion.

When asked about the family purity laws, these newly Orthodox women almost unanimously used the "graceful" rather than the "demonic" to characterize their experiences and feelings about niddah and mikveh. Most eschewed the understanding of themselves as "unclean" and referred to the counting of the postmenstrual days as the "white," not "clean" days. "During niddah," explained one particularly articulate woman, who, although a ba'alat teshuvah, had come so far in her own studies that she taught seminars on the laws of niddah, "the woman falls between categories of life and death." She noted that she often calls upon nonlegal but traditional sources of explanation to frame discussions of niddah and mikveh. "For instance, when it is questioned why women and not men are still subject to impurity rituals, I look to traditional explanations. . . . [Y]ou can find one that suggests that women are closer to God because of their ability to create life and that they are therefore subject to purity rituals . . . still another views the woman's body as a 'holy' temple.[13] I like to think of a woman's cycle as part of all the sacred time rhythms in Judaism—the Shabbat, holidays. . . . "

The following quotations underscore how important and meaningful the laws of *niddah* are to these women: "Even before I became religious and was living with my boyfriend (now my husband), we began to practice the laws of niddah. I thought it the most wonderful thing, it made good sense."

A Ph.D. in psychology who lived with her then lover, now husband,[14] in Jerusalem noted that the laws of niddah most fully interested her when she was introduced to orthodox Jewish law, while occasionally attending a ba'al teshuvah institute in Israel:

> I had counseled many young people about sexual practices when I lived in the United States. When I first read about taharat hamishpacha they made absolutely good sense to me . . . psychologically speaking, that is. I leaned over in bed and shared with Daniel [a fictitious name] what I was reading. We made a commitment to try this practice for at least one month. We got separate beds. I went to the mikveh and when next we made love it was wonderful. I smile now, really not because I am embarrassed, but because of how much I have grown since then. You see, then it seemed like a lark; it made good psychological sense to me. Now it has so much more meaning. . . . I practice niddah with other women and we share in a sacred ritual that connects us to our past and with our children and their children.

But not all introductions to sexual orthodoxy are so sanguine. Another woman recalls her first introduction to the laws of niddah:

> I was terrified of water and immersion. I knew I could not be an Orthodox mother and wife if I was not able to use the mikveh. I went for counseling and it did not help. My boyfriend [now husband] said that we should marry anyway and that this would somehow be resolved. We loved each other and would live like sister and brother if necessary until I could overcome my fear. I tried going to the mikveh several times before we were married. The first time I

went to the mikveh, the attendant talked with me for several hours; I could not immerse myself. After several tries over the first few months, I finally decided to try it slowly, very slowly. As I went under for the first time I concentrated on how this one act linked me to generations of other women. . . . I lost my fear completely. I truly felt renewed, like a new woman capable of anything I really set my mind to. I'll also say that my friends were especially supportive in this. . . . we all had a big party at my house afterward.

Almost all women noted the positive functions of the family purity laws. Most frequently cited were claims of increased sexual interest and pleasure within the marriage. Although newly married women were more likely to complain about sexual separation, those married over longer periods of time and with more children found the laws quite positive over the adult life cycle. One woman notes:

When we were first married I found it hard to consider sexual separation as a positive thing. In fact, during my menstrual cycle I felt I wanted to be held and loved more than at other times of the month. But I must admit over the years it truly serves as a renewal . . . it is really like being a bride again . . . well, almost.

Even among the newly married, many claimed that forced separation heightened desire.

Others referred to the autonomy and control they experienced when practicing the laws of niddah. Invoking Virginia Woolf, one woman noted, "It allows me a bed of my own." Others referred to the increased time for themselves: "I can curl up with a good book during niddah and not feel in the least bit guilty." Other women emphasized the increased time for themselves, and still others spoke of a kind of control over their sexuality. "I can say no with no pretense of a headache if I wish," claimed one newly married woman. Other women suggested that the family purity laws provide a sexual rhythm to marriage for both partners.

Because these women have to attend intimately to their bodies to engage in sexual activity according to religious law, many speak of an increased awareness of their bodies they had never known before, evident in the following response:

> At this time of the month I am acutely aware of myself, everything is heightened because I am paying attention to what is happening inside of me. Over the years it is building a cycle for me; it's a rhythm that is related to me and my body alone.

While most of the women seem to enjoy the rejuvenation and spiritual uplifting of going to the mikveh, not all were uniformly happy about the length of time they were separated from their husbands during the month. Indeed, if anything, it was length of time, not the practice of the laws, about which women complained. However, even their complaints were expressed in positive terms. A good number of women suggested that the practices surrounding the period of niddah force them and their husbands to learn new forms of communication and, perhaps more important, to use those newly found skills.[15] "Most men don't know how to talk things out," claims one woman, "but since approximately one-half of my year is spent in niddah, I have found that we are forced to talk about things more and that he has learned to show his love in ways more important than just physical contact."

From the earliest literature on marital satisfaction (Bernard, 1971) to the more recent (Schwartz and Blumstein, 1983), it is clear that communication (sexual and otherwise) is a major problem for middle-class women. Specific data on the frequency of sexual intercourse and sexual satisfaction and experimentation were not forthcoming. Modesty rules inhibit truly open discourse about such details. However, when discussing the marital purity laws, almost all women made some references to the laws of onah. They told me that women are entitled to an active and satisfying sexuality in marriage.[16] Perhaps because they are ba'alot teshuvah and not frum from birth, as they often categorize other Orthodox women, these women may have been more forthcoming than other Orthodox women about their sexuality. "Do you know that a husband cannot abstain from sex without regard to his wife's feelings and needs?" noted one woman. "Onah," suggested one ba'alat teshuvah who had studied in a yeshiva in Israel, "concern a woman's sexual pleasure, not her procreative functions." One woman noted that even in "ancient times a woman could seek a divorce if her husband did not properly support her or sexually satisfy her." "Do you know," claimed one woman, "according to halakhah, my husband is commanded to kiss *every* part of my body?"[17]

In Jewish orthodoxy, men are commanded to marry, to procreate, and to perform their conjugal duties at regular times.[18] The main obligations for women are to observe the laws associated with a menstruant woman. They are not commanded to marry and they are explicitly exempted from the duty of procreation. As Biale writes: "Other than the general obligation not to consistently and unreasonably refuse sexual relations with the husband, women do not really have 'sexual obligations' in marriage" (1984, p. 122). On the other hand, men are specifically instructed to please and satisfy their wives.[19]

Feldman (1974) notes that a man can deny himself, but not his wife, pleasure.[20] Moreover, he says, a man cannot force his attentions on his wife, but must be attentive to her needs and cues for sexual intercourse. Since the legislation around onah is concerned with a woman's sexual pleasure, not her procreative needs, husbands' obligations to satisfy their wives sexually are detailed in the Talmud and the Code.

While I do not believe that all of these women are sexually satisfied, in control of their sexuality, or personally happy with marriage, it is quite clear that they believe that the laws of niddah and mikveh function positively for women within marriage. Frequently women would state, "My husband cannot take me for granted" or, as one woman put it, "My husband's sexual desire is not the only consideration." One woman who had been married to another man before her current marriage bluntly acknowledged that her heterosexual life prior to this marriage was a disaster:

> To put it crudely, my former husband's main interest in life was in his pockets and what's between them. Money and sex. We communicated about nothing and had a lot of sex. After a while I found

that he was having affairs with at least two other women. By then I
didn't care, I just wanted out of the marriage and I didn't want my
children growing up with him as their father. . . . Even before I
remarried, I knew that a marriage in the Orthodox community was
one in which I could have faith. I mean that literally. Every aspect
would be a part of something larger than just us . . . something
spiritual and holy.

These twentieth-century women use female-linked religious
symbols as a way of limiting and controlling males.[21] Like those in
the social purity movement of the nineteenth century, who de-
plored the sexual double standard and wished not to extend men's
sexual privileges to women, the ba'alot teshuvah speak of niddah
and mikveh as a way of sexually constraining *both* men and
women. Therefore, modesty and the family purity laws are
double-edged. Although they serve as a means of social control,
particularly of women, they are also a means of obtaining
control—by restraining oneself and others.[22]

However, the experiences these women describe are more than
responses to controlling males or accommodation techniques.
While they do believe that the laws encourage men to respect them
as sexual beings, increase their own self-respect (particularly toward their bodies), and heighten sexual desire, there seems to be
more than that. The symbolic framework emerging from their
language, imagery, and experiences moves beyond the self and the
dyad to the community at large. Indeed the pride with which one
leader of her community took in taking me on a tour of the newly
completed mikveh was unmistakable. The women had raised the
money in their own sisterhood and helped the architect with the
design. The more affluent the community, the more commodious
and luxurious the mikveh. One mikveh I visited was constructed
all in redwood with a sauna and an elaborate dressing room. Blow-
dryers and vanity tables were also available. One community
boasts the only solar-heated mikveh in the country.

Without the mikveh the community of believers that calls itself
Orthodox could not be reproduced. Therefore, the immersion in
the mikveh is more than personal sanctity. It also represents the

sanctity of the community. The mikveh, although legally required for women only, has deep symbolic and communal meaning. It is sued as the final step in conversion to Judaism. A groom sometimes uses the mikveh before his wedding, some Jews purify themselves before the Sabbath or holy days, and it may be used by men and women whenever they want to renew or establish a deeper commitment to Judaism. No woman doubted the importance of the mikveh to the community. As one woman put it: "There is no doubt about it . . . if a choice has to be made, a community has to build a mikveh before it can build a shul or even acquire a Sefer Torah."

But it is to yet another larger community that mikveh unites these women. "I feel connected to history and to other women," says one ba'alat teshuvah who has practiced the laws of niddah since her marriage twelve years before. Feeling a sense of history, one woman mused: "The Jews at Masada used the mikveh." "Each time I use the mikveh I feel I come back to the center of Judaism and to my own core," a woman married fifteen years proclaimed. What became clear after several years of interviewing was that for these women the core of Judaism emanates from activities and obligations shared with other women even, and perhaps most ironically, when speaking of the religious ritual surrounding their heterosexuality.

A heightened air of sensuousness and intimacy surrounds the practices of niddah and mikveh. These rituals create a world in which women, not men, are the central actors despite the heterosexual goals. "I have been to the mikveh all over the world," stated one ba'alat teshuvah, "and there is a sense of togetherness. There are unspoken codes among women . . . no one ever counts or questions another woman's use of the mikveh." Indeed there is something private, almost secretive, and emphatically intimate about the ways in which the women describe their experiences. "I feel closer to all women who share in the practice of mikveh," claimed one woman. "We share all kinds of unspoken secrets with one another. After all we celebrate our bodies, our sexuality, our regenerative powers in the same way. . . ."

After immersion in the mikveh, women and men are allowed to

resume sexual intercourse. Forgetting that completion of the mikveh ritual is often a prelude to sexual activity, I once almost overstayed my welcome at one respondent's home. I had accompanied one woman to the mikveh, where we met others from the same community, including the woman with whom I had the next interview. My next interviewee and I spoke for a while at the mikveh and then I accompanied her to her home to continue the interview. As we concluded the interview, she smiled at me and said that although she was enjoying the conversation she really did not want to make it a long night. She then hesitated, and I, belatedly picking up her cue, left soon thereafter.

Nothing attests to the social construction of sexuality and the true meaning of the erotic better than how these women describe the religious rituals which heighten their sexuality. Many find erotic fantasies in the social act of "cleansing the body" for purity purposes. A woman married three years states:

> All the connotations of being a bride again are brought back. It is even more than the anticipation of making love but the whole secret sharing of it with other women, a friend I may meet at the mikveh or the friend who might take care of the baby when I go, that makes it all more, I don't know, sort of sexy.

By maintaining and preserving appearances of chastity and not talking directly about their sexuality, the ba'alot teshuvah seem to stimulate and deepen their sense of sexuality.[23] Although head-coverings and hemlines may vary from community to community and from woman to woman, all women abide in some way by the code of modesty in dress, conversation, personal habits, and in public displays of affection with men. Prior to their entrance into the Orthodox community, most would have found tzniut an alien concept; or as one woman put it, "'Victorian'—you know, 'prudish.'" Eschewing prudish and Victorian reasons for abiding by these modesty customs, one woman compared them to the values of a sexually liberated society. The same ba'alat teshuvah who taught seminars on the family purity laws notes: "I find that those things we consider so intimate—like a kiss or a hug—meaningless if you give them to everyone. It's easy to 'turn on' in this community, hard to do so out there."

The practices of niddah and mikveh celebrate the woman, body and soul. The ritual both constrains and extends. For the ba'alot teshuvah, the family purity laws represent the purity rites surrounding the entrance to the Second Temple. Renewal and regeneration of life forces are themes that run throughout these women's commentaries. The themes of sexual and sacred are concomitant for them. Immersion in the mikveh nullifies their state of impurity and gives rise for them to another cycle of sexuality and generativity.

Wechsler argues that the ritual cycle of niddah and mikveh help women recover the deep, spiritual meaning that accompanies their recurring cycles. She writes:

> The women who can enter this ritual and participate in such a fullness of meaning may experience an affinity and a powerful reconciliation with the source of all that is. This is, at a deep level, the dynamic of atonement.[24] Rather than being outside the sacred circle, this dynamic oscillation places her firmly within it (1981, p. 24).

Women's separateness, apartness, and even otherness are microcosmically emblematic of the Orthodox community itself—a community separate, apart, and "other" from the larger "gentile" society.[25] As noted earlier, one ba'alat teshuvah suggested that women represent the values attached to the "community as a whole." Menstrual impurity for these ba'alot teshuvah is experienced as part of the symbolism of death and rebirth through the cycles of their own bodies. For most, their recurring impurity is connected to holiness. Jewish marriage, and consequently, conjugal relations are seem as "holy"—the "sanctuary here on earth"—as many women voiced it. These women's association with the purity cycle becomes for them a symbolic claim upon the community at large.

Faye Ginsburg provides one of the few empirical examples of the practices of the laws of niddah and the use of mikveh. Reporting on her data from two upwardly mobile Syrian Jewish communities, she demonstrates how the rituals transform the most explicitly private and individual of relationships into matters of public concern and even collective pressure (1981, p. 9):

> In the most delicate and seemingly individual of social arenas, these rituals give Syrian Jewish women authority and collective strength in shaping male sexuality. Using a potent symbolic vocabulary, women are actively creating a situation in which their biological and social experience of being female is integrated gracefully and powerfully into communal life (1981, p. 18).

For Ginsburg, these rituals allow women to maintain social power, moral authority, and control over the sexuality of men. The laws, she notes, provide a symbolic barrier that women impose not only on themselves and their daughters, but, more important, on men.

Although many of the ba'alot teshuvah under study appreciate or at least allude to the ways in which the laws surrounding sexuality protect women, there is evidence that this is not the only appeal of the laws of family purity. The many remarks about heightened sexuality and a better sense of their own bodies bespeaks more than simple control or restraint over men within marriage. Eschewing an open and uninhibited approach to sexuality, these ba'alot teshuvah refer to the sensuous, emotional, and evocative features of sexuality. Many believe they are reconnecting sexuality to something more sensuous and spiritual than what they experienced prior to their return to orthodoxy. The experience and meaning of sexuality supersedes, for them, the dyad alone. These ba'alot teshuvah connect their most private experiences to a wider social and communal setting where sexuality is socially defined, not individually developed. For many of these women, sexuality and, as we shall see in the following chapter, mothering are communal acts, more extensive than self-experience, thereby linking women beyond themselves, or the dyad, to the larger religious community.

Keeping with the theoretical orientation of a double hermeneutic,[26] we shall see in the next few chapters how these women place their "born again" choices in the larger context of contemporary society and how the patriarchal context of sex-segregated living yields systems of action and meaning that are both the result and the medium of men's and women's cultural practices.[27]

CHAPTER FOUR

•

Revaluing Domesticity

Ba'alot Teshuvah and Religious-Right Women

Religious and political social movements are more likely to flourish if they explain problems of everyday life and provide possible resolutions (Liebman, 1983). The roots of the crisis of meaning which led many of these women on what they perceive as their homeward journeys are reflected in more than the absence of community and an ideology of individualism.[1] Historical changes in the family, and, consequently, in the nature and meaning of personal life, have also set the stage for a "return."

The "normative order" which once bound individuals to marriage, childrearing, and the many constraints and obligations required of family life has weakened. In *The Hearts of Men*, Ehrenreich claims that the contemporary moral climate endorses "irresponsibility, self-indulgence, and an isolationist detachment from the claims of others." This irresponsibility, she reasons, is most clearly seen in a flight from family commitment, particularly by men (1983, p. 169).[2] For many scholars, industrial capitalism provides the key component in analyzing this emphasis on self and personal fulfillment. Trask argues:

> [E]xtended kinship relations which had joined productive labor to subjective experience and had brought the individual a communal rather than a private existence dissolved under the impact of capitalism. With the decline of communal relationships came the tightening interactions of the conjugal unit. The bourgeois family (reduced to the preservation of property) and the proletarian family

(reduced to the reproduction of the labor force) both began to concentrate their increasing leisure time on a search for personal fulfillment (1986, p. 34).[3]

Stripped of its productive functions, argues Zaretsky, the family "threatens to become a well of subjectivity divorced from any social meaning" (1973, p. 122). He concludes:

> The "individualist values," generated by centuries of bourgeois development—self-consciousness, perfectionism, independence—have taken new shape through the insatiability of personal life in developed capitalist society. . . . [T]he internal life of the family is dominated by a search for personal fulfillment for which there seem to be *no rules*. Much of this search has been at the expense of women (1973a, pp. 122–123, emphasis mine).[4]

The choices ba'alot teshuvah make must be placed within a specific historic context. In Chapter One I argued that most of the ba'alot teshuvah came to orthodoxy during a period of cultural confusion and confrontation, described by many analysts as a time of normative breakdown and increasing moral ambiguity (Robbins, Anthony, and Richardson, 1978), a time, writes Bellah (1976), when Americans could no longer trust or find a complex of symbolic meanings to unite them in a moral community. In that the women under study feel that liberal individualism has failed to provide a basis for moral discourse, the pursuit of personal fulfillment over commitment and obligation becomes particularly threatening.[5] If contemporary family life is dominated by a search for personal fulfillment for which there are few rules, it becomes increasingly difficult for women to expect men to honor the claims of traditional family living.[6] A liberal tradition stressing individualism, personal autonomy, and personal fulfillment does not work well for those who are primarily dependent upon others, as women are, for their economic and social well-being.

The postindustrial economy and its political ideology of individual rights affect men and women differently.[7] Half of women with children under the age of three work. However, we are the only advanced industrial nation that has no public policy of family support, either as a family allowance or as publicly sponsored child care. Skyrocketing United States divorce rates have stabilized in the eighties, but remain among the highest in Western industrialized countries. Forty-three percent of those households maintained by a woman alone live in poverty, compared with 8 percent of those maintained by a man alone or in a married couple (Women's Economic Agenda Working Group, 1985, p. 13). In 1985, 18 percent of white and 57 percent of black families were headed by women (Ginsburg 1989, p. 214). Of those, only 18 percent were awarded and received child support allowances (Ginsburg, 1989, p. 214). To be a single mother in our society often means joining the ranks of those in poverty or, at the very least, to drop precipitously in income (Weitzman, 1985; Arendell, 1986). Even most of those relatively few women who hold high-paying jobs and who therefore can afford child care and domestic help earn less than similarly situated men despite their education, training, and experience (Kaufman, 1989).

If the exact economic conditions do not immediately apply to the generally well-educated middle-class Jewish women under study, the contours of postindustrial life in American for heterosexual marriage and motherhood are clear. By the 1970s, Jews had become so well integrated into American life that the trends affecting the rest of the society affected them as well. Although American Jews have a lower divorce rate (Goldscheider and Goldstein, 1985; Tobin and Chenkin, 1985; Cherlin and Celebuski, 1982),[8] there is a growing consensus among rabbis and other Jewish communal workers that the number of American Jewish divorces has risen dramatically over the past decade (Waxman, 1983).

A political ideology of individual rights, moreover, is often at odds with family values. Lasch thinks that "liberal societies tend to undermine family life, even though most of them profess a sentimental attachment" (1989, p. 95). He suggests that the ideology of liberalism is incapable of making sense of the family, which is "an institution that appears irrational in the sense that its members ideally do not think of their own interests and of the rights designed to protect them, and that they promise to sustain each other through a lifetime" (1989, p. 96).

It is not surprising, then, that since the mid-1970s many women have found their way to patriarchal religious communities where they can find what Stacey (1987) refers to as a "patriarchal profamilialism." Women appear to find in these religious communities places where intimate relationships and the personal side of life can be stabilized, places where women can make claims upon men that will be supported by structural and cultural institutions, places where women believe the sex/gender system is organized around family-centered and woman-oriented values.

The ba'alot teshuvah claim that in Orthodox Judaism they are able to make demands upon men as husbands and fathers in ways they believe less possible in the secular world. Adopting the stance that many values traditionally associated with women, such as mothering and the capacity for connectedness, are undervalued in society, these ba'alot teshuvah link the feminine and the female with the sacred and spiritual meaning of life, turning their devalued status in the secular world into a high-status aspect that the Orthodox community confers. In the religious world, these women claim, the female and the family and whatever is associated with them are seen as a positive source of value, not only for the self, but for the community as well.

Although embracing the fundamentalist arm of Judaism reinforces traditional understandings of "femininity" and the female, orthodoxy also makes a statement about male gender roles. As we have seen in Chapter One, the ba'alot teshuvah claim that Jewish orthodoxy replaces the "masculine ethos" of aggression, self-importance, and individualistic orientation with a "feminine ethos" stressing modesty and a collective orientation. Humility, self-restraint, and collective orientation are important religious (cultural) values for the entire community. In the following sections of this chapter, I will explore the structural arrangements, particularly the gender organization of the domestic sphere, that reinforce the "feminine ethos" that these women claim is the cultural value system of Orthodox Judaism.

Chapter Four

ORTHODOXY'S PROFAMILIALISM

In Orthodox Judaism, both men's and women's priorities are focused on childbearing and -rearing. Orthodoxy requires only men to procreate and considers only children born of a Jewish mother to be Jewish. Since Judaism is an ascriptive religion, childbearing and -rearing are especially important. Farber (1984) notes that in ascriptive religions the purity of the group must be sustained from one generation to the next. Rearing children who will help sustain the Orthodox community is of special concern. "By way of contrast," writes Farber,

> religious groups which rely for membership upon acceptance of a particular creed are not under special pressure to protect and nurture "the seed" of existing members. Instead, in every generation, these religions must replenish their numbers by spreading the faith to all nonadherents—outsiders as well as their own children. As a result, creed-based religions need not give special prominence to nurturance in childrearing; offspring provide only one means of recruitment (1984, p. 2).

Orthodoxy, therefore, takes an unambivalent profamily stance, creating a priority and purpose for both men and women. Men's involvement with their children is readily apparent. Interviews held during the day and especially on Sundays would inevitably find a father and child (of either sex) reading or discussing a story or doing some school preparation. One particular scene has stayed with me. During the Succot holiday, I joined one family before the interview for a breakfast in their sukkah (a hut built for the holiday). The five children, the oldest of whom was thirteen, had decorated the sukkah with laurel branches, cranberry strings, popcorn designs, and many cutouts of the six-pointed Star of David. Each child was busily telling me what he or she had contributed. The father, who was a computer analyst, engaged the children in computer games and graphics based upon appropriate holiday themes, while his wife and I were left in the sukkah to have our interview. The gales of laughter and sense of fun that punctuated the interview revealed that the interaction between father and children was not simply a baby-sitting routine.

Another time I arrived late in the morning for an interview with a mother of three, the youngest five weeks old, and the oldest six. Although she had been trained as a performing artist, religious custom did not allow her to perform in public (except to an all-female audience). Her creative talents were channeled into a business enterprise she and her husband had begun for Orthodox communities. They were quite well known in the community for their renditions of folklore and their presentations of children's shows (this is a fictitious account of what they do, in order to maintain their anonymity). Now she could do creative writing at home while he ran the production. Once all her children were in school, she planned to return to the business. Her husband arrived home for lunch, played with the children, put them down to nap, delivered some groceries, and then returned to the office. I asked if he came home for lunch everyday and she replied, "Yes."

Yet despite their profamily stance and their emphasis on gender differences, these women are not restricted only to practices traditionally associated with familial roles. Fifty-one percent (77) of all the ba'alot teshuvah I interviewed currently work, and almost all intend to participate in the paid labor force at some time.[9] All but three of the working women with children under the age of six held either part-time jobs or jobs with flexible hours. The flexibility needed to maintain dietary laws, the many holidays, and the Sabbath encourages both men and women either to take part-time jobs or positions in Jewish institutions and agencies where their religious needs can be accommodated. Almost all of the women who did not have advanced degrees intend to retrain and/or obtain more education before returning to the labor force.

Almost all of those women with children living at home use some form of child-care or day-care services regularly, whether they work or not. One-half of those women who work full-time have someone living in the household to help with child-care responsibilities and/or housekeeping. Many of the live-in helpers

91

are young women who are in the process of "converting" to Orthodox Judaism. Of the remaining women, almost all have at least
weekly help with housekeeping.[10]

Despite their work status and irrespective of other child-care
arrangements, these women feel they can and do make claims
upon their husbands for child-care services and responsibilities.
Of the women who worked full-time, all husbands had some, and,
in one case, close to half, the responsibility for the care of children. An interesting combination of reasons accounts for this situation. Because of their religious commitment to prayer, study,
the Sabbath (Saturdays), and the many religious holidays, both
men and women require flexible work patterns. They and their
husbands, claim these women, give priority to family and religious community over all secular pursuits, including work.[11]
Men's presence in the home, often during the day, allows them frequent contact and often responsibility for child care. This is especially true in the Hasidic communities, where secular pursuits
have very low priority (Sharot, 1982). Hasidic men tend to work
either in the community as teachers, administrators, small businessmen, or money collectors, or as ba'alei teshuvah recruiters.
Many of these ba'al teshuvah men abandoned corporate careers
for more flexible work settings.[12] Some became consultants or
computer analysts with a base at home. Even for husbands of non-
Hasidic women, and even for those with professional jobs, child
care was a part of their daily responsibilities. Even lawyers and
doctors were clearly involved with family and child care, most especially, on the Sabbath. They were the ones who often escorted
the older children to synagogue and spent the day in leisure with
their families.

In general, the division of labor in the household was variable,
but husbands were nevertheless held responsible for household
chores. Although women do the majority of the cooking for the
family, almost three-quarters of them reported that their husbands did the heavy weekly grocery and meat shopping. While
the wives did most of the child care, husbands had distinct roles.
When the husband's Hebrew school and/or Judaic background
was superior to the wife's, he was responsible for helping with the

children's homework. Mothers usually assumed the responsibility for their children's secular studies, although they claim that their husbands will help when their special areas of expertise are needed.

Irrespective of their work status, these women claim that family and religious community are their priorities. Most of the ba'alot teshuvah believe that the association between their religious and domestic roles gives them an edge in domestic decision making at home and an important social status within the community. The structure of religious observance reinforces this belief. Nurturance, for instance, like feeding and eating, assumes an important place in the Code of Jewish law. Farber suggests that halakhah "sublimates feeding and eating into ritualistic acts [and] extends the concept of nurturance to the giving of gifts and charity (tzedakah), and . . . specifies the priority of family and kin in nurturant activities" (1984, p. 4). He suggests that the concept of nurturance plays an important function in structuring Jewish family and kinship relations.

In Judaism, food enforces a distinction between the sacred and the profane. Before consuming food, even the youngest of children is expected to say a blessing. Most of the activities surrounding eating and feeding are women's major responsibilities. Each mother I observed made her children say the blessings before eating. One woman noted: "I know this sounds awful, but the thought of my children eating tref literally makes my stomach turn." Farber argues that given the ritual significance of food in Judaism, nurturance is a mitzvah.

Likewise, almost every major holiday demands a form of feast giving. The rhythm of the passing weeks is marked by the Sabbath, a time when the community is encouraged to "partake generously of fruits and delicacies" (Farber, 1984, p. 4). So, too, the passing of the seasons is marked by major holidays: Simchat Torah, Sukkot, Purim, Pesach, and Shavuot—all calling for feasts. Indeed, all ritual ceremonies, weddings, circumcisions, and the conclusion of Yom Kippur are times when Jews are commanded to "eat and drink and rejoice." Farber claims that food, gifts, and charity are all different kinds of sustenance governed "under the rubric of nurturance" (1984, p. 4). He notes that the occasions for giving feasts are also occasions for giving gifts and charity. In short, by associating feast making with gift giving and charity, the Jewish code implies that all such acts are governed by the norms of altruism and nurturance often associated with women's roles in Judaism (Farber, 1984).

The holiday of Purim provides a good example of the way in which women are involved in important religious activity—and where their private and public religious roles converge. In her study of modern Orthodox suburban Jewish women, Sacks (1986) shows how women command a certain amount of social power through the management of food. *Mishloach manos*, or, as many women in this study referred to it, *shalach mones*, is a gift exchange by observant Jews on Purim. To observe the holiday properly, one is obliged to send "portions" (usually delicacies) to one another and gifts to the poor.

Sacks (1986) notes that although husbands are consulted, women make the decisions about the production and distribution of mishloach manos. They, not men, represent the entire household in this activity. Sacks (1986) describes the creativity and individuality that goes into producing the portions for distribution and the managerial skill necessary in making sure everything is delivered on time. Although the law only requires delivering gifts containing more than one kind of food to more than one recipient, the distribution of these Purim treats has also become a time for reasserting the extensive network of exchange among the households and can include, writes Sacks, up to as many as thirty families, depending on the community size and women's active community participation. Those most involved in the community are expected to exchange the largest number of Purim portions.

None of men's activities, such as communal prayer, writes Sacks (1986), normally incur social obligations like women's volunteer work and active community participation. Comparing their production of mishloach manos to folk art, Sacks notes that female-controlled symbols, in contrast to male ones, are subject to much individual variation.[13] In linking their domestic and religious roles, women represent their households to the community[14] and, Sacks concludes, "by going beyond the lawful requirement, women amplify and multiply the messages and meanings invested in Purim portions. They co-opt the male-created law and make it their own" (1986, p. 10).

PATRIARCHAL PROFAMILIALISM AND CONTRACEPTION AND ABORTION

Orthodoxy's focus on the family and its unequivocal profamily stance provides a sense of direction and purpose for many of these women. Yet despite this emphasis on childbearing and -rearing, these newly Orthodox women do not automatically dismiss the use of contraception. Including many of the Hasidic women, a little over 85 percent of this sample have used contraception at some point in their marital life cycle. Of the twenty-two who have not used contraception, only two were non-Hasidic. As one woman revealed to me: "Family planning doesn't necessarily mean small families."

Because the Talmud describes contraception in a somewhat ambiguous language and without a clear prescriptive formulation, Biale (1984) suggests that the halakhic literature which has evolved around contraception encompasses a wide spectrum of opinions and highly complex and subtle argumentation.[15] At least two very different interpretations emerge concerning contraception. The more restrictive limits the categories of women who may use contraception and the acceptable methods of contraception and the more permissive allows greater flexibility to more women.[16] However, in general, there is agreement that since they are exempted from the obligation to procreate, women may use contraception.[17] The use is delimited, however, in that it cannot interfere with the "proper" emission of male seed. Therefore, writes Biale, contraception can be used as long as there is no "wasting of male seed."[18]

Not unexpectedly, the majority of the ultra-Orthodox women in this study called upon the restrictive interpretations in their discussions about contraception, and most of the Modern Orthodox the least. Except for many of the Hasidic women, most were able to distinguish between continual childbearing and the need for good-quality family relationships and a healthy family environment.[19] Most women believed that as mothers they were safeguarded by halakhah against extreme pain or danger in pregnancy or childbirth.[20] Even for some in ultra-Orthodox communities, as long as the husband "casts his seed properly," contraception (for example, use of a diaphragm or the pill) is a possibility.[21] For the majority of women, the mental and physical anguish for the mother as well as the quality of life for the unborn child and other members of the family were legitimate reasons for the use of contraception.

Abortion presents another highly controversial issue. There is general consensus among halakhists, writes Biale (1984), that an abortion is permitted when it is necessary to save a mother's life. However, other possible reasons for abortion are highly contested. The biblical sources for the discussion of abortion do not directly address an elective abortion. I shall elaborate a bit on the complex issues in halakhic interpretation, because it may help explain why Orthodox Jewish women have not been particularly active in the "right to life" campaigns for which women of the religious Right are generally well known.

The biblical source for the reference to abortion occurs in Exodus. The case in Exodus is that of an accidental abortion caused by a man's striking a pregnant woman in the course of a fight with her husband (Biale, 1984). If the woman suffers a miscarriage, the man is fined; if the woman loses her life, the man must pay with his. In this ruling, Biale points out, there is a clear distinction between the woman and her child. The woman, writes Biale,

is a living person, . . . and anyone who harms her body or kills her must pay in kind. The fetus is not a person in this sense. Destroying it through causing an abortion is not a capital crime and carries no capital punishment. Rather it is a crime of causing loss and destruction, analogous to property damage. The damage is inflicted on the husband, not on the pregnant woman, since he loses his progeny. Why is it the husband who suffers the loss of progeny and not the woman? Because in biblical law, while the woman herself is not quite the property of her husband since she is a person and not

an object . . . any of her products, whether through work or pregnancy, are the property of her husband. The text in Exodus 21 in-
dicates that in biblical law a fetus has the status of an object, not of a
person. This fundamental principle informs the discussion of abortion in Jewish law even when the abortion is intentional and not
accidental.[22]

As long as the fetus has no independent status, it appears that
abortion is permitted to save a mother's life. However, subsequent
argumentation complicated this interpretation, culminating in the
twelfth century with Maimonides' discussion. Maimonides brings
a totally new justification for aborting the fetus to save the
mother's life.[23] In his view, a fetus which endangers its mother is
analogous to a "pursuer." Biale explains:

> The Halakhah permits anyone who sees a person pursuing another
> in order to kill him (indicated by a weapon in his hand, etc.) to kill
> the pursuer in order to save the victim. The normal rules pertain-
> ing to manslaughter are suspended: one may kill the pursuer with-
> out warning and due process. Furthermore, Maimonides states
> that it is prohibited to take pity on the pursuer and refrain from
> killing him. He must be killed in order to save the victim. This law
> is Maimonides' justification for killing a fetus when the birth
> threatens the mother's life (1984, p. 230).

The contradiction between Maimonides' view and the views of
earlier Talmudists poses problems for contemporary interpretations.[24] Most contemporary Talmudists walk a fine line between
Maimonides' interpretation and earlier talmudic intention. The
most regressive interpretations permit abortion only on the
grounds that the fetus endangers the mother's life (therapeutic
abortions can be performed as long as they are done before the
baby's head emerges). The most lenient interpretations maintain
that the fetus is inferior to the mother in its claim to life (Biale,
1984; Rosner, 1972).

In Israel, where Orthodox law applies to all family matters, the
Knesset put into practice (1977) the following: abortion in cases of

serious hazard to the mother, conception from adultery or rape, or child pregnancy; suspicion of severe birth defects and congenital disease; and pressing socioeconomic factors. Biale writes that the "last item was a subject of great controversy because the religious party Agudat Yisrael opposed it vociferously. In 1979, as part of the coalition agreement between the Likud party and Agudat Yisrael, the last category was repealed." (1984, p. 237).

Despite the conflicting interpretations, there is a strong recognition in halakhah that it is the right and duty of a woman to preserve herself. Strict interpretation limits such self-preservation only to situations in which the fetus threatens the mother with death; the more lenient interpretations include "self-protection against other hazards: pain, mental anguish, and disgrace" (Biale, 1984, p. 238).

Again, not unexpectedly, the ba'alot teshuvah reflect these differing interpretations, depending on their Orthodox identification. The ultra-Orthodox reflect the more stringent, the Modern Orthodox the more lenient. Three Hasidic women in my study invoked the mystical concept that the Messiah will not come until all souls waiting to be born are brought into this world.[25] For them, neither contraception nor abortion was a viable alternative. However, for the majority of women, including Hasidic women, the issue of abortion, while never taken lightly, was a possibility. Few women couched their views on abortion in terms of fetal rights. Most did speak, however, of the sanctity of human life. Most also placed the issue of contraception and abortion in the aftermath of the Jewish Holocaust and the almost total destruction of the world's Orthodox Jewish population during World War II. For the majority, abortion had to be placed in the context of communal responsibility and an ethical code.

PATRIARCHAL PROFAMILIALISM AND CHILDREARING

It is evident that these women's ties to orthodoxy and community are clearly linked to their roles as mothers. Almost all of the women nurse their children. Certainly there is no religious sanction to do so, yet many believe that nursing is yet another tie to Judaism. "My mother," notes one new mother,

> frowns upon my nursing Sarah. I suspect I would not have nursed my children if I was not part of a community that values children so much. The times I nurse make me so aware of my giving to my daughter, of my relationship to her as a mother and all that I hope to give to her in the years to come. That's my job: to nurture, to give, to enrich.

Others spoke almost reverently about the births of their children. Indeed, as several women were quick to tell me, in Hasidut, the Jew's spiritual striving is compared to labor and childbirth. As most of these women nursed, so did many bear their children through natural childbirth. While some husbands trained for coaching their wives during labor, many Hasidic men, because of the religious rules of modesty, did not take classes with other couples. Although husbands did share to some extent in the process, other women, rather than husbands, served as coaches for those women preparing for natural childbirth.

Moreover, it is not uncommon for women to organize around child care and food preparation for a week or two following a woman's return from the hospital. Food for the entire family and care for those children not in school or otherwise cared for is often done on a rotating system by members of the immediate community. The need for such support is often more true for ba'alot teshuvah than other members of the Orthodox community:

> You know, I cannot depend on my family to help me when I cannot do the cooking and caring. You see, my family is not Orthodox, don't understand the laws of kashrut, and—probably more the case—they really are angry with me for making it so difficult for each of us to spend much time with one another. . . . The children are often asking why Grandma doesn't cover her head or why Grandpa doesn't make a blessing over the food. . . . On the Sabbath it is almost impossible, since they [the parents] ride on the

Sabbath, turn on lights, and do all the things we cannot do. . . . The holidays are the worst time, since unless they were to do what we do, it would be impossible to share those times with them. Anyways, when I had my last baby, my mother made it really clear to me how she felt. "If you expect me to come help you and take time from my work, you are wrong," she said. "You made your bed; now lie in it." I know she cares, but she really is angry with me.

The focus on childbearing presents many unanticipated problems for ba'alot teshuvah. Women who do not marry, who are divorced, separated, or deserted, or who cannot have children are marginal in orthodoxy. There is virtually no role for unmarried women, except as grandmothers or the equivalent. Unmarried women, and those without children, cannot make the same claims on the community that their married sisters can. Celibacy is not valued in either the legal or customary tradition of rabbinic Judaism. The demographic profile of these women reflects this. Over 97 percent of the women between the ages of twenty-one and thirty-five who were interviewed were married or engaged to be married. While Hasidic women bear the most children (3.6 on the average), the average number of children for all the ba'alot teshuvah is 3.2.

Despite indicators that divorce is on the rise among Jews in general, the rate is still lower among Orthodox Jews than among other Jewish denominations (American Jewish Committee, 1983; 1985). I interviewed only one ba'alot teshuvah who had been divorced since her return to orthodoxy. Her ba'al teshuvah husband had, as she said, "cheated on" her with another Orthodox woman. When I asked if this made her wary of orthodoxy, she simply replied: "They weren't truly Orthodox." Although hers had been a matched marriage, she fully expected to be married within the next few years again through a matchmaker. One woman, now remarried, but divorced upon her return to orthodoxy, noted: "When I first came here I had one small baby and a part-time job as a social worker. I knew it was just a matter of time before I would remarry. All I needed was one good *shidduch* [arranged marriage]."[26]

Childlessness might be the most difficult problem for women within the Orthodox community.[27] One particularly poignant story was told by a woman who, with her husband, had become Orthodox after they had had two children, but after he had had a vasectomy:

> I cannot tell you the pain we experience now. . . . We have not been able to reverse my husband's vasectomy and we want more children. . . . It is so difficult to adopt. Do you know that Jewish agencies discriminate against us because we are Orthodox. They let us keep foster children but won't let us adopt. I don't know what they think we will do to children . . . beat them, not feed or clothe or love them . . . no, it's because they are afraid we will brainwash them. We'll force religion down their throats. . . . Maybe just maybe they would love religion the way we do . . . Its a real *shanda* [Yiddish for disgrace].

Because the Orthodox prefer children who are Jewish, and, therefore, born of a Jewish mother, there are very few children eligible for adoption. Moreover, births out of wedlock are virtually unknown in these Orthodox communities.[28] One ba'alat teshuvah who had been trying to conceive for several years admitted that she was experiencing a good deal of depression. She and her husband had been to several fertility clinics. She admitted that conception was now the primary concern of their life. Another woman told me that she had had three operations over the past five years for fertility problems. She felt confident that this time she might be able to conceive. She says she simply will not give up hope, although she had been in therapy for several years after her first two unsuccessful operations.

Despite the often weakened ties with their families of origin, and the problems orthodoxy presents to women without children, these women have found a setting that addresses their concerns about family and gender roles and about commitment and connection

101

in modern society. The ba'alot teshuvah view spousal and communal commitments as lasting. They have found a community that reinforces men's active involvement in home and childrearing responsibilities. Indeed, compared to national quality-of-life studies they seem to fare no worse, and, perhaps even a little better, than the majority of married middle-class American women (Pleck, 1977; 1981; 1982).[29]

RELIGIOUS-RIGHT WOMEN AND PATRIARCHAL PROFAMILIALISM

The ba'alot teshuvah regard the daily activities surrounding their domestic tasks (the maintaining of food, dress, and Sabbath and holiday laws) not only as a way of distinguishing the Orthodox Jewish community from the gentile world, and indeed even from other Jewish denominations, but as sacred ritual. The social practices associated with the everyday activities of domestic life are deeply intertwined with women's religious lives. These women equate religious values with a coherent set of symbols which, they claim, value the "feminine." In addition, they see these values as rooted in a stable social setting which, according to them, honors the social practices associated with the female. They equate their religious duties with their everyday activities as women, mothers, and wives. This congruence provides many of them with an ethical system that connects their public and private lives. They have, as Tipton (1982b) might describe it, bridged the gap between their moral religious and their everyday lives.

Setta (1983) has identified other contemporary women of the religious Right who equate their domesticity with sacred rites and rituals as well. For instance, the home has become an important issue in the religious faith and belief of women who are part of Women Aglow, a white middle- and upper-middle-class cross-section of women demographically similar to the ba'alot teshuvah.[30]

Aglow women, like many of the social conservative women in Klatch's study (1987) of New Right women, reaffirm gender hierarchy. However, they believe that male authority will end in heaven, since the locus of men's powers here on earth, in family, business, and politics, have "no other-worldly implications" (Setta, 1983, p. 16). For Aglow women, women's earthly ministry, like that of Jesus, is one of self-sacrifice. Setta argues that Aglow women see themselves as engaging in action that will lead to the coming of God's kingdom. This is not unlike the implicit belief among many ultra-Orthodox women (Hasidic) that they are morally superior to men and that through their actions the Messiah will come.

Although we have no data on how the Aglow women actually practice their domestic lives, they seemingly subscribe to many of the positions put forth by the Christian religious Right. The religious literature for both ba'alot teshuvah and Aglow women supports their beliefs that their everyday lives are also their religious lives. Many Orthodox Jewish women subscribe to journals and newspapers written for them by the Orthodox community. In those magazines and journals, such as the *Yiddishe Heim* (The Jewish Home), questions about proper childrearing and ritual issues often arise. Biblical text is often cited and interpreted to exhort women and men to live up to their religious ideals.

Tips on homemaking and cooking are often shared among women, especially around the many Jewish holidays. Setta notes that Aglow's national organization offers texts on meal preparation (*Aglow in the Kitchen*), advice on home decorating and housecleaning, and money management. Pohli's research on women members of conservative Protestant churches yields a portrait of the Evangelical woman as "circumscribed by institutional supports for her faith-centered life." She writes:

> The Evangelical woman can begin her day by turning on a local, twenty-four-hour Christian radio station, or turn the television on the Christian Broadcasting Network's Morning Talk Show. She can curl up with an Evangelical magazine such as *Virtue*, and *Eternity*, or reach for a book published by a flourishing Christian publishing house (1983, p. 541).

As Pohli notes, through the Christian Yellow Pages the Evangelical women can find anything from prayers to plumbers.

However, despite the portrait of women, either Jewish or Christian, of the religious Right as "circumscribed by institutional supports" for their traditional choices, there are some surprises. To label, for instance, all of the literature they dispense as reactionary or antifeminist in purpose is not entirely accurate. Describing the data from their fieldwork among participants in a small charismatic Christian ministry in the Silicon Valley (Global Ministries of Love), Stacey and Gerard (1988) are surprised by what secular feminists can find in Christian women's magazines, including "information on rape self-defense, a criticism of social pressures for thinness and youth, and reviews for books celebrating friendships between women" (1988, p. 19). For secular feminists, women's active involvement and leadership in the religious Right is also surprising.

In *Women of the New Right*, Rebecca Klatch characterizes one of the "distinguishing characteristics of the new conservative movement" as the leadership and prominence of women (1987, p. 4).[31] Moreover, Klatch cautions that just as the New Right is not a cohesive movement, neither do right-wing women share a single set of beliefs and values.[32] She distinguishes between two constituencies among right-wing women: social conservatives and laissez-faire conservatives. The social conservative group is rooted in religious belief and considers the family the key and sacred unit of society; the laissez-faire constituency goes back to the classical liberalism of the nineteenth century, which believed that the rational, self-interested individual is the primary element of society.

The ba'alot teshuvah resemble more closely the social conservative women of the New Right than the laissez-faire women of Klatch's study. The social conservative women are mainly concerned with the sexual mores and familial patterns of society.[33] With some irony, Klatch (1987; 1988) notes that while laissez-faire conservative women actually support part of the feminist agenda,[34] by eschewing social conservatives' views of male authority, female submissiveness, or women's "natural" orientation toward others, they do *not* recognize their collective interests as women. On the other hand, social conservatives, like many ba'alot teshuvah, act to protect their interests as women, wives, and mothers within traditional patriarchal boundaries. Gender identity is central to the political involvement of these social conservatives:

Nofault divorce laws . . . have liberated many men from the obligation to support their wives and children. Women placed in these unfortunate circumstances are touted by the feminist movement as its most valiant "heroines." However, it is the feminist movement's strident insistence on eradication of all sex-related distinctions that has contributed so greatly to the present predicament of divorced women with children who must support the family unit alone [a profamily activist cited in Klatch, 1987, p. 138].

All I can see is women with careers who then have to come home and clean their house, so all day Saturday or Sunday they are doing housework. All I see is women taking on men's roles, but not men helping. On one side of the feminist's mouth they call for universal daycare, and on the other they say, "Don't worry. Men will help." But I don't see men helping [another pro-family activist cited in Klatch, 1987, p. 138].

Interestingly, what belies this hostility toward feminism is an implicit distrust of men. These women are especially wary of feminism when they believe it supports men's irresponsibility. Mrs. Bill Graham notes that the women's liberation movement is "turning into men's liberation because we are freeing them from their responsibilities. I think we are being taken for a ride" (cited in Klatch, 1987, p. 137). Phyllis Schlafly sums it up:

Consider a wife in her 50's who husband decides he wants to divorce her and trade her in on a younger model. . . . If ERA is ratified, and thereby wipes out the state laws that require a husband to support his wife, the cast-off wife will have to hunt for a job to support herself. . . . The most tragic effect of ERA would thus fall on the woman who has been a good wife and homemaker for decades (cited in Klatch, 1987, p. 137).[35]

Klatch notes that "in social conservative eyes, when individuality and freedom of self extend to women as well as to men, marriage, the family, and society itself are threatened" (1987, p. 128). She goes on to quote Connie Marshner, a leading figure in the profamily movement, on "macho feminism." Marshner claims that "macho feminism has convinced women that they would be happy only if they were treated like men, and that includes treating themselves like men."

Women who have returned to Orthodox Judaism resemble the religious Right in several ways, although for Jewish Orthodox women this does not mean active political involvement in the secular arena as it often does for the Christian New Right.[36] Jewish Orthodox women, like the social conservative women in Klatch's study, reject a secular humanist outlook and have returned to biblical religion as a moral guide. They, too, seem preoccupied with reclaiming traditional domestic values. Although their depth of religious commitment should not be minimized, the phenomenon of "return" may also express their quest for revalued domesticity, a literal "coming home." By reviving a focus on women's domestic roles, which every national survey suggests young women intend to play, these women refocus an area of women's lives they claim contemporary feminists disregard and devalue. Both ba'alot teshuvah and Christian women of the religious Right seem intent on reestablishing traditional "feminine" values and female-linked symbols and activities. In part, they do so by celebrating and emphasizing a woman's stereotypically "feminine" traits and functions; and for some, as among the ultra-Orthodox Jewish and social conservative right-wing women, her superior moral sensibilities.

In Defense of Home: Ties That Bind

Feminist historians have pointed to the ways in which the defense of the domestic sphere and "femininity" have served feminist as well as antifeminist purposes.[37] There are numerous precedents in American history when women have mobilized in defense of the traditional family in the hope of reorganizing their relationships to men and to society in general. All during the nine-teenth century, women in the temperance, suffrage, antisuf-frage, and other movements often used their positions as "guard-ians" of home and family to argue for their respective political causes.

In *The Politics of Domesticity* (1981), Barbara Epstein traces the emergence of a popular women's culture through four stages of women's religious activity, from the mid-eighteenth through the late nineteenth century. Like Ann Douglas (1977), Epstein be-lieves that the conflicts between the sexes were played out in the arena of culture, especially religion, and that in that arena, middle-class women were able to exert some influence. Epstein notes that the broad nineteenth-century social spectrum that can be called the middle class identified with the cause of Protestant orthodoxy, rather than liberalism. It was that orthodoxy that they turned against those men whom they saw as trying to escape from genuine piety (1981, p. 8). Epstein describes these women as pit-ting themselves against the "bastions of male culture" as they rec-ognized their difference from and antagonisms toward men. The development of their religious activity alongside a particular set of female concerns and values, argues Epstein, helped elucidate and revise their relationships to men. [38]

In the latter half of the nineteenth century, women's evangelism became focused on "home values" and was transformed into a form of social morality. The Women's Christian Temperance Union is a good example of this transformation. [39] While morality was still defined in Christian terms, the WCTU's main activities centered around the defense of the family and "home values." It attempted to rectify private abuses against women such as intem-perance and the sexual double standard. Drinking was associated with the strand of "masculinity" that was seen as hostile to women and the family. Implicit was a criticism of male culture; the at-tempt to bring both men and women under the "sway of Victorian morality" (Epstein, 1981, p. 127). Throughout this period, writes Epstein, women were increasingly widening the definition of re-ligious activities to include secular concerns.

Although such values were indeed part of a religious tradition steeped in patriarchy, Epstein notes that the religious revivals gave women legitimate opportunities to voice their concerns based on their own experiences and their own sensibilities. In other words, it gave them the opportunity to define their own situations by framing issues from a woman's perspective. Even such outrightly antisuffrage proponents as Catharine Beecher had a place in the intellectual feminist tradition of the nineteenth century. As one of the most outspoken proponents for women's sphere and culture, Beecher provided arguments for feminists later in the century. According to her early treatise on domestic economy, Beecher believed that women's greater ability for self-sacrifice entitled them to claims of a superior morality. These claims were used not only as a way of holding men responsible to women and family obligations, but of changing the moral climate of society in general. For instance, Beecher believed businessmen should imitate the self-sacrificing and self-denying ethics of mothers and wives (Banks, 1981). Hayden argues that Beecher's strategy for domestic reform was enhanced by two new metaphors of female authority: woman as "home minister" and as skilled "professional." Writes Hayden:

> Women were to do their own housework without help from domestic servants. Rather than indicating a diminution in status, this work was to provide the opportunity for gaining power through self-sacrifice (the ministerial role) and skill (the professional role) (1981, p. 56).[40]

We should not be surprised, then, that the personal and familial have been of great concern to women and at the heart of several social movements spearheaded by women. Nor should we be surprised that profamily religious-Right activists of the twentieth century, like profamily religious activists of the last century, have taken collective action in defense of their status as women. Epstein (1983) contends that "over the last one hundred years of American history, there have been two periods during which issues of family life and sexual morality have been central concerns of popular movements: the decades around the turn of the century and those from the 1960s to the present" (p. 117).[41] The closing decades of each century have some interesting parallels.

The Women's Christian Temperance Union, closely related to other social reform movements and considered one of the largest organizations of women in the United States (Bordin, 1986), focused on domestic problems. Using religion as a base of protest, in this century we see some women of the New Right concerned with "home problems." Although there are no accurate statistics, the purported membership of some of these groups suggests a large membership base. The "born again" attitudes of the religious Right, Evangelical, or Orthodox Jewish, cannot be easily ignored. Whether the women are Jewish or Christian, antagonisms with men in an "individualist" culture frame the concerns of many contemporary women. They voice profound worries about family, sexuality, women, and commitment.

Different eras present different contexts for women in framing their concerns about the familial and the personal spheres of life. The political direction taken also varies. Contraceptive information was available to middle-class women throughout the nineteenth century, but public support for contraception, argues Epstein, would have directly contradicted the aims of the social purity movement, a movement widely and energetically supported by middle-class women of the time (Gordon, 1977; Bordin, 1986). Freely available contraceptives would have reduced the risks for men in visiting prostitutes, and would have made it easier for men to put off or entirely avoid marriage (Epstein, 1983, p. 123). Epstein writes:

> The social purity and related women's temperance movements . . . undoubtedly reflected mainstream sentiment among women in their defense of the family and their view that any separation between sexuality and marriage threatened that institution and therefore threatened women. The movement regarded a restricted, even anti-sexual, morality as in the best interest of women (1983, p. 123).

Epstein argues that, given women's position in the labor market and their general dependence upon marriage for survival, the valorization of motherhood was seemingly made "the only basis for anything remotely resembling female autonomy" (1983, p. 123). If the separation of sex from procreation had made marriage less compelling for men and infidelity easier, it was reasonable, she argues, for these nineteenth-century women's movements, "including feminist ones, to shy away from support for contraception" (p. 123).

And, as at the end of last century, it is not surprising that some contemporary women fear sexual liberation; nor that, as in the last century, some use religious arguments to make their demands, to hold, as it were, impious men to pious rules. Ehrenreich, Hess, and Jacobs (1986) note that women's fear of sexual liberation is not unfounded. They write:

> The fear is not irrational or neurotic, for if sex is disconnected from marriage, childbearing and family commitments, women stand to lose their traditional claims on male support. The teasing, instrumental sexuality prescribed for single women before the sexual revolution had a purpose, after all: to "land" a man, and to claim him as one's breadwinner for life. If sex is "free," then so, potentially, are men; and women are left to fend for themselves in an economy that still drastically undervalues women's labor. This was a dilemma that the radical feminists of the late sixties and early seventies, who boldly proclaimed the link between sexual liberation and women's liberation, did not always seem to grasp (1986, p. 199).

Epstein suggests that by the 1920s new definitions of middle-class marriage and sexual morality gave couples a new degree of control over family size and the problems caused by prostitution and venereal disease. Indeed, the family literature of the time clearly notes the emergence of the mobile conjugal family, separated from extended familial ties and focused on the husband-and-wife dyad. The importance of the husband-and-wife bond and new emphasis on sexual intimacy, Epstein astutely notes, may have compensated for the loosening of extended familial and community ties. However, she also notes that valorization of women's sexuality did not bring about any major familial changes. In fact it may have added new strains to couple relationships, especially for women.[42] Women could not rely upon their helpmate and motherly qualities alone but now had sexual attractiveness and ability to maintain intimacy added to the marital expectation list.

According to Epstein's social history of the family, it was not until women's steady and increasing entry into the labor force, after World War II, that familial and sexual issues emerged again as important popular concerns. Women's entry into the labor market, without changes in the sex-segregated patterns of participation and clear sex-discrimination patterns (both overt and covert), put new strains on women, many of whom had little choice but to work. Without structural and normative changes either in the work world or in the family, many women were under major strains and in impossible circumstances. From Constantina Safilios-Rothschild's early critique (1970) of the egalitarian marriage studies to more contemporary ones (Hochschild, 1986), it is clear that marriages are not egalitarian, either in decision making or in domestic workload.

The women who had embraced orthodoxy in their young-adult or adult years are well aware of these issues. They develop images of women as responsible mothers and citizens; as active agents and decision-makers in the private sphere. Even more interestingly, they reject the materialistic claims of the "male" success ethic for both sexes. Both men and women, in their view, should make religion and family their priorities. They wish to break from a work ethic that is too demanding in order that they may have more time for religious study and practice. They approach the public sphere of synagogue and study from their private roles as wives, women, and mothers. In some senses, the ba'alot teshuvah bridge the often alluded-to distinctions between private and public spheres by adopting orthodoxy. The family, "their" sphere, and the private sphere are placed in a larger supportive context, the Orthodox community. Many claim that in this larger context, personal and lasting ties can be nurtured and maintained.

As we have seen in the last two chapters, the ba'alot teshuvah

111

negotiate their familial and marital roles in ways that they claim help them maintain control over their bodies and their sexuality. Like some feminists of last century, they claim strong family-centered values for the community at large and hold men accountable to them and family life on those grounds. They symbolically reconstruct the sex/gender system not only to enhance female status, but also to bring men's aspirations and value systems more in line with women's. Therefore, while most of these women openly reject feminism or what they perceive feminism to represent and advocate, their focus on raising women's status, promoting female interests, and focusing men's behavior on their roles as fathers and husbands resonates with issues long in feminist lexicon and history.

In a world as highly segregated as Orthodox Jewish communities, women engage in a daily round of activities dominated by familial concerns and by other women. Through their sex-segregated roles, these women engage in a tradition of female institution building (Freedman, 1979), which, although it does not and cannot formally challenge male hegemony in synagogue and study, does establish nurturing, caring, and interconnected relationships as the primary bases for their everyday lives and, they claim, for the community at large. In the next chapter we'll explore more fully that woman-centered world.

CHAPTER FIVE

•

Sex-segregated Living

Women's Culture in the Making

The ba'alot teshuvah share the "official" patriarchal belief system of Orthodox Judaism and a belief system that emerges organically from their everyday lives as women in a highly sex-segregated community.[1] They believe that community is critical if Orthodox Jewish life is to be preserved.[2] For them, female activities and systems of meaning are as vital to Orthodox Judaism as are men's. They do not see their sphere as inferior, but rather as a place where, as we shall see in this chapter, they are free to create their own forms of personal, social, intellectual, and, at times, political relationships. Whether intentional or not, sex-segregated living may provide women with the resources on which they can build a community of meaning and action. As we have seen in the past few chapters, by accepting and elaborating on the symbols and expectations associated with gender difference, these ba'alot teshuvah claim they have some control over their sexuality and marital lives.

Although their values and beliefs are less formally articulated than those of men, these ba'alot teshuvah have developed, in the highly sex-segregated world of Orthodox Judaism, a strong women's culture.[3] They seem to expand the domestic limits set by patriarchal living, not by entering a man's world, but by creating a world of their own.[4] The solidarity, self-esteem, and strength they receive from this world reinforces them in their celebration of difference and woman-centered values and in making claims upon the community as a whole for care, commitment, and connectedness.

The Hebrew world for "holy" means "set apart." Liebman (1979) suggests that it is symbolic of the split between the sacred and the secular. He writes: "From the ancient Near East to Durkheim and his students, people who reflected on the nature of holiness understood that its basic component was its apartness, its radical differentness" (1979, p. 23). The ba'alot teshuvah celebrate their difference both as women and as Jews. However, they are differentially attached to the religious community and to sex-segregated living, depending on the number of nonreligious affiliations they claim, their work patterns, the kind of work they do, and the amount of time and attention they pay to activities outside the religious community.

How Segregated from Secular Living Are These Newly Orthodox Women?

The attachment of the ba'alot teshuvah to the religious community is tempered by work patterns in the paid labor force. Over 51 percent (77) of all the women in this study were currently employed in the paid labor force. One-fifth (30) of all the ba'alot teshuvah had earned less than a bachelor's degree. Of those, only five were employed. These women tended to work as teachers' aides or secretaries. All but two were employed part-time. Of the 120 women who had received at least a bachelor's degree, one-third (40) had earned or were in the process of earning a master's degree, and 12 percent (18) had earned or were working toward a professional degree. If they worked, those studying for master's or professional degrees tended to be employed part-time. Generally, only those with advanced degrees work full-time in what might be classified as male-dominated professions. However, even in these positions, women, like the men, create the flexibility needed to maintain dietary laws, the many holidays, and the keeping of the Sabbath. In this study there were four lawyers, two doctors, and seven university-affiliated teachers or researchers, and three women in executive-managerial positions.

Except for several computer analysts, the remainder of all those who work are in female-dominated, semiprofessional occupations (teaching, library jobs, social work, nursing), and two were real-estate brokers. Flexibility in work arrangements were critical for these women, since they had to accommodate both Orthodox obligations and, for many, child-care arrangements as well. In general, the higher her educational degree, the more likely the woman was to work full-time and to have fewer children. The average number of children (2.9) for those working was less than for those who were not working (3.4).

Hasidic women were less likely than the others to have completed a bachelor's degree or to have earned an advanced or professional degree. Therefore, fewer Hasidic women were employed, and even when they worked, they were more likely to be employed part-time, irrespective of their job status. On average, Hasidic women enjoy a smaller combined annual household income ($31,000) than that of non-Hasidic women ($48,800). For the most part, the Hasidic women were less likely to partake in activities or work outside the religious community. They fully expect to live their lives as insulated from the secular world as possible.

This pattern of isolation from secular activities and thought is evident in other ways as well. For instance, while both Hasidic and non-Hasidic women were almost equally identified or affiliated with synagogue and religious women's organizations, non-Hasidic women were more likely than other ba'alot teshuvah to affiliate with political, civic, and cultural activities. The most common secular interest had to do with environmental issues. In contrast, one Lubavitch woman told me that she had no time or interest in activities other than those that are part of her religious life. She participates in the annual conventions of Neshei U'Bnos Chabad (a Lubavitch women's organization of about 3,500 women from abroad and from fifty states), and with her weekly meeting with other women to study *Tanya*. "Who has time," she asked me, "for any *nareshkeit* [Yiddish for foolishness], when there are so many more important things to do?"

Hasidic women, more than other ba'alot teshuvah, spent more

115

time in informal communal women's groups studying Torah and its implications for parenting, family, and psychological well-being. One such group was called Emotional Maturity Through Torah (its initials almost form an acronym for the Hebrew word for Truth). When Hasidic women are involved in secular cultural activities, they often participate in order to screen those activities (movies, theater, music) for their families. "Sometimes I will go with another woman friend to see a movie," said one Hasidic woman. "If I think it's all right," she continued, "I'll suggest that the children might enjoy it. If it's something I think he'll like, I tell Chaim [her husband] to go see it, too. But to tell the truth, there is very little over the last few years I find appropriate. Mostly, we stick to our own."

Lubavitch women are very dependent upon the opinions of their rebbe. Since he has publicly announced his disdain for commercial television and much of what the secular media have to offer (Rebbe Schneerson has sanctioned the use of cable television for recruitment purposes and to enable him to reach larger populations with his speeches), most Lubavitch homes do not have televisions and most families do not regularly engage in any secular cultural events. Although most Hasidic families (including Boston Hasidim) do not watch television, almost all have electronic equipment (sometimes rather advanced equipment, such as computers) for formulating their own video games, stories, or songs and/or recording and listing to tapes and other self-selected materials. On the other hand, while the non-Hasidic women are more likely to attend concerts, the theater, movies, and civic events, they also claim that they censor most of their families' entertainment.

Most of these ba'alot teshuvah, it appears, are the monitors of the community's moral sensibilities. Although the whole community is expected to engage in activities that hold to the standards of modesty, women, it seems, are the guardians of those standards. However, while these women see women's actions and relationships as the cornerstone for morality and moral behavior, they do not identify with any secular groups that also see themselves as the guardians of morality. For instance, they do not actively support any of the antiabortion groups nor are they members of any anti-pornography groups. None of them seemed aware of any of the assorted national groups such as Happiness of Womanhood, Feminine Anti-Feminists, or League of Housewives.[5] Neither were they members of the League of Women Voters, NOW, or any feminist groups.[6]

As pointed out earlier, stricter boundaries exist for Hasidic women than for other ba'alot teshuvah. These include reading materials. Hasidic women subscribe to a much more limited selection of Jewish magazines, newspapers, and journals.[7] These differences are even more striking in their secular subscriptions. While both Hasidic and non-Hasidic women were as likely to subscribe to their professional journals and/or alumni magazines, Hasidic women were less likely to subscribe to or read the broad array of books, magazines, and newspapers that their other Orthodox sisters did. Newspapers such as the *New York Times*, the *Wall Street Journal*, and the *Boston Globe*, frequently found in non-Hasidic homes, were generally absent in Hasidic ones. Similarly, news magazines such as *Newsweek*, *Time*, and *Life* appeared more frequently in non-Hasidic homes. Interestingly, while not frequently found among any group of ba'alot teshuvah, women's magazines (such as *Redbook*, *Parents' Magazine*, *Family Circle*, *Vogue*, and *Woman's Day*, and even *Ms.* and *Savvy*), appeared in some Hasidic and non-Hasidic homes. Specialty magazines (such as *Archaeology Journal*, *Whole Life Times*, *Organic Gardening*, and *Vegetarian Times*) were equally subscribed to by both Hasidic and non-Hasidic women.

Hasidic and non-Hasidic women differ both in the kinds of secular ties and in the types of institutions with which they identify in the religious community. Although both Hasidic and non-Hasidic women are involved in religious community activities, either with their synagogues or with their children's schools, Hasidic women are more likely to identify with the goals and values of the more extreme institutions than the other ba'alot teshuvah do. Hasidic women were more likely to indicate that they agreed with the goals of the extreme right-wing Jewish Defense League and the more right-wing Israeli party, Agudat Israel than non-Hasidic women were. On the other hand, the latter were more likely to mention the more "modern" Yeshiva University and the Rabbinical Council of America as reference groups.[8]

Despite non-Hasidic women's "less traditional attitudes" and their greater contact with secular institutions, the everyday demands of Orthodox living ensure that religion and the Orthodox community remain the major focus in their lives. Every aspect of orthodoxy serves to separate Jews from the larger society— keeping kosher, the Sabbath, rituals, dress, and even the lunar calendar. Orthodoxy's strong antisecular component militates against its members' active political, social, or civic secular engagement. Their political engagement, outside the immediate Orthodox setting, tends to take the form of attention to political conditions affecting Soviet Jewry and to Israeli politics.[9] In general, the ba'alot teshuvah do not seek social reform; rather, they nourish ways of remaining isolated from the secular world and its "immoral" influences. In this sense, they are not out to save the world, but individuals, and just Jewish ones at that.

Perhaps one of the most important boundaries for ba'alot teshuvah that help to hold them into the Orthodox community and that ensure a tight bonding among them as women is their difficulty in maintaining close relationships with those outside the Orthodox community. This is particularly true for newly Orthodox Jews in relationship to their families of origin. Tensions between ba'alot teshuvah and their parents are inevitable, forcing many of the former to rely heavily on one another and the Orthodox community for support. In this context, many of them admit to the downside of their choices. Ironically, many are forced to distance themselves from their extended families and families of origin, even as they celebrate familial life in the Orthodox community.

As noted in Chapter One, many ba'alot teshuvah have rejected the life-styles and, in many cases, the political values and principles of their parents. Ten of the women interviewed were once "red-diaper" babies, coming from families where both parents were "old lefties." While they did not necessarily see their parents as materialistic and/or "phony" or "shallow" as did others, they initially embraced Orthodox Judaism because they wanted a well-articulated set of beliefs that transcended a political analysis of the "here and now." For others, it was a rejection of what they called the "shallow" and "phony" life-styles some had come to associate with middle-class suburban living. And for still others, it was simply an extension of what they believed their parents already had committed themselves to, as in the case of those who had come from Conservative Jewish backgrounds. Even here, report some of the ba'alot teshuvah, it appeared to some parents that their children were trying to "one-up" them.

Whatever their stated reasons and motivations—and these are at best reconstructed explanations—it is clear that the ba'alot teshuvah are committed to something different from what they experienced while growing up. They have made choices different from those of their parents. Since the life patterns are so dramatically different, tensions with families of origin are inevitable. One Hasidic woman reported that after the birth of her third child in four years, her lawyer mother shouted to her: "Take that *shmata* [a Yiddish word for rag, referring to the woman's head covering] off your head and use the talent you have for thinking, not baby-making. Is this why we spent so much money on your Ivy League education?"

And while it is a bit easier for non-Hasidic Orthodox families to relate to their families of origin, the tensions are still clearly there. The laws of kashruth and other ritual practices are often as foreign to the parents as they were to the ba'alot teshuvah when the latter first embraced orthodoxy. Dietary laws are particularly destructive to non-Orthodox family relationships. Family visits are generally limited to no-eating and nonholiday situations. This, of course, is particularly difficult for those with families out of town.

One ba'alot teshuvah (Modern Orthodox) recognized this with some sadness when she noted that although she and her family visited her own family at least once a year, it was growing more difficult. She laments:

> We have to drive, not fly, because we have to bring our own utensils and our own food. We cannot visit over the weekends or Jewish holidays because we will not drive on Shabbat or on *yom tovim*

[holidays]. We also then have to explain to the children why Grandma and Grandpa use the lights on Shabbat, heat the food, and ride in a car [Orthodox Jews will not generate electricity on the Sabbath]. You can image how difficult it is for us. We don't want to hurt my parents, but of course it is inevitable. My mother loves to cook and tries to buy the right food and all, but it almost always presents a problem.

Although some parents have accommodated to their children's orthodoxy by changing their household patterns when their children visit, or converting to orthodoxy themselves,[10] others remain openly hostile and disapproving. As one perceptive young woman said: "By becoming Orthodox, my parents feel I am saying to them, 'I am a better Jew than you are.'" And, although the arrival of grandchildren may soften some attitudes, it frequently presents problems as well. "Why doesn't *Zeda* ("Grandpa" in Yiddish) wear a yarmulka?" one mother claims her son asks each time they visit her parents. Since honoring one's parents is a valued norm in the Orthodox community, the issues are complicated for many of these ba'alot teshuvah. The issues that create tensions between them and their parents are the ones that are of critical importance to these women. Trying to find neutral areas of communication and visitation are almost impossible. The very things that separate these women from the secular world also separate them from their parents. Despite "creative compromises" (she still attends baseball games with her father) with her parents, one woman admits that her relationship with her mother still is the most troubling part of her life. As she says, "I have come to accept the fact that we will never share our lives in the important ways."

Many recognize that their conversion has come at a high price. For many, there is even more disruption and pain in dealing with their siblings. One-fifth of these newly Orthodox Jews have siblings who have married outside Judaism or who have openly rejected it. "Although I see my sister on occasion," states one woman, "we now have very little in common. She has married a man outside the faith and our life-styles are quite different. We were once very close. We pretend it doesn't matter, but we both know that it does." Their often weakened ties with their families of origin make these women feel even more tied to the religious community and one another.

While many of the women maintain ties to non-Orthodox friends, most conceded that unless their friends were eventually interested in "converting" to orthodoxy, they did not believe they could continue with those relationships. Thus they rely on women within the Orthodox community, especially other ba'alot teshuvah, for their primary friendships and activities.

MECHANISMS FOR MAINTAINING SEX-SEGREGATION WITHIN THE ORTHODOX COMMUNITY

In general, all Orthodox communities require, at least in the practice of public religious ritual, a separation between men and women. In one ultra-Orthodox community, I often found myself during the daytime to be the only woman in the local Orthodox restaurant. Despite the limited seating, men would not share a table with me, but preferred to wait until I finished my food, or they crowded around tables with other men.

The informal codes of proper behavior and modesty rules also restrict the kind of contact in which men and women can engage. Within Modern Orthodox communities, there is an easier relationship between men and women than there is for those who are more traditional. Danzger (1989) claims that the "modernists" in orthodoxy have become more traditional. For instance, among the Modern Orthodox (except for religious services) men and women used to sit, dance, and swim together. Now, he claims, there seems to be a trend away from doing those things together.

Newly Orthodox women's leadership roles and formal representation in the Orthodox community are usually limited to areas labeled as women's, such as day-care facilities, early grade-school education (decision making about secular, not religious, content), extracurricular children's activities. Their public religious roles are also limited to what are considered to be women's concerns: the sisterhood of the synagogue, the building and maintenance of the local mikveh. In their secular roles, the services of ba'alot teshuvah are preferred over those of others who are not religious. This is particularly true for what are considered to be sensitive areas of service, such as counseling and/or therapy.[11]

Study groups, recreational activities, and support groups are often done for and by women. Many women reported frequently attending some type of all-female religious study group. Even the topics studied revolve around what are considered women's topics (for example, ethics as opposed to the logic of legal codes). Most of the women are involved in some form of sisterhood or women's auxiliary within their local communities. Their activities are almost endless, because of the many Jewish holidays and orthodoxy's dependence for most of its entertainment and culture on the community itself.

IN THE COMPANY OF OTHER WOMEN

There is a correlation between Hasidic and non-Hasidic women's isolation from the secular community and attachment to the religious community, but for all, religious life is a priority. Despite non-Hasidic women's broader contacts with the secular world, they, like Hasidic women, measure the outside world through their experiences and values as Orthodox Jewish women. These women claim that they approach the secular world with a firm sense of what is moral, and with a sense of self-worth and confidence in their female sensibilities. For many, but especially for the Hasidic women who are most attached to the religious community, the sex-segregated world of Jewish orthodoxy has provided strong female identities. Sex-segregated living sets the stage for many of these women's perceptions and sensibilities.

Many women spoke freely of the support they often found in the company of other women. "Not since my days at [a small women's college] can I remember being so close to other women. We do go out as couples, but the main part of my life is spent in the company of other women. I like that." Another woman states: "We don't compete with one another for men's attention . . . we really like one another." "I could not do without the help of my friends," claims another; "someone is always home, someone is always there to count on. When I had my last baby our meals were taken care of each night for one full week."

"I've discovered something I never knew before," another woman told me, "that women can be friends with one another. Before it was always competition and comparisons . . . it made it hard to be real friends." Even the currently unmarried women in the sample felt similarly. "You know we don't believe in dating a whole lot just for fun," says one nineteen-year-old. "You begin to date when you are serious about getting married. If, after three or four dates, you are not interested in the person as a mate, then you should not lead him on or he you. I've found something wonderful with other women . . . friendship; it's wonderful." Another woman described a *forshpil* she had just attended, an all-female gathering on the Sabbath before a woman marries; a "leave-taking," as it were, of her unmarried life. Female friends, usually unmarried, although the married women who may have been instrumental in introducing the bride and groom may also attend, gather together to sing and dance. One community established a choir that performed frequently in religiously sanctioned, all-female environments.

Newly Orthodox Jewish women bring to their communities secular talents and knowledge. Those most involved in child-rearing find themselves in the company of other women in a variety of religious and communal contexts. Child care, child-care arrangements, and carpooling are almost always shared with other women. In some communities, ba'alot teshuvah with some psychological expertise integrated the principles of Torah with issues of parenting and marriage, in courses for other ba'alot teshuvah. This is one of the clearest examples of how these women adapt their secular training and skills to religious life. This also provides a forum for women to air their concerns and to resolve them according to values important to them as women and as Orthodox Jews.

In one Hasidic community, many of the ba'alot teshuvah met once a week to discuss problems they might be having as newly Orthodox women, with the group providing support in helping them work out their responses. While deferring to the Orthodox community on matters of religious content, ba'alot teshuvah with expertise, especially those with psychological training, are often asked to give guest lectures and/or to lead discussion groups. Knowing where to find the needed secular resources, ba'alot teshuvah often organize get-togethers that focus on discussions about such diverse topics as body image, dieting, and nutrition. Often such groups explicitly counter the devalued images of women frequently found in the secular media.

Since much of their daily living is conducted in the company of other women, the focus on femininity, family, and, most certainly, on gender differences, is not surprising. Generally, it is in the company of other women that these ba'alot teshuvah learn, define, and refine their understandings of Jewish orthodoxy. Their study groups are led either by women teachers in the community or by others who have recently taken continuing-education courses in the community or who have returned from a "refresher" course at a yeshiva. It is in the company of other women that they learn how to apply the "feminine principles" of orthodoxy they so frequently alluded to in their interviews.

Because these newly Orthodox women depend upon specialized services for food, clothing, religious institutions, and, to some extent, recreation, they often live in communities geographically close to one another. Since they are not as distinguished from one another in dress as are men, nor are their religious duties limited to specific synagogue and study, the women often cross Orthodox lines—through joint sisterhood meetings, the use of the mikveh, and even such events as fashion shows. The women often shop together in specific bakeries, butcher shops, groceries, and fishmarkets that cater to the Orthodox population. In some large urban areas, there are book stores and arts-and-crafts shops that feature only Jewish themes and work. Women will often visit wig and dress shops together in preparation for the holidays and the many weddings they attend. The contact with women from other communities reinforces their sense of connectedness to a world of women and reinforce women-centered values.

In Jewish orthodoxy there are clear prescriptions about all the key life-cycle events: marriage, birth, death, illness. The ba'alot teshuvah often bring a new energy and fervor to the community. They are less likely to take tradition for granted. Consequently, they bring to orthodoxy not only new areas of expertise, but also a fresh perspective. For instance, several women from different Orthodox communities, including a few Hasidic ones, told me that they were involved in writing naming ceremonies when their daughters were born. Since there is no halakhic proscription against such a ceremony, they are using traditional texts in an innovative way. While this cannot serve the same religious function as the naming of the firstborn son or circumcision, it is an attempt to acknowledge publicly the value and worth of the female to the community at large.

Almost all of the women interviewed were involved in some charitable activity. Indeed, orthodoxy's obligation to take care of the community's poor, to visit the sick, and to care for the elderly falls to women. Caring for the sick, the elderly, and the young, and delivering food and clothing to centers or specific homes are done primarily by women and are seen as part of a woman's obligation to do good deeds. The ba'alot teshuvah view the religious woman's major communal responsibilities as those tasks involving connectedness, care, and nurturance. Nurturance and affiliation are more than just a way of thinking; they are a way of being for women in the Orthodox community. The social practices associated with nurturance dominate their lives. Consequently, their definitions of orthodoxy "resonate" with charity, commitment, and care.[12]

For many ba'alot teshuvah, daily religious ritual enforces a homosocial world of shared activities with other women. The practices associated with that world emphasize altruism and connectedness. The social organization of life around affiliative needs, so characteristic of Orthodox sex-segregated living, suggests that the values, modes of communication, and language of nurturance that emerge in these women's interviews are not based upon women's unique sensibilities or differences (as most of these women suggest), but rather on the mode of organizational life inherent in sex-segregated living. What emerges from that shared action are shared meanings, unique not to women, but to the activities and relationships involved in their homosocial activities. The social structural arrangements of sex-segregated living help to explain the similarities in attitude and feelings these ba'alot teshuvah express. Many of these women suggest that being in the company of other women has increased their own sense of self-worth and confidence.

The lives that women actually live in the patriarchal setting of Jewish orthodoxy reveal an energetic community of women, strong in their commitment and belief that the female, and those symbols and activities identified with the "feminine," are vital and highly valued in the Orthodox community. The ba'alot teshuvah share a culture which builds upon the strengths of that which is associated with the female and female-linked symbols. Buoyed, perhaps, by the collective consciousness of themselves as women and perhaps strengthened by the solidarity and high self-esteem a strong women's community provides, these women demand that the male community acknowledge and respect the "feminine principles" they have discovered within that tradition. Perhaps the strong ties with other women reinforce their woman-centered consciousness and help provide the knowledge (through study groups) and social pressure necessary to make those demands a reality.

ANALYZING PATRIARCHY FROM WITHIN

Feminist anthropologists have contributed to a burgeoning literature describing the ways in which women have actively negotiated their own social and physical space within patriarchal societies. In a world as highly segregated as Orthodox Jewish communities, women engage in a daily round of activities concerning gender-related and communal areas of concern dominated by other women. These sex-segregated roles encourage a tradition of female institution building, which, although it does not and cannot formally challenge male hegemony in synagogue and study, does establish nurturing, caring, and interconnected relationships as the primary basis for their everyday lives and, they claim, for the community at large.[13]

The anthropologist Michelle Rosaldo (1980) summarizes the historical and ethnographic data which strongly suggest that everywhere, from those societies we might call egalitarian to those in which sexual stratification is most marked, men have had some authority over women; that they have had a culturally legitimated right to their subordination and compliance. Rosaldo also notes, however, that whether or not their influence is acknowledged, women exert important pressures on the social life of the group. In certain circumstances, she argues, male authority "might be mitigated," and perhaps "rendered almost trivial," by women's informal influence and power (1974, p. 21). As Rosaldo points out, while authority legitimates the use of power, it does not exhaust it. Giving rewards, controlling information, exerting pressure, and shaping events are not limited to men.

In those societies where domestic and public spheres are firmly differentiated, Rosaldo asserts that

> women may win power and value by stressing their differences from men. By accepting and elaborating upon the symbols and expectations associated with their cultural definition, they may goad men into compliance, or establish a society unto themselves" (1974, p. 37).

She cites examples which show how women use the very symbols and social customs that set them apart, and seem to circumscribe their activities, to establish female solidarity and worth.[14] Rosaldo further argues that when men and women are highly segregated, men unwittingly provide women with the symbols and social resources on which to build their own systems of meaning. She hypothesizes that the extra-domestic ties that women have with other women may prove to be important sources of power and value to women in societies that create a "firm division between public and domestic, or male and female, roles" (1974, p. 39).

Cynthia Nelson (1974) suggests that segregated social worlds may not be as severe a limitation on women as they first appear. For instance, segregation may also be viewed as a way of excluding men from a wide range of contacts which women have among themselves. Not limiting descriptions of women's worlds merely to the activities and perspectives of men provides another view of the social order. Citing various ethnographic studies, Nelson writes:

> Instead of an image of segregated social worlds of men and women, in which women are relegated to the private domestic sphere, we find all-female institutions responsible for the sanctioning of breaches of social norms—certainly a most public concern (1974, p. 557).

She concludes that women do approach public affairs but that they do so from "private positions" (1974, p. 558).

Koskoff (1986) cites some of the ethnographic work of Sue Roark-Calnek on Native American ritual dance performances and writes that

> women, appearing to take a secondary role by moving quietly on the sidelines are actually subtly displaying the creative handiwork of their shawls, competing for prestige and power, not with men, but with other women. Although it may appear that the women are "allowing" the men to "assert" their "superiority," in reality, the values of the male music/dance performance are irrelevant for the women (Koskoff, 1986, p. 15).

The historian Ellen DuBois raises some interesting questions about the relationship between a woman's culture, which for her refers to the "broad-based commonality of values, institutions, relationships, and methods of communication, focused on domesticity and morality and particular to late eighteenth- and nineteenth-century women" (1980, p. 29) and feminism. She suggests that while women's culture did not "constitute an open and radical break with dominant sexual ideology," women could develop in such a culture "group solidarity and some degree of psychic autonomy from men" (1980, p. 29). Most important, DuBois argues that the "pressing historical questions about the concept of

women's culture center on its relation to feminism" (1989, p. 30).
She asks:

> At what point can we say that feminism surfaced out of women's
> culture? How was feminism in conflict with, as well as a develop-
> ment of, women's culture? What was the impact of feminism, and
> particularly of the emergence of a women's politics, on the course
> of women's culture? (1980, p. 30).[15]

DuBois warns, however, that we should not confuse women's
culture and feminism or "assume a simple and direct development
out of one into the other" (1980, p. 30). Separatism does not necessarily lead either to self-identity or cultural hegemony. Certainly
sex-segregated living does not automatically produce a women's
culture nor provide women with a feminist consciousness and a
wish to transform collectively the larger culture of which it is a
part. More important, it certainly does not automatically provide
women with the resources necessary to make any significant
changes. In fact, it may do nothing more than limit women to their
own sphere of activities, networks, and rituals, thereby reinforc-
ing the status quo. However, it may unintentionally stimulate
among women a consciousness of themselves as a group with interests of their own.[16] Some historians (Cott, 1977) suggest that
women's consciousness of themselves as a group is a prerequisite
for the development of a feminist movement. If one assumes, as
does Smith-Rosenberg, that "cosmological and symbolic systems
develop in relation to social structure" (1980, p. 61), then it would
not be surprising to find that sex-segregated living both contributes to women's accommodation to the status quo and promotes
among women the development of values and visions of the world
different from those of men. For instance, it was the strong community of woman-identified women, irrespective of their specific
political or religious causes, that some feminists believe served as
the backbone of the suffrage movement. Indeed, Estelle Freedman (1979), among others, argues that the decline of feminism

after the suffrage victory in 1920 resulted from the loss of a woman's culture.[17]

Freedman suggests that even today feminists face the kinds of problems that have been part of the feminist past; the experiences of an oppressed group which needs both "to affirm the value of its own culture and to reject the past oppression from which that culture in part originated" (1979, p. 526). Rather than imitating the male-dominated world of synagogue and study, the ba'alot teshuvah are enmeshed in a woman's world with its own sphere of activities. These women seem to enter into what Rayna Rapp (1979) might describe as a "dialectic of tradition" with the larger Orthodox community; retrieving and reclaiming for support and affirmation the feminine principles many claim are at the heart of orthodoxy and simultaneously refusing to reject that which still oppresses them within the community. Perhaps, strengthened by the solidarity and self-worth derived from a collective consciousness of themselves as women, these newly Orthodox Jews actively make claims upon the community, not as individuals, but as a community of women. Separatist living may serve as a way for these ba'alot teshuvah to feel they have control over what they define as theirs in the Orthodox community.[18]

The problem Freedman (1979) identifies not only has some parallels among these newly Orthodox Jewish women, but among some contemporary feminists as well.[19] The former are trying to claim the "feminine" from a patriarchal tradition, the latter from a feminist one. In the closing chapters, we will end where we began, by exploring the paradox of how ba'alot teshuvah seem simultaneously to accept and to negotiate patriarchal interpretation and process. I shall also explore the similarities of these women's traditional choices to different waves of feminism.

CHAPTER SIX

•

Paradoxes

Feminism and Religious-Right Women

*Rachel weeping for her children; she refused to be comforted for her
children, because they were not. Thus says the Lord: Keep thy voice
from weeping, and thy eyes from tears: for thy work shall be rewarded, says the Lord; and they shall come back again from the land
of the enemy. And there is hope for thy future, says the Lord, and thy
children shall come back again to their own border.*

Jeremiah, 31:14–17

Ample evidence attests to women's second-class status within Jewish orthodoxy. In the early 1970s, many American Jewish feminists
turned their attention inward, subjecting Judaism and the American Jewish community to the same critical analysis they had used
outside that community.[1] Umansky (1988) notes that Jewish feminism emerged as a means of asserting both Jewish visibility within
the feminist movement and feminist self-consciousness within the
American Jewish community. It reached its peak in 1974 with the
creation of the Jewish Feminist Organization, but was on the wane
by 1976 when the JFO disbanded (Umansky, 1988, p. 352). Feminists challenged theological interpretations of Jewish law in every
aspect of Jewish living. Jewish orthodoxy has responded negative-
ly to virtually all such feminist challenges. It has maintained a
religious-legal system that supports only heterosexual marriage,
recognizes only the husband's right to divorce, and leaves public
religious leadership and devotion in the hands of men.

Yet the ba'alot teshuvah describe their experiences within orthodoxy in ways that suggest a range of feeling and experience many feminists have not anticipated. Ironically, many of the ba'alot teshuvah claim that their "return" to the sex-segregated community of the patriarchal world of Jewish orthodoxy has put them in touch with their own bodies and the so-called feminine virtues of nurturance, mutuality, family, and motherhood. Paradoxically, these women claim to have found in the very branch of Judaism most resistant to feminist challenge a strong female consciousness and a community which values what they feel is "uniquely" theirs.

In the preceding chapters I have presented these newly Orthodox Jewish women in their own voices and from their own perspectives. I described their everyday world "by taking it up from within," from the standpoint of them as "knowers actually and locally situated" (Smith, 1987, p. 3). Had I not presented these ba'alot teshuvah in their own words and voices the reader might not appreciate, nor perhaps even recognize, the paradox their situation presents. Despite their rejection and often caricature of feminism, many of these women use the rhetoric and values of contemporary feminism in their everyday lives as members of the Orthodox Jewish community. Moreover, by telling their own stories in their own voices, I find it difficult to caricature them easily as only or simply another example of oppressed reactionary religious-Right women.

I began my research with feminist epistemological and methodological assumptions. I assumed these women were "minded" social actors, capable of constructing their own systems of meaning and of negotiating both their individual and collective social identities and realities. Many readers may believe I have given too much credence to the women's own words, that, like many researchers, I have "fallen in love" with my subjects, and that I am unable to see them objectively or analytically. Therefore, it is now time for me to take up their narratives from the standpoint of a feminist social scientist. I have already revealed my methodological assumptions by suggesting that we must derive our theories from the actual lives women lead.[2] My feminist orientation, as

Paradoxes

Smith (1987) might observe, compels me to place these women's narratives in an ongoing dialectic between history and the present and between institutions and the individual.

INSTITUTIONS AND THE INDIVIDUAL

No matter where they are on the Orthodox continuum, for all Orthodox men and women the core of religious authority is halakhah. Customs and community practice codified into religious law by a majority of scholars in the past are obligatory for all Orthodox Jews. Yet despite the fact that halakhah is the source of authority for all Orthodox Jews, there are distinctive differences in style, dress, and attitudes among them. Danzger (1989) identifies the three subcommunities of orthodoxy as Hasidic, "black hat" (or the *yeshivishe velt*, those who consider themselves loyal to the heads of yeshivot), and Modern (p. 53).[3]

For the ultra-Orthodox, such as the Hasidic, the rebbe of the community is the ultimate authority. Those who are traditionally Orthodox, but not Modern Orthodox, such as the Agudah, are expected to seek Torah authority from the Council of Jewish Sages. Modern Orthodox, such as Young Israel, do not defer to an Orthodox rabbinate, and, therefore, religious authority lies primarily with the rabbi of an individual synagogue or with another recognized male rabbinical *posek* (person recognized as a competent formulator of Jewish law). Danzger emphasizes that a critical distinction between the modernist and the traditionalist in orthodoxy is *"the nature and scope of the authority to which each is committed"* (1989, p. 164, italics his). He writes:

Traditionalists allow their leaders authority in political and personal matters, and the leadership attempts to exercise authority beyond the specifics of halakhah. They achieve this by developing powerful communal ties and customs. Modernists, in contrast, seek maximum scope for personal decision making, and their leadership limits it authority to halakhah. Communal ties and customs are weaker among modernists (1989, p. 164).[4]

133

Torah authorities are essential to understanding how Jewish law is interpreted. Therefore, no matter how much interpretive control these newly Orthodox women claim they may have over the meaning and symbols of nurturance, domesticity, mothering, and sexuality, it is always limited by a male authority. While they may claim that positive values are associated with the "feminine,"[5] and therefore have at their disposal a very powerful ideological tool, they do so without the mechanisms or legitimacy to contest decisions made by halakhic authority.

As noted earlier, unlike the other Jewish denominations, orthodoxy will not accept women as rabbis, refuses to count them as part of the minyan, and does not allow women to say the Kaddish (prayer for the dead) publicly for their loved ones. Even when women form separate female prayer groups and do not violate Orthodox Jewish law, they have evoked a hostile response from the authoritative Orthodox community. Sylvia Fishman writes that in 1985 a responsum on the appropriateness of female minyanim ruled that it was

> a "falsification of Torah," a "deviation," and a product of "licentiousness" of feminism. The responsum, condemned by more moderate modern Orthodox figures for its startling, undocumented brevity and blatant lack of halakhic objectivity, was followed by a more scholarly but no less inflammatory 17 page article by Rabbi Hershel Schacter (1989, p. 47).

The religious discourse,[6] be it about the body, sexuality, marriage, mothering, or prayer still resides in claims to knowledge embodied in institutions such as the yeshiva and the councils of rabbinic authority. Orthodox women confront significant problems in Jewish orthodoxy, because it is not within their power to control the discourse, even in those areas they consider the most important to them. One of the best examples of their institutional powerlessness is that of divorce. If a husband refuses to give his wife a get, or divorce contract, she cannot remarry. If she does remarry she is considered an adulteress, and any children from that marriage are considered illegitimate. Fishman points to the clear inequality of the law since under certain circumstances "the husband can legally marry again even without a get." "Because women have far more to lose than men do if no get is obtained," writes Fishman, "some men have used this as a means to blackmail their wives during divorce proceedings" (1989, p. 59).

Despite the fact that some Orthodox lay leaders have formed the organization G.E.T. (Getting Equitable Treatment), many feel most Orthodox leaders have not responded adequately to the problem.

> Despite the attention get blackmail has been given in the Jewish media . . . the Orthodox establishment has not responded. Ostrich-like, some Orthodox rabbis have even suggested that there is no problem. They maintain that they are dealing satisfactorily with the individual cases that come before them . . . they gently shoo from their presence "feminist" troublemakers, with condescending assurances that they too are deeply troubled and suffer sleepless nights but cannot change the law (Rackman, 1988, p. 38).

While the ba'alot teshuvah claim that halakhah supports them in their views of reproduction, infertile women and women married to infertile men are limited in the kinds of reproductive decisions they can make.[7] Whenever the "natural act" of sexual intercourse is interrupted, issues about paternity arise. Is the child truly the issue of the father? What about the possible consequence of incest when the child of such arrangements eventually marries? It brings into question, according to Jewish law, inheritance rights and the unintended consequence of labeling the mother as an adulteress. My telephone conversations with different Orthodox religious authorities around the country indicated that there is variation among and even within communities on the issue of artificial insemination and in vitro fertilization.[8] The use of a case-by-case decision-making process complicates challenges to such decisions.

The remainder of this chapter will explore paradoxical issues which relate to the ongoing dialectic between history and the present: how feminist rhetoric and values have entered into the narratives of women of the religious Right; how apparently conflicting arguments (relational and individual) have been at the heart of feminist discourse both past and present; how, for instance, both newly Orthodox Jewish women and some contemporary feminists, despite radically different politics, argue for celebrating women's culture, women's biological processes, and the affirmation of the nurturant qualities of women.

In the next section, I shall place these Jewish Orthodox women's stories in the context of other "born again" narratives. These narratives tell us something about current social texts which may become tomorrow's historical and cultural texts about religious-Right women in the closing decades of the twentieth century.

BA'ALOT TESHUVAH: LOOKING LIKE THE RELIGIOUS RIGHT?

Early scholarship about the American New Right political movement drew sweeping generalizations from the rhetorical and visual portraits presented by conservative politicians, prime-time preachers, commentators from the conservative think tanks, and other representatives of the male-dominated Moral Majority. Andrea Dworkin (1983) was one of the first to write a full-length book about the New Right's appeal to women. Dworkin acknowledged that men controlled the New Right political movement by building on women's fear, ignorance, and dependence. Her major contribution was showing how male violence against women contributes to many women's need for a conservative world order.

Other scholars have broadened our perspectives of both the roots and the theoretical issues of right-wing women's antipathy toward feminism (Conover and Gray, 1983; Ehrenreich, 1983; Eisenstein, 1982). Recently, some feminists have drawn a nuanced and ambiguous portrait of conservative, religious-Right women (Pohli, 1983; Stacey and Gerard, 1988; Stacey, 1987; Ammerman, 1987).[9] They have explored popular myths about religious-Right women, revealing subtle differences among "antifeminist" women. In doing so, they have also contributed to a more inclusive feminist analysis of contemporary American women's problems and concerns. Carol Pohli (1980) was among the first to question the ideological unity among Evangelical women. In a research poll of women members of conservative Protestant churches, Pohli demonstrates that there is a small but significant percentage of Evangelical women who carry the tradition of Protestant individualism to its logical conclusion—independent thinking (Pohli, 1983, p. 549).

Like other women of the religious Right, the ba'alot teshuvah articulate their uneasiness about the quality of secular life, particularly for women. In general, most claim that orthodoxy enhances women's status, protects women as a group, and focuses both men and women on familial life. Other "born again" women have made similar claims for an enhanced status for women and for greater claims upon men as husbands and fathers within patriarchal religions.

Elizabeth Brusco's Colombian field research traces how converting to Evangelical Protestantism affects converts' domestic lives. Her data reveal that conversion serves to reform gender roles in a way that enhances female status. She writes:

It promotes female interests not only in simple practical ways, but also through its potential as an antidote to machismo (the culturàlly constructed emphatic masculinity which constitutes a variant of the male role in Colombia as well as in other parts of Latin America) (1986, p. 3).

The Evangelical movement provides a powerful ideological tool which, in Brusco's words, "radically alters sex-role behavior, promotes female interests and raises the status of women" (1986, p. 4). She writes that it does so in two ways: practically, by improving the material circumstances of the household, and strategically, by culturally reshaping "aggressive masculinity" with the Evangelical belief that places husband-wife relations at the center. Colombian Evangelicalism, writes Brusco, alters patterns of status acquisition and consumption by placing greater value on the standard of living of women and children in dependent households. Brusco argues that "[a]ggression, violence, pride, self-indulgence, and an individualistic orientation in the public sphere are replaced by peace seeking, humility, self-restraints, and a collective orientation and identity with the church and the home" (1986, p. 6). "One outcome of conversion," writes Brusco, "is that the boundaries of public male life and private female life are redrawn and the spheres themselves are redefined" (1986, p. 6).

American researchers have found similar patterns among "born again" women in the United States. Judith Stacey discovered that "a significant tendency in contemporary fundamentalist thought incorporates some feminist criticism of patriarchal men and marriage into its activism in support of patriarchal profamilialism" (1988, p. 15). She contends that the term *postfeminist*, rather than the usual *antifeminist*, characterizes the dominant gender ideology of some contemporary Evangelicals. Describing their fieldwork, Stacey and Gerard (1988) supply ample evidence of the way in which the director of the Global Ministries of Love and many of her followers selectively employ and revise Christian theology to reform and strengthen heterosexual marriages, as well as to develop a variety of viable alternatives to nuclear family life.[10]

Some evidence exists to support that what is preached among fundamentalist groups is also practiced. Nancy Ammerman's investigation of the Southside Gospel Church found that fundamentalist men do not have the power to impose their authority unilaterally on women. She notes:

> In a variety of ways, Christian wives are both powerful and powerless. Within their households, they have enormous powers of persuasion that are based in part on their intimate involvement with the details of the everyday family's life. They simply have more information, more emotional investment, and often more skill than their husbands (1987, p. 140).

Although a husband theoretically has all the authority and makes the important decisions for the family, decisions are actually made by a consensus between the husband and wife (1987,

p. 139). "The "ideal" of male domination is thus subtly accommodated to the reality of modern expectations for equality" (1987, p. 139).[11]

Rebecca Klatch (1987) suggests that the portrayal of right-wing women, based on involvement in anti-ERA or antiabortion organizations, is too limited. Like the ba'alot teshuvah, the social conservative women Klatch describes view the world through a religious lens with the family at its focus. And again, like ba'alot teshuvah, they believe in gender differences. Connie Marshner, a spokeswoman for the New Right, sounds similar to some ba'alot teshuvah when she speaks of women's nature:

A woman's nature is, simply, other-oriented. . . . Women are ordained by their nature to spend themselves in meeting the needs of others. And women, far more than men, will transmit culture and values to the next generation. There is nothing demeaning about this nature: it is ennobling (quoted in Klatch, 1987, p. 45).

Social conservatives, observes Klatch, view feminism as an antifamily force and as a symbol of narcissism, a remnant of the "Me Decade." Phylis Schlafly's fundamental distrust of individuality and freedom of self resonates with concerns similar to many of the ba'alot teshuvah:

An extraordinary emphasis on self is happening today across our nation, and this is why we continue to tear our marriages apart, splinter our families, and raise our divorce rates to new heights every year. The very core . . . is the enshrinement of individuality, the freedom of self, at the expense of marital union and social compromise (quoted in Klatch, 1987, p. 128).

However, while social conservative women blame feminists for attacking the homemaker's status and degrading the traditional female role, their fundamental distrust of men underlies that attitude. According to Klatch, it is this distrust of men that motivates their anti-ERA stand, since these women fear that homemakers will be left vulnerable if legal controls are lifted. Like the ba'alot teshuvah, social conservative women of the New Right believe that the divinely structured religious community holds men responsible to women.

Both social conservatives and feminists are concerned about women's economic dependence upon men. Rather than encouraging women to be independent, social conservatives seek security through trying to ensure women's rights and entitlements within marriage, thereby binding men to a stable family unit. Klatch writes:

> It is not, then, that social conservative women suffer from "false consciousness" in not recognizing their own self-interest as women, as some feminists charge. In fact, social conservative women are well aware of their interests as women and act in defense of these interests. The difference between social conservative women and feminists, rather, is rooted in the fundamentally different meanings each attaches to being female. . . . [S]ocial conservative Women . . . seek to extend and secure female rights within the context of marriage and the family. In this way, social conservative women are women for themselves; they act for themselves as traditional women (1987, p. 139).[12]

Although social conservative women protest male values, they do so on different grounds from that of feminists. The social conservative woman

> fears that a gender-free society will mean a world enveloped in self-interest, devoid of qualities such as nurturance, altruism, and self-sacrifice associated with the female role. If women become more like men, she reasons, there will be no one left to instill moral values in the young, to ensure that passions are controlled, to guard against a world besieged by self-interest. Social conservative women, then, act as an extension of their role as women—as mothers, as nurturers, as caretakers, as the upholders of moral values (1987, p. 206).

Characterized this way, these social conservative women appear quite similar to ba'alot teshuvah and some of their Evangelical forebears in the "woman movement." Prompted by concerns in the private arena, these religious-Right women choose communities with religiously based authority. Thus, husbands and wives are exhorted to relate to one another the way Jesus does to the Christian church. A "saved man," writes Ammerman, takes responsibility for the physical, emotional, and spiritual needs of the household. In so doing he is bound to the household. Ammerman notes:

> The people at Southside argue that their way works, that they do not suffer from divorce and unhappy homes precisely because they abide by rules for a clear division of labor and authority. To support their success claims, Southside couples often point to their own marriages; there is, in fact, little divorce in the congregation. In addition, a remarkable number (20 percent of those currently married) claim that Fundamentalist beliefs have saved their marriages (1987, p. 142).

The ba'alot teshuvah claim much of what attracts and holds them in Orthodox Judaism is the nature and description of the "feminine" and the female. Feminine spirituality and moral virtue represent not merely a criticism of excessive individualism, but of other male-linked symbols and activities often associated with Western culture as well. Antagonisms between the sexes are not settled simply or solely according to gender hierarchy, but rather according to implicit cultural rules embedded in religious practice. Such practices are regulated by traditional rules and values. These values, the ba'alot teshuvah claim, are humane and closely aligned with a "feminine" ethos which stresses a collective orientation over individual rights and quality of familial life over public achievements.

Dolores Hayden (1981) states that contemporary feminists offer the housewife few alternatives to home life. Paradoxically, increases in women's civil rights and the entry of women into male areas of work have increased women's responsibilities without any major changes in either the home or the workplace to compensate significantly for those increases. For many of the women under study and other "born again" women, the women's movement, and consequently feminism, has not defined a profamily agenda, nor proposed any realistic alternatives for transforming their private lives, particularly as heterosexual women. Indeed, as Brusco contends, private and domestic life seem to be intractable, difficult to reach through most kinds of social reform. She writes:

> [E]ven the most well-intentioned and vigorous legislative reforms aimed at promoting gender equality often fail to bring about real changes in male and female status and role behavior, particularly within the context of the family and household. Although many would argue that the "private" world of the family is ultimately shaped by wider political forces, the intimate world of courtship patterns, marital roles, and who washes the dishes seems to be one of the most conservative areas of life, or at least one of the areas which is [sic] the most difficult to police (1986, p. 5)

Because many ba'alot teshuvah have personally experienced or feared the familial and economic instabilities of our times, they reject secular liberation movements and quasi-religious communities which don't adequately address these issues. For these women, Jewish orthodoxy's concrete rules and expectations, especially about their lives as women in a community of believers, constitute an improvement over the abstract ideologies of political and social liberalism. In the next section, we shall see that feminists also have been concerned about the abstract ideologies of political and social liberalism. Moreover, their contemporary arguments have a long feminist history.

THE LIMITATIONS OF LIBERAL FEMINISM FOR BOTH FEMINISTS AND RELIGIOUS-RIGHT WOMEN

Some contemporary feminists have also become wary of the ability of liberal ideologies to reconcile individual rights and a collective identity. Barbara Rothman believes that "the difficulty in reconciling the image of people as 'atomized parts' with our very real desire for community, for interconnectedness between people, remains one of the ongoing problems of liberal society" (1989, p. 59).

Liberalism articulates the values of a technological society, "with its basic themes of order, predictability, rationality, control, rationalization of life, the systematizing and control of things and people as things, the reduction of all to component parts, and ultimately the vision of everything, including our very selves, as resources" (Rothman, 1989, p. 53). Liberalism, therefore, suggests that all ends and goals are ultimately a matter of personal taste, and leads, to our knowing, to quote Oscar Wilde, "the price of everything and the value of nothing."[13] The ba'alot teshuvah defend traditional femininity in a religious patriarchy where they claim that neither commodity nor production is the key to everyday living.

Since liberal feminism's roots are deeply embedded in American liberal culture, it necessarily shares both its virtues and its weaknesses.[14] Liberal feminism, writes Rothman, "works best to defend women's rights to be like men, to enter into men's worlds, to work at men's jobs for men's pay, to have the rights and privileges of men." But the limits of liberal feminism are most evident, she argues, "when we look at women who are, or are becoming, mothers" (1989, p. 24). Since motherhood is the very embodiment of connectedness, Rothman feels that

> every pregnant woman [is] the living proof that individuals do not enter the world as autonomous, atomistic, isolated beings. . . . In pregnancy the private self, the sexual, familial self, announces itself wherever we go. Motherhood is the embodied challenge to liberal philosophy, and that, I fear, is why a society founded on and committed to liberal philosophical principles cannot deal well with motherhood (1989, p. 59).

The liberal argument falters on those issues that women who become mothers must face. As Rothman puts it: "How can uniqueness be made to fit into an equality model?"[15] She writes: "Liberal feminism does not challenge the mind-body dualism posited by and embedded in liberal philosophy, and so falters on the same grounds. . . . [I]t has no place for the inherent physicality of gestation and lactation, and no respect for the 'menial' work of body maintenance" (1989, p. 249). Because liberalism denies the "connectedness and relatedness of individuals," liberal feminists are forced to minimize precisely those feminist priorities which reflect "an understanding of the social nature of woman's oppression" (Rothman, 1981, p. 191). Feminist politics, Zillah Eisenstein (1981) argues, requires a social collectivity that simultaneously recognizes the independence and interconnectedness of women. Elshtain puts the issue into sharp perspective when she writes that "the notion of freedom flowing from an absolutizing of rights and choice (to the exclusion of granting any similar status to principles of belonging or obligation) is a deeply flawed and impoverished one" (1984, p. 12).

It is the limitations of liberal feminism, not feminism itself, I believe, that most of these ba'alot teshuvah, and perhaps a good number of other "born again" women, reject. Women who choose to be mothers and wives under current capitalistic and technological conditions and definitions of the personal sphere of life face challenges liberal feminism has not yet adequately addressed. A focus on rights, as Rothman suggests, ignores needs. "For those people . . . who want to see women—our bodies, ourselves, our sexuality, our motherhood—treated with respect, liberal feminism fails" (1989, p. 250).[16]

Betty Friedan's *The Feminine Mystique* represents the hallmark of liberal feminism. Although Friedan's work appeared radical in 1963, it is clear that she built her understanding of the women's movement upon mainstream liberal ideology.[17] Using the dominant values that define American consciousness, Friedan helped create a feminism based on the liberal values of independence, equality of opportunity, and liberal individualism (Eisenstein, 1981). This is the feminism with which many of the women under study were most familiar.

As Eisenstein (1981) notes, claims for equality in education and work through political action did not address the unequal relationship between men and women in the domestic and familial spheres or, for that matter, in personal and emotional life in general. Women were and still are held mainly responsible for domestic, child-care, and nurturance responsibilities (Fox and Hesse-Biber, 1984).

Friedan's focus on equality and self-realization to encourage women to enter the world of work allowed the media to caricature the early stages of the contemporary women's movement as hostile to the family. Feminists' support of day care and reproductive choice for women was often characterized as hostile to children. The struggle for equality was frequently confused with embracing the male ethic of achievement based upon individualism, competition, and aggression, or simply with man-hating.

Many of the ba'alot teshuvah had been frustrated by liberalism's direction and slow reform policies. In their interviews the ba'alot teshuvah stressed the specialness of women and the importance of their sphere of activity and often juxtaposed those attributes to their conception of what was described as feminism. Most of the ba'alot teshuvah understood feminism as the liberal tradition associated with the "early" Betty Friedan and the National Organization of Women.[18] Feminism, for most of these women, is defined as the women's liberation movement, a movement they believe to be primarily focused on dismissing differences between men and women in order to achieve equal pay in the world of work. For many, Friedan's liberal feminism represented the same focus on individualism and public achievements they had rejected in the secular culture.

But in the early 1980s, Friedan again captured popular attention. In *The Second Stage* (1981), she suggests that the challenge of the 1980s would be to create new family patterns based on equality and full human identity for both sexes. Friedan now identifies the "feminist mystique" to be as debilitating as the "feminine" one. By adopting a male model of careerism and public achievement as female goals, she claimed that the feminist mystique denied women's needs for intimacy, family, and children.[19]

The shift in focus among such feminists is not as radical a break from the feminist past as it might initially seem. New feminist historiography has broadened our understanding about the evolution of feminist thought and politics. While the liberal tradition minimizes the discussions of sex-linked qualities or contributions, especially those related to childbearing and its attendant responsibilities, there is another tradition emphasizing women's rights as women (defined principally by their childbearing and/or nurturing capacities in relation to men).

Cott's aptly titled article, "Feminist Theory and Feminist Movements: the Past Before Us," reveals that women's-rights advocates in the nineteenth and early twentieth centuries pursued both the sameness and the difference (two logically opposing) arguments to advance women's causes. She writes:

> The coexistent . . . emphases, on women's full and equal human capacity, and yet on women's unique strengths and potential, reflected the fact that "woman's sphere" was both the point of oppression and the point of departure for nineteenth-century feminists. "Womanhood" was their hallmark and they insisted it should be a "human norm" too (1986, p. 51).

She notes that the American suffragist Harriet Burton Laidlaw "captured the dual message most succinctly in her 1912 assertion that insofar as women were like men they deserved the same rights, and insofar as they differed they ought to represent themselves" (Cott, 1986, pp. 51–52).

These deeply ingrained, conflicting arguments reemerge in very different forms during different periods of time, according to different sets of women's needs and historic conditions. The vote, for instance, "was pursued for different reasons by socialists and by members of the Daughters of the American Revolution, by black women and white racists; 'sexual politics' has been differently understood by, though equally central to, radical lesbians and middle-class wives" (Cott, 1986, p. 59).

Offen (1988) suggests that two modes of analysis run through feminist thought: relational and individualist. She writes:

Both the relational and the individualist modes of arguments have historical roots in what historian Temma Kaplan has called "female consciousness," or consciousness of the "rights of gender." The evidence also suggests incontrovertibly that proponents of the relational position possessed a "feminist consciousness": they viewed women's collective situation in the culture as unjust, they attributed it to social and political institutions established by men, and they believed that it could be changed by protest and political action. Nevertheless, they insisted that women had a special role, a role distinct from that of men (1988, p. 141).[20]

Offen (1988) claims that virtually all the reform efforts labeled "social feminism" during the Progressive era in the United States were based on relational feminist analysis. Revisionist historians have broadened our view of what feminism encompassed in the past and consequently what it might include in the future.

Olive Banks contends that no one was more important than Catharine Beecher among Evangelical feminists.

By arguing that women had a special reforming role in society, . . . [Beecher] provided the rationale for the entry of large numbers of women into moral reform, whether in the cause of purity, or temperance, which eventually led feminism into the attempt to use the vote to transform society itself (1981, p. 88).

Banks demonstrates how later feminists reflected Beecher's work in their writings. Elizabeth Blackwell, for example, based her claim for the need of women doctors on the notion that woman's nature "is the spiritual power of maternity . . . the subordination of the self to the welfare of others" (Banks, 1981, p. 89). Margaret Fuller emphasized "the special genius of women" (Banks, 1981, p. 89). But perhaps Beecher's most "feminist" exhortation was her belief that men should act upon "feminine" virtues. She wanted businessmen to imitate the self-denying ethics of the wife and mother.

Banks states that by the second half of the nineteenth century,

Chapter Six

the "woman movement" (as it was then called) had gone beyond the doctrine of male-female equality (liberal Enlightenment) to emphasize the notion of female superiority (1981, p. 84). A dominant theme in the movement was that women have "unique" feminine attributes based on their domestic and maternal roles. The home became a haven, an antidote to the harsh reality of the competitive male world. By the end of the nineteenth century, what we now refer to as the feminist movement in the United States was an alliance among suffrage, temperance, and social purity associations (Banks, 1981, pp. 80–81).

At the start of the twentieth century, feminist reform causes became less evangelically inspired. American middle-class women involved in social reform reached an unprecendented number (Buhle, 1980). Many of these feminists firmly adhered to the ideal of women's moral superiority rather than abstract notions of equality. Even when they argued, as did Jane Addams, "for economic independence and political rights," they "tended to base their arguments on women's moral superiority" (Banks, 1981, p. 97). Even such staunch feminists as Charlotte Perkins Gilman talked about women as mothers, whose task it was to "remake humanity . . . to rebuild this suffering world" (quoted in Banks, 1981, p. 97). Some feminists believe that the "woman movement," as a product of separate spheres, provided women with a collective self-consciousness, and, eventually, the resources to act on those issues.[21]

Women discovered that their belief in their special nature and moral superiority was a powerful ideological tool. Their difference from men was a way to develop their own organizations and argue for leadership opportunities to "clean up the world" according to their "unique" sensibilities. Rather than privatizing their concerns, they could publicly articulate their collective problems—prostitution, rape, sexuality, alcoholism, or the vote—from the perspective of woman-oriented values and goals. Many writers agree that the affirmation of women's human rights and women's unique needs and differences dominated feminism at the beginning of the twentieth century.[22]

Feminism's diverse origins yielded different, and often disparate, images of women and their "proper" place in society. It should not be surprising, therefore, that the contemporary feminist movement reflects these disparate images and arguments. Indeed, attempts to change women's position or conventional ideas about them may be viewed, depending on the sociohistoric moment, as either reactionary or radical (see Cott, 1986; Rosenberg, 1982).[23]

All through the nineteenth century, many women in the "woman movement," including those whom we now call feminists, used the metaphor of the home and a homelike world to argue for their respective causes. They appealed to women's "unique" sensibilities, and "moral superiority" to urge a "feminine" antidote for a world run amok with masculine notions of competitive achievement and individualism. Among some contemporary feminists, women's "unique" and "superior" spiritual qualities are once again emerging as a theme in feminists' respective arguments for social change.

Ba'alot Teshuvah: Looking like Contemporary Radical Feminists?

Current clashes among feminists mirror the difference-and-sameness arguments to which Cott refers.[24] Hester Eisenstein recounts two distinct phases of thinking in the United States among what she calls second-wave contemporary feminists. The earliest of second-wave feminists built on the work of Simone de Beauvoir[25] and argued that socially constructed differences between the sexes were the primary source of female oppression.[26] Generally, such writers deemphasized differences, and, in various ways, wanted to replace gender polarities with some form of androgyny (Eisenstein, 1983).

Catharine Stimpson calls this the minimalist stage of recent feminist history. Whether intentional or not, the minimalists' criticism of the gender difference theories and their emphasis on the commonality of women's experiences focused on women as a "generic grouping."[27] By the mid-1970s, feminists such as Gerda Lerner, Adrienne Rich, and Jean Baker Miller took this focus in a specific direction. They held the view that female experience ought to be the source of dominant values for the culture as a whole (Eisenstein, 1983, p. 47).[28]

A second phase in contemporary feminist thinking rejected androgyny in favor of a woman-centered perspective. This theoretical turn, like its nineteenth-century predecessor, celebrated the female and the "feminine." This woman-centered perspective was not intended "to minimize the polarizing between masculine and feminine," but "to isolate and to define those aspects of female experience that were potential sources of strength and power for women" (Eisenstein, 1983, p. xii).[29] Although this theoretical turn deepened and expanded earlier feminist thinking, Eisenstein is deeply troubled by a subsequent development, which equated female superiority with women's physicality and spirituality. In the work of Adrienne Rich and Mary Daly, for instance, a woman's body and her greater relational capacities often are associated with higher moral sensibilities than men's.

Like Daly, Rich locates women's power to change the world for the better in their bodies and in their woman-centered consciousness. Recovering the virtues of the female body has the possibility for Rich "of converting our physicality into both knowledge and power" (1976, p. 284). If women could overcome the mind-body split, "*to think through the body,*" Rich believes that many of our most entrenched patriarchal relations, ideas, and thoughts could be changed, and we could "connect what has been cruelly disorganized" (Rich, 1976, p. 284).

According to Eisenstein, Daly (1978) urges women to "reject reformism and co-optation of the women's movement, and to embark upon a further journey toward liberation" (Eisenstein, 1983, p. 107). But such a journey, Eisenstein warns does not actually challenge the status quo, but represents an inner, psychological voyage. "Without a grounding in the realities of race, class, and history, the radical feminist voyage became a metaphysical or spiritual journey, rather than a political one" (Eisenstein, 1983, p. 135).[30]

The political implications of the extreme woman-centered

feminists—variously referred to as radicals, neo-conservatives, maximalists, revisionists—were soon manifest. Eisenstein insists that a "return" to women's unique biological, emotional, temperamental, psychological, and/or spiritual qualities obscures the important contributions of the first phase of second-wave feminism.[31] Eisenstein sees the second-wave feminists' extreme position as shifting woman from agent, actor, and subject to eternal essence. One possible and unintended consequence is to reinforce patriarchal assumptions that women's bodies and their capacity to bear children relegate them universally and forever to the roles of wife and mother as patriarchy defines those roles.

Jaggar (1983) expands on Eisenstein's political analysis of radical feminists. Although she recognizes that radical feminists hold a variety of views, she believes that they all seem to agree that the basis of women's subordination has something to do with sexuality, childbearing, and childrearing. Therefore, rather than organizing around conventional political and economic issues, "they concentrate their main efforts on transforming sexual and procreative practices" (Jaggar, 1983, p. 105). Consequently, reasons Jaggar, contemporary radical feminists' criticisms of patriarchy are often offered in terms of alternatives, especially to heterosexual sexuality and familial living. Theirs is generally a separatist strategy. In this sense, it is, as Eisenstein refers to it, a retreat from confrontational politics.[32]

There are interesting parallels between radical feminists and the ba'alot teshuvah.[33] The first radical feminists, like the early "holy hippies," represented a relatively small group of predominantly white middle-class college-educated American women in the late 1960s. Like the countercultural ba'alot teshuvah, these older radical feminists had political experience in Left institutions, NOW, civil rights organizations, or in movements opposing American involvement in Vietnam. Sometimes other traditions from astrology to Zen Buddhism informed their radical feminism (Jaggar, 1983, p. 84).

Jaggar (1983) argues that radical feminism has changed since its inception.[34] Most of the younger radical feminists "are not identified by adherence to an explicit and systematic political theory. Instead, they are part of a grass-roots movement, a flourishing women's culture concerned with providing feminist alternatives in literature, music, spirituality, health services, sexuality" (Jaggar, 1983, p. 84). The contemporary radical feminist movement is characterized by a general celebration of womanhood. Jaggar writes: "This celebration takes many forms. Women's achievements are honored; women's culture is enjoyed; women's spirituality is developed; lesbianism is the preferred expression of sexuality" (1983, p. 95). Significantly, as Jaggar notes, these feminists "glorify women precisely for the same reasons that men have scorned and sometimes feared them" (1983, p. 97). Their writings abound with references to "the creative power associated with female biology" and "the native talent and superiority of women" (Jaggar, 1983, p. 95).

For each, the ba'alot teshuvah and the radical feminists whom Jaggar describes, women are a class whose membership is defined by sex. Like women-centered feminists, many ba'alot teshuvah and women of the new religious Right celebrate gender differences. For many radical feminists and for newly Orthodox Jewish women, women represent a source of special strength, knowledge, and power. Jaggar contends that radical feminists give "special value to women's reproductive functions and to the psychological characteristics that have distinguished women and men" (1983, p. 97).[35]

Other interesting similarities exist between ba'alot teshuvah and some radical feminists. Jaggar (1983) notes that radical feminists believe that the ways in which women understand the world are distinctly different from "patriarchal" approaches to knowledge. Radical feminists, she writes, believe that men see the world from a dualistic viewpoint, rationally attempting to analyze and exploit nature, while women trust their intuitive mode of knowing (p. 96). So, too, do ultra-Orthodox Jewish women claim that there are natural differences between the sexes, and that women's superior moral sensitivities arise from their greater intimacy with the everyday physical world.

These newly Orthodox Jewish women derive a great deal of strength from their highly sex-segregated living. Women-centered groups define and reinforce their sense of identity and worth. Significantly, Jaggar notes that a distinctive feature of radical feminist strategy for social change is to extol separate and autonomous women's organizations as the best means to accomplish women's liberation (Jaggar, 1983, p. 102). She acknowledges that they tend to focus their energies into developing alternative social arrangements, rather than organizing direct confrontations with patriarchy (1983, p. 104). Both newly Orthodox Jewish women and radical feminists see women's culture as the source for transformation of values for humankind.

There are, however, clear differences between newly Orthodox Jewish women and those radical feminists Jaggar describes. Significantly, radical feminists *choose* sex segregation as a way of resisting male dominance and as a way of shaping society. Sex segregation and separatist institutions are a result of their feminist demands to be autonomous. On the other hand, the ba'alot teshuvah accommodate themselves to sex-segregated living established by patriarchal tradition. Therefore, the latter develop a female consciousness limited by the parameters of patriarchy. The former develop a feminist consciousness shaped by their resistence to patriarchy. Another way in which the two differ is the way each refigures the relationship between women and men. Radical feminists admire women's strength, particularly in resisting male dominance. Although they value woman's nurturing capacity, they understand that the nurturing of the self is as important as the nurturing of others. The ba'alot teshuvah stress traditional understandings of women's nurturing capacities. Both newly Orthodox Jewish women and radical feminists emphasize the significance of sexuality, procreation, and mothering, but in significantly different ways. Where radical feminists challenge the patriarchal definitions of sexuality and maternity, the ba'alot teshuvah do not.

Here lies the fundamental distinction between the two. Radical feminists have politicized the reproductive sphere, believing that it determines how economic production as well as other forms of culture are organized (Jaggar, 1983, p. 105). The ba'alot teshuvah have no analogous understanding of the politics of sexuality. They reclaim the value of sexuality and procreative practices, but within the limits of patriarchal definition.

•

Conclusion

If these newly Orthodox Jewish women appear to the reader to have omitted from their stories the "real" oppressiveness and personal disappointments of religious patriarchy, both in the private and public spheres of life, they do reveal a very "real" concern about the loss of community and a moral discourse in contemporary secular living. Such themes have surfaced in a number of empirical investigations over the past few decades, especially in the works of those writing about the rise of "new religions." At the end of the seventies, Robbins and Anthony (1979) wrote that the West had witnessed "an explosion of heterodox religiosity entailing a transplantation to the United States and Europe of Oriental mystical traditions, the emergence of a quasi-religious psychotherapy subculture, and a surge of Christian evangelical sentiment" (1979, p. 75). Indeed, the proliferation of cults and revivals was so great that the period has been referred to as "the age of conversion" (Robbins and Anthony, 1979). Debates about whether this spiritual ferment represents religion's last gasp or its revitalization are not central to this book. Explanations for this spiritual ferment, however, do provide a backdrop to the stories of conversion these Orthodox and other "born again" women tell.

Robbins and Anthony describe the increase in spiritual ferment as occurring in a "climate of deepening normative ambiguity" caused by the "erosion of a cultural tradition of moral absolutism in a highly differentiated and pluralistic society" (1979, p. 75). Glock (1976) writes of a "crisis in meaning" that had been long in

Conclusion

the making. In particular, Glock points to science and the "scientific world view" as undermining "old imageries, the cultural values and social arrangements informed by them, and the inherent ability of these world views to give life meaning and purpose" (p. 362). "At the same time," he argues, "a scientific world view offers no clear alternative formula either for organizing society or for living one's life" (p. 362). While the scientific world view could expose the myths of old world views, it could not "contribute an alternative myth as a substitute for the old one" (p. 365). Consequently, "Old ideas were brought out, dusted off, and made available either in their original or in amended forms" (p. 365). It is the lack of satisfaction with the everyday, claims Glock, that has led to a "widespread exploration among youth of alternative ways of interpreting their worlds and living their lives" (p. 353). For Anthony and Robbins (1982) the traditionalist resurgence, "as witnessed by the growth of conservative Protestant denominations, evangelical movements within liberal denominations, and the Catholic charismatic movements, as well as the surge of neoorthodoxy within American Judaism, are all evidence of widespread repudiation of cultural modernism" (p. 235).

Conversations with these ba'alot teshuvah help to provide some of the concrete dimensions of such abstract concepts as "cultural modernism" and a "crisis in meaning." Their stories focus us on the everyday concerns that many women face, given the particular organization of political, economic, and familial arrangements in our contemporary postindustrial liberal patriarchy. Their stories help us to refigure realities many of us believe we know and therefore have taken for granted. Those stories help bring to life tomorrow's understanding of history and culture (Bordo, 1990). Gender figures importantly in their understanding of "cultural modernism" and a "crisis in meaning." These so-called antifeminist women focus clearly and decidedly on gender as the predominant principle in their lives and as the cornerstone of their ideological and political stances. More important, they add dimension and challenge to contemporary feminist discourse. For those of us who wish to build a radical future for liberal feminism (Eisenstein, 1981a), their stories are instructive.

156

These women have found in Jewish orthodoxy a sense of community and a moral discourse to be used for everyday living. While their narratives may have omitted what they have lost, they have no difficulty in recounting what they have found in Jewish orthodoxy. For most, the personal costs of coversion were and still are well worth the price. And while religious orthodoxy may not provide the answers for most of us, these women have raised important questions about the meaning of family, the politics of gender identity, and feminism in the closing decades of the twentieth century. Their stories, and those of other "born again" women, reveal more than the antipathy of an antifeminist religious Right. Their voices are the voices of women trying to cope with what they perceive to be the inequities and imbalances of postindustrial living and liberal patriarchal culture.

Feminist sociology begins with the premise that women's experiences are central to the construction of social reality. Loosely structured interviews allowed me to uncover those issues and concerns that were significant to these newly Orthodox women, rather than those events community leaders might consider important. Smith-Rosenberg notes that when we insist on "men as the central actors in women's past, and thus transform women's history into a subcategory of the history of male values and behavior" (1980, p. 56), we risk losing an important part of that historical narrative.[1] Therefore, I have not begun this narrative about newly Orthodox Jewish women from a patriarchal discourse— that is, from its historically social and institutionally specific structure of statements, terms, and categories. Rather, I have begun by relating the ways in which this particular set of women think and talk about their lives and the ways in which they do or do not make claims upon others.

Interpretive models of sociology encourage us, as Max Weber claimed, to understand "social action insofar as the acting individual attaches a subjective meaning to it" (1964, p. 88), or, as Blumer puts it, to "get inside their worlds of meanings" (1969, p. 51). The epistemological and methodological bases of most feminist and interpretive sociology call for analytic categories as complex as the lives people actually live.[2] Feminist models focus on how women understand their own value systems. We cannot, then, limit the world to male images of women nor assume that the parameters of women's experiences are set by male exploitation alone (Smith-Rosenberg, 1980, p. 56).[3] For, as I have argued, even within the most rigid patriarchal parameters, women seem able to develop some interpretive control.[4] A feminist framework does not begin with the assumption that what goes on in the public world of men's relations is the most important focus in an analysis of female relationships or of community relations in general. As "minded" social actors, women are capable of constructing their own systems of meaning and of negotiating their social reality.

The women's culture described in these past chapters is a composite of female-defined values and processes within an overall male-defined context. Therefore, an analysis of women's culture should end with some discussion of the complex relationship between female and male cultural forms within the context of Jewish orthodoxy.

In the orthodox Jewish community the shared belief system for both men and women is steeped in patriarchy. Feminists are not incorrect in their recognition that this serves as a powerful social-control mechanism in consigning women to public religious activities which are subordinate in importance and power to those of men. Yet there is another set of belief systems which affects the everyday actions of men and women as separate groups.[5] In this specific sense, women's mutually shared meanings of the religious community serve simultaneously as an accommodation and resistance to patriarchy; they simultaneously ignore those institutions important to men and to what maintains male dominance, while creating and/or maintaining their own more relevant systems of meaning (Koskoff, 1986). In turn, these systems help them negotiate their familial and marital roles and, in limited ways, to recast patriarchal definition and practice.[6]

What are the issues and concerns of newly Orthodox Jewish women? How do they react to the world of Jewish orthodoxy and reflect upon the meanings of phenomena, wield symbols, and communicate about them? These women claim that much of what attracts and holds them in this traditional life-style is the nature and description of the "feminine" and the female in Jewish orthodoxy. Both Hasidic and non-Hasidic women invoke classical Jewish sources to express their positive identification and participation in orthodoxy. Ironically, it is through their "return" to the sex-segregated conditions of patriarchal tradition that many of these women claim they have developed a consciousness which values their reproductive and spiritual selves.

Recognizing that social movements and/or ideologies which promise self-fulfillment and personal autonomy over familial and communal values almost always leave women at a distinct disadvantage,[7] these ba'alot teshuvah negotiate their familial and personal status within Jewish orthodoxy through the positive and sacred use of the symbols and structure associated with the female and the "feminine." In so doing, they claim they hold men and the community accountable to them. For many, the formal world of patriarchy in Jewish orthodoxy is preferable to the informal secular patriarchal one they have rejected.

These ba'alot teshuvah focus on "feminine" qualities which the community as a whole expects of both men and women. For example, such qualities as modesty and charity are seen as normative for the community at large. For instance, men and women are not expected to present themselves in an aggressive or self-important manner. Charity is described by some Jewish authorities as a character trait that is the basis for all Jewish ethics (Meiselman, 1978). The concept goes beyond charitable work to mean a concern for the welfare of others out of an identification with others' concerns and problems.[8]

Many ba'alot teshuvah began their journeys toward Jewish orthodoxy partly in reaction against feminism or any "liberation" movement they perceived as placing individual freedom above social responsibility. While they do not adopt feminist politics, the data suggest that almost all of them selectively incorporate and adapt woman-centered values. Therefore, while most of these women openly reject feminism or what they perceive feminism to represent, they nevertheless maintain a gender identity deeply informed by attitudes and values some contemporary feminists hold. Like some second-wave feminists,[9] the ba'alot teshuvah celebrate the female and female-linked qualities and traits. Not only do they contrast the "feminine" ethos of nurturance, connectedness, and caring with what they see as the "masculine" ethos of "materialistic" success, aggression, and individualism, but they view it as a source of power and strength for themselves as well. They symbolically negotiate their familial and marital roles in ways that they believe help them maintain control over their bodies and their sexuality. They also feel they maintain strong family-centered values for the community at large and can hold men accountable to them and family life on those grounds.

Feminist anthropologists have illuminated the ways in which women actively negotiate their own social and physical space within patriarchal societies (Rosaldo, 1974). Feminist historians have shown how the defense of the domestic sphere and "femininity" has served feminist as well as antifeminist purposes.[10] And even more recently, some feminist sociologists have suggested that "evangelical theology and institutions may be flexible resources for renegotiating gender and family relationships, and not exclusively in reactionary or masculinist directions" (Stacey and Gerard, 1988, p. 2).[11]

Such negotiations, however, reflect the powers of the weak.[12] Although these newly Orthodox Jewish women have little doubt that they are theologically equal to men, they do not directly challenge the sociological and legal sources of gender inequality. At best, some have made attempts to reform, but certainly not transform, some of the laws associated with divorce.[13] They do not forthrightly challenge male hegemony in the public, legal community that is identified as Jewish orthodoxy (the world of synagogue and study). They accept as the very premise of orthodoxy that men are to be at the center of the religious community as rabbis, leaders, and those who study and interpret the heart of orthodoxy—religious law. They do not explicitly acknowledge that the "feminine" virtues they celebrate also support a gendered religious division of labor that clearly helps to maintain their subordinate status to men—in public religious ceremony and in religious law. In this sense, they do not use their gender identity for confrontational politics with patriarchy.

Therefore, although these women share some attitudes and values in common with some feminists, their female-consciousness[14] is limited, at best to mild reformist tactics and most certainly to the concerns of primarily other Orthodox heterosexual Jewish women. Since these women's most important roles involve their functions as wives and mothers, unmarried, divorced, widowed, separated, and childless women face clear problems within such communities. Furthermore, while they may express positive values associated with the "feminine," they do so without the mechanisms or legitimacy to reject what is still oppressive to them and others, and thus "fail to extend moral authority so that it becomes a part of social institutions beyond the family" (Lipman-Blumen, 1984, p. 32). Their gender strategy does not directly address the politics of religious patriarchy or the division of labor that helps to maintain it.

While the feminine principles of which the ba'alot teshuvah speak may serve well at an ideological level, these women lack the mechanisms to enforce or to institute the practices associated with such principles for the Orthodox community as a whole. In this sense, those social practices which extol the "feminine" emanate from the world of women, not from the community of men and women. As of now, these women do not use their strong gender identity (itself, at least partially, derived from sex-segregated living) to challenge directly a system of inviolable law defined and continually refined by men.

However, as suggested earlier, a female collective consciousness is a product of both social conditioning and human agency. By virtue of their own historic placement, it is not unreasonable to argue that some of the values, goals, and strategies of these newly Orthodox women can be presented as a variation on both contemporary and past feminist rhetoric and strategy. The focus and the language of these, and other Orthodox women, set at least some of the terms for ongoing discussions within the Orthodox community. That there is a collective movement within orthodoxy around divorce suggests that the case-by-case decision making of authoritative rabbinic decision makers is not working. That the issue of women's prayer groups has forced a virulent attack against "feminist troublemakers" within the Orthodox ranks suggests again that the patriarchal discourse of religious orthodoxy is forced "not to forget the ladies."

Different historic times, like different life-cycle stages, demand different strategies. Because those strategies and the discourse presented in the support of those strategies change, no patriarchal setting is quite the same or continues to be the same over time. There is a tension between Jewish orthodoxy's most oppressive and more flexible argumentation. Each historic moment presents its own challenges to Jewish law and creates its own discourse in response to those challenges. The entire collection of reponsa reflects those changes. That some challenge has emerged to the patriarchal law is clear from both the slow, incremental changes for women in public rites and private rituals, and from the way feminism may have helped to set some of the terms of contemporary halakhic discourse (Fishman, 1989).

As the dimensions of the private sphere of life change for these ba'alot teshuvah and as the female community continues to grow more knowledgeable in halakhah, perhaps they will be able to articulate more definitively and authoritatively the clear contradictions between what orthodoxy preaches and what it practices (for example, the community coming down hard on the women forming prayer groups, the potential for blackmail and coercion of husbands against wives in granting a divorce, the equivocation among Torah authorities on the use of forms of technology surrounding childbearing, such as artificial insemination, and in vitro fertilization). It remains to be seen how orthodoxy might be forced to accommodate these newly Orthodox Jewish women, especially as they grow more knowledgeable and secure about their choice to perhaps challenge Orthodox interpretation and operation.[15] Interestingly, it was two leading Orthodox figures, Hafetz Hayyim and the Belzer Rebbe, who pointed out that women receiving sophisticated secular education, but rudimentary Jewish education, were likely to abandon orthodoxy. Fishman writes:

Conclusion

Today, intensive Jewish education of girls is widely accepted by all Orthodox elements as an absolute necessity. In day schools ranging from Satmar's Bais Rochel system, which eliminates the 12th grade to make sure its graduates cannot attend college, to coeducational Orthodox schools such as Ramaz in New York and Maimonides in Boston, which provide outstanding secular education and teach both boys and girls Talmud, a rigorous Jewish education for girls has become an undisputed Orthodox communal priority. During the past decade, it has also become increasingly popular for Orthodox young women to spend a year of religious study in an Israeli yeshivah between high school and college (1989, p. 49).

Their initial ignorance of Jewish law and custom requires that most ba'alot teshuvah undergo a rather intensive religious education. As revealed earlier, many continue with their religious educations. Because many of these women have been well educated prior to their return to orthodoxy, it is not uncommon for them to bring that same kind of critical curiosity to their Jewish education as well. As we have seen, in some of these Orthodox homes a daughter's birth occasions a special welcoming ceremony, although it cannot equal in significance the circumcision rite of the male offspring.[16]

In all likelihood, time will alter many of these women's experiences with Jewish orthodoxy, especially those which tie their private and religious lives so closely. If the expression of their spirituality is so closely tied to the lives they lead as wives and mothers, what might happen when those roles are completed or substantially diminished as they move along the life cycle from young wives to widows? Their choices have been made at a particular point in time and at a particular time in the life cycle.

While their female collective consciousness may now mesh well with their overall definitions of themselves within the sex-segregated world of orthodoxy, what will happen when there is a disjuncture between what is culturally given and subjectively experienced? The close connections the ba'alot teshuvah make between their domestic and religious lives may continue to affect the

163

way they collectively interpret the symbols and rituals of the Orthodox community. As women live longer and spend more time without children and without husbands, as most demographic projections suggest (Giele, 1982; Lopata, 1973), will the issues concerning their spirituality in the public religious community, as opposed to the private sphere of home, become more important to them? Will the virulent attacks against the women including Orthodox women, who attempted to pray at the Western Wall in Israel (without violating halakhic law),[17] for instance, become more problematic for women when they find more time for public rituals and spirituality? Will the aggressive stance taken against the Palestinians and the vigorous defense of Israeli settlements in the West Bank lead these women to question their belief that a "feminine ethos," as collectively defined, is at the heart of Jewish orthodoxy?

Women committed to heterosexual marriage, sexuality, and motherhood have found in religious profamilialism one answer to the instabilities associated with familial and occupational arrangements for women in the closing decades of the twentieth century. Newly Orthodox Jewish women emphasize their uniqueness and difference from men in their efforts to rectify what they see as injustices and failures within liberal patriarchy to provide a clear set of moral values other than those related to individual rights, and to bring public remedy to private injustices, especially those that exist between men and women.

That women are the same as and different from men complicates the formulation of feminist politics. As Cott states it:

Feminism is nothing if not paradoxical. It aims for individual freedoms by mobilizing sex solidarity. It acknowledges diversity among women while positing that women recognize their unity. It requires gender consciousness for its basis, yet calls for the elimination of prescribed gender roles. These paradoxes of feminism are rooted in women's actual situation, being the same (in a species sense) as men; being different, with respect to reproductive biology and gender construction, from men. In another complication, all women may be said to be "the same," as distinct from all men with respect to

Conclusion

reproductive biology, and yet "not the same," with respect to the variance of gender construction. Both theory and practice in feminism historically have had to deal with the fact that women are the same as and different from men, and the fact that women's gender identify is not separable from the other factors that make up our selves: race, region, culture, class, age (1986, p. 49).

The question remains whether these newly Orthodox women and feminists can learn ways of using the vantage point of difference without stumbling on its limitations.

The time it has taken to write this book, from research to final editing, has encompassed almost a decade of ferment and excitement in the feminist community of scholars. We are exploring the similarities and differences between a postmodern and a feminist stance. Like postmodernists, feminists have questioned the objectivity of the academy and most particularly have shown that "claims put forth as universally applicable" are generally "valid only for men of a particular culture, class and race" (Nicholson, 1990, p. 5).[18] Feminists have situated in time and place the construction of theory itself. As Nicholson suggests: "Feminist theorists have not attempted, by and large, the construction of cross-cultural theories of the true, the just, or the beautiful. On the contrary, feminist theorists have most frequently claimed to base their theories in observation and to acknowledge their construction as rooted in the concerns of the present" (1990, p. 5).[19]

Gender identity is key to these newly Orthodox Jewish women. It has been crucial to different constituencies in the feminist movement. Women have used their gender identity culturally to resist or challenge aspects of patriarchy, capitalism, technology, and even feminism, as each is commonly understood at a particular sociopolitical moment in history. Gender identity has been used both for political accommodation and resistance.

I have presented these newly Orthodox Jewish women's narratives in hopes of constructing what constitutes nurturance, sexuality, domesticity, family, and public and private arenas according to certain women's needs at certain sociopolitical points in time.

Comparisons to other groups of women, both past and present, are predicated on the assumption that similarities are artifacts of similar social constructions, not universal definitions.[20]

It remains to be seen whether the infusion of feminist "rhetoric" by some of these newly Orthodox women will eventually present challenges to the patriarchal discourse that determines the kinds of opportunities they enjoy. As of now, these women cannot make claims which transcend collective patriarchal interpretation. But what of their daughters? If identity and politics are a by-product of both social conditioning and human agency, and if no patriarchal setting is ever the same as another in time or location, then we can speculate that the very conditions for changes in the way claims are made and the ability to enforce them may currently be in the making.[21]

The long history of the women's movement suggests that the two strands of argument, sameness and difference, were generally not seen as mutually exclusive, but were often dialectically juxtaposed to one another. Same and different, individual and relational, gender and sex are not always mutually exclusive, and, for theoretical and political reasons, often have to be juxtaposed.[22] The political arena of academic knowledge-making requires similar strategies: gender/sex categories have raised our consciousness and have helped to change the very epistemological processes whereby we have come to understand those terms.[23] It is not contradictory, it seems to me, to keep a foot in each camp: to understand that women as a whole differ from men as a whole and that there is great diversity among us as well.

In this book I have tried to maintain a wariness toward generalizing beyond the boundaries of the white, female, primarily middle-class urban dwellers under study. I have tried to base my theories "in observation" and to acknowledge that they are "rooted in the concerns of the present" (Nicholson, 1990, p. 5). But I am also aware that the narratives these newly Orthodox women recount resonate with other stories of women from the past and in the present, different from them in religion, class, and ethnicity. Acutely aware of assaults on essentialism, I conclude that gender makes a difference. I have one foot in the modern camp of a "woman's perspective" and another in the plurality of conditions which give voice to "women's perspectives," for while I am not able to present a "truth" about women in the closing decades of the twentieth century, I hope I have added to a less false[24] set of narratives about gender, identity, feminism, and politics.

Notes

Introduction

1. Much of the debate about religious renewal is contained in renewed discussions about the meaning and direction of the secularization thesis commonly subscribed to by the founding fathers of sociology. See especially Robbins, Anthony, and Richardson (1978) for a comprehensive review of the issues and arguments about "new religions."

2. Some caution about assessing revivals is in order. For instance, Barbara Hargrove cautions:

> A good deal of the apparent increase of evangelical Christianity is in reality an increase in media and scholarly interest in the evangelicals. For example, a 1976 Gallup poll showed 34 percent of the American population claiming to have had a "born again" experience. However, the poll is not particularly useful for ascertaining trends, since it was only in that year that the question had seemed worth asking. A significant percentage of those claiming the experience were older people who might be expected to have been converted many years ago. There is, however, little doubt about an increase in public awareness of evangelical Christianity and in its respectability. That in itself could be considered a new movement. (Hargrove, 1979, p. 282)

3. And again, as with religious renewal in general, there is controversy about numbers and the meaning of Jewish Orthodox revival. In particular, there is some question about whether the indicators of growth are signs of numerical growth or a byproduct of increased organizational

coherence and affluence among Orthodox Jews (and therefore an increase in institutions serving that population).

4. The term *teshuvah* can be interpreted in several ways. It can mean "repentance from sin" or "return to the past." The past can represent one's own past or one's ancestral past. It can also mean an abrupt change or turning. Since most of these women had never been Orthodox, "return," in the literal sense, is a misnomer. See Steinsaltz (1982) for a fuller discussion of *teshuvah*.

5. For instance, in a six-part series by H. D. S. Greenway on Islamic revival in nearly all of the radical Arab countries, the *Boston Globe* reports that even in comparatively liberal countries such as Egypt, Kuwait, and Jordan, some educated women are turning to the veil, which many of their mothers fought to discard. Indeed, notes the *Globe*, women were in the vanguard of the fundamentalist takeover of the student union at Kuwait University (*Boston Globe*, March 6, 1986, p. 20). In the United States, Concerned Women for America, headed by a fundamentalist, Beverly LaHaye, boasts 500,000 members, more than the combined following of NOW, the National Women's Political Caucus, and the League of Women Voters (*Time*, September 2, 1985, p. 50). However, in a personal communication to me, the political scientist Denise Baer suggests that the claims made by Concerned Women for America are somewhat suspect. She suggests that most of the members are probably checkbook members drawn from the televangelist audiences, not true grassroots members. She believes that the small budget of $6 million for a membership of 500,000 is nowhere near what it should be unless the dues are quite small (unlike the usual $25 for most national women's organizations).

6. The five cities include Boston, Cleveland, New York City (including Crown Heights), Los Angeles, and San Francisco. The choice to interview in these cities was based on several considerations. All five cities have a visible Orthodox Jewish population, ranging from 5 percent in Los Angeles to 13 percent in New York City, claiming Orthodox affiliation; see also Tobin and Chenkin (1985). Interviewing also occurred in cities where I had Jewish communal contacts who could help me map the Orthodox communities and provide contacts, and where there were known newly Orthodox Jews. Finally, this was not a study of Orthodox Judaism nor of Orthodox communities.

7. In most social science studies, the Orthodox Jewish community is generally explored and then analyzed through the perspectives and experiences of men, especially through the male-oriented activities associ-

ated with synagogue and study. Even some of the most recent books published on Jewish orthodoxy, despite their rich detail and keen insights, fail to give us any compelling sociological explanation of orthodoxy's potential appeal to women. In *The World of the Yeshiva* (1982), William Helmreich confines his study to the all-male world of the yeshiva. In highly sex-segregated religious communities, it is difficult for men to gain access to the institutions relevant to Orthodox women's lives or to explore their experiences within them. Neither Helmreich (1982) nor Mayer (1979) focuses exclusively on newly Orthodox Jews. Given women's different location within the community, it would be unexpected if the attraction to orthodoxy or the mechanisms which held them to that traditional life-style were the same for women as for men.

Other works about Orthodox communities in general and Hasidic sects in particular were helpful in situating the material on newly Orthodox Jews: Kranzler (1961, 1978); Poll (1962); Liebman (1964); Rubin (1972); Levy (1975); Pinsker (1975); Mayer (1973, 1977, 1979); Mayer and Waxman (1977); Mitchell and Plotnicov (1975); Katz and Katz (1977); Gutwirth (1978); Heilman (1977, 1978); Shaffir (1974); Wallach (1977); Singer (1978); Bosk (1979); Mintz (1979).

8.   For a fuller discussion, See Kaufman (1985a, 1985b, 1987, 1990).

9.   Eighty-five percent of the women returned a questionnaire left with them in which they detailed their demographic histories.

10.   Only 8 of the 150 women were "lapsed" Orthodox Jews and therefore had any previous knowledge or familiarity with Orthodox Judaism. Ten were converts to Judaism. The majority identified themselves, as one woman phrased it, as "bagel and lox" Jews.

11.   The havurot of the 1970s took two forms, writes Heilman (1982): as a separate fellowship of religious seekers and as a concentrated fellowship or quasi-kin group within a large synagogue.

12.   In this book, *halakhah* refers to traditional Jewish law as observed today (with minor variations) by Orthodox Jews throughout the world. As Judith Wegner notes: "Departures from the *halakhah* by progressive Judaism, whether Conservative or Reform, are not called 'Jewish law' even by those adopting them, but are recognized as accommodations to changed social circumstances" (1982, p. 1).

13.   Lynn Davidman (1986) compared ba'alot teshuvah in a Lubavitch yeshiva to those in a modern Orthodox setting. I know of no other research that focuses solely upon newly Orthodox Jewish women. Virtually all studies to date focus on a ready-to-hand population either in yeshivot or in specific synagogue settings.

14.   Aviad (1983) estimates that two-thirds of her sample of 1,200 students in ba'al teshuvah yeshivot in Israel were American. Moreover, males outnumbered females by about four to one. Glanz and Harrison (1978) estimate that since the early seventies, several hundred youthful and relatively assimilated Jews are thought to have entered Hasidic communities. More important, estimates by either rabbis of Orthodox synagogues or heads of yeshivot in the United States are at best guesstimates. Initial interviewing of several Orthodox rabbis revealed that knowledge of ba'alei teshuvah within their own communities was often limited—especially in modern Orthodox communities. No records or statistics are kept of persons in such a category. Moreover, I was told by one head of a yeshiva in the United States that he is in the habit "of counting souls, not bodies." When statistics are offered, they seem quite inflated. "We are witnessing thousands who are returning to orthodoxy," offered a leading outreach recruiter for ba'alei teshuvah in the United States. Interestingly, number estimates are difficult to obtain for almost all religious-renewal phenomena. For instance, although the American church (believers in the Unification Church of the Reverend Sun Myung Moon), writes Arthur Parsons, "has no more than 10,000 members and perhaps as few as 2,000, it has been the object of extensive sociological and psychological analysis" (1985, p. 1).

15.   Once within these settings, the referral method or snowball technique of sampling (Coleman, 1971; Taylor and Bogdan, 1984) was employed, thereby identifying smaller interactive groups of ba'alot teshuva within each community. Interviewees were asked for names and addresses of people they knew about, rather than friends' names or names of people they knew personally (although such names were also permissible). In this way the population under study was more than a network of friends, but also a population who, for religious reasons, live in easily identified communities and/or who share common religious institutions. Interviewing ended when no new names were generated. No claims are made that the women under study were randomly drawn as a sample of a defined universe nor can the interviewed by considered statistically representative of those who return to Orthodox Judaism or of orthodoxy itself.

16.   See also Sarah Bunim (1986). For her dissertation research, Bunim compared three groups of Orthodox mothers representing the continuum just described. She chose her population from three synagogues or study settings: Kollel (most stringent), Agudah, Young Israel (least stringent). She suggests that Young Israel (modern Orthodox) rep-

resents the church end of a church-sect continuum and Kollel (ultra-Orthodox) the sect end of such a continuum.

17. In her summary of secular education of Jews in New Jersey, by sex and age, Fishman (1989, p. 21, table 2) found that 56 percent of the females between the ages of twenty-five and thirty-four had completed their bachelors' degrees, 24 percent their masters' degrees, 3 percent their postgraduate degrees, and 1 percent their Ph.D's. The data are fairly similar to the data cited for other major urban areas in other population studies I found at the Center for Modern Jewish Studies at Brandeis University. Janet Aviad (1983) reports that 45 percent of those she studied had had at least some college education.

18. Data obtained from virtually all population studies in the 1985 *Jewish Yearbook* reflect that employed Jews are more likely to be found in the solidly middle-class professional and manager-administrator occupational categories than in any others. Written correspondence with Janet Aviad confirmed that the ba'alei teshuvah she studied fell solidly within the middle-class socioeconomic category.

19. In Aviad's study 56 percent of the American ba'alei teshuvah ranged between twenty and twenty-five years of age.

20. Generally, these newly Orthodox Jews match the profile of those entering religious cults as well—fairly well educated, white, middle class, and of college age or slightly older (Melton, 1983).

21. Interestingly, Dr. Rasha al-Sabah, and Yale-educated vice rector of Kuwait University, notes that the new conservatism and return to the veil among college-educated Moslem women are due to a feeling that Westernization threatens the family. He writes:

This has led to a conflict among our young women . . . where do we stand with our Moslem and Arab ways? They see in Western society a high divorce rate, alcoholism, drug addiction, herpes, even AIDS. Girls here say to themselves, "what are we"? Perhaps if we return to Islamic ideas we will be able to protect ourselves and our future families from the negative winds that are coming from the West" (cited in the *Boston Globe*, March 6, p. 20).

22. Some writers suggest that it was women, not men, who argued for the extension of the period of niddah from seven to twelve days (adding to the minimum of a five-day menstrual flow another seven "clean" or "white" days) before the resumption of sexual intercourse. In

this way, women could maintain more control over their sexuality by making certain that enough time had passed so that they had actually come into "clean" days (thereby avoiding the need to have the rabbi determine, by examining the stains, if it is a "clean" or "unclean" time). See Biale (1984) for further elaboration.

23.   See especially Straus, Gelles, and Steinmetz (1980), Russell (1982), and Hoff (1984), for corroborative data.

24.   For a historical and sociological analysis see, in particular, Berger and Berger (1983). Many ironies resonate in the New Right's assault against feminism. Historically, the word *feminist* originally referred to early twentieth-century women's rights advocates who asserted the uniqueness of women and the special joys, even mystical experiences of motherhood (Gordon, 1977). Interestingly, the social conservative women in Klatch's (1987) study often echo the rhetoric and tactics of those feminists involved in the moral, educational, and social reform movements of the late nineteenth and early twentieth centuries. In addition, there are some among contemporary feminists who contrast what they perceive as women's "unique" qualities to a dominant "masculine" ethos.

25.   See Klatch (1987, p. 9) for a more extensive discussion.

26.   See especially Stacey and Gerard (1988); Stacey (1987); Brusco (1986); Ammerman (1987), and Klatch (1987) on social conservatives among New Right women.

27.   Klatch (1987) makes this point about social conservative women of the New Right.

28.   Postfeminism's dominant mood, argue Rosenfelt and Stacey (1987), is the "loneliness of women without families, the frustration and exhaustion of mothers who also must or wish to work, and the anxiety of single mothers trying to reconcile heterosexual adult relationships with maternal responsibilities" (p. 343). Aware of the controversial nature of this term, the authors write:

> Because it seems to imply the death of the women's movement, and because of the revisionist and depoliticizing aspects of the ideology it promotes, the term "postfeminism" itself troubles many feminists. . . . Although we share the concerns of those who recoil from its usage, we believe that there are important distinctions between the ideologies and constituencies of postfeminism and those of antifeminism, distinctions that make it worthwhile to grapple

with rather than simply dismiss the literature and issues of the former (1987, p. 341).

29.   Stacey uses the term *postindustrial* in a descriptive sense, "to designate a form and period of capitalist social organization in which traditional industrial occupations supply a small minority of jobs to the labor force, and the vast majority of workers labor in varieties of clerical, sales, and service positions" (1987, p. 24).

30.   Zaretsky (1973a and b), Sennett (1974), and Bellah et al. (1985) are among many authors who argue from different perspectives that Americans need to reconnect to public, communal life if they are to avoid the excessive individualism that leads to a preoccupation with self and with private interests.

31.   In fact, feminists have been most aware of this problem. Among the earliest to address this concern, without losing a feminist politics, was Zillah Eisenstein (1981, 1982).

32.   I am playing with the motto associated with the feminist movement: "The personal is political."

33.   Carroll Smith-Rosenberg writes:

In hundreds of cultures around the world and across time, women have lived in highly sex-segregated communities; spending their time with other women; developing female rituals and networks; forming primary emotional, perhaps physical and sexual ties with other women. Such women develop visions of the world, values, and indeed, I would argue, even symbolic and cosmological systems different in highly significant ways from those of the men with whom they shared sex, food, and children. Indeed even in response to the same instances of economic and institutional change, women and men of the same class, ethnicity, and religion develop quite distinctive symbolic and metaphoric systems (1980, p. 61).

Chapter One. Youth and Its Discontents

1.   Danzger (1989) notes that for at least a decade before the "hippie" interest, students with little background had been interested in Jewish orthodoxy. By 1972, he notes, the term *ba'al teshuvah* did not

mean what it had meant throughout the twentieth century—those "lacking in background" or "late starters"—but rather it referred to those who were "struggling with commitment" (p. 94).

2. Hasidism is a pietistic movement that originated in the eighteenth century among the Jews of Eastern Europe. The founder of the movement was Israel ben Eliezer (circa 1700–1760), called the Baal Shem Tov (Master of the Good Name), who emphasized zeal, prayerful devotion, and humility as a religious expression (Sharot, 1982, p. 148). The Hasidim restructured what were then traditional Jewish values by placing prayer, mysticism, dancing, singing, storytelling, and the sanctification of daily life on an equal footing with talmudic scholarship. Central to the founder's teachings was the concept of *devekut* (cleaving to God). If the intention was to "cleave to God," writes Sharot, then any act, even the most material and pleasurable, could become a religious act.

Schneur Zalman was the founder of Chabad Hasidism, which became known as Lubavitch Hasidism when its leaders moved to the Belorussian town of Lubavich, two years after Zalman's death. Zalman (1745–1813) was a blend of talmudist and mystic. Handelman notes that his writings were a "unique synthesis of Rabbinical Judaism, Kabbalah, Rationalism, and applied Mysticism" (1984, p. 3).

3. What distinguishes Hasidim from other Orthodox Jews is their devotion to their rebbe. The rebbe is considered a moral instructor and spiritual leader. Ba'alei teshuvah, in particular, and Lubavitch specifically, rely heavily on the judgments of the rebbe, whom they consider a sage and holy man. Shaffir (1974) writes that the recognition of the *tzaddik* (righteous man) as a central figure in their lives and a willingness to conform to his views and directives are the distinguishing characteristics of the Hasidim.

4. Bellah explains that at this same period of time most mainline Protestant denominations reflected the culture's dominant ethos in being virtually devoid of anything like "ecstatic experiences" (1976, p. 340). Similarly, Reform and Conservative Judaism, the more progressive branches, were identified with mainstream American values. Therefore, the more assimilated wings of Judaism were not suited to those youth who wanted a spontaneous and ecstatic religious experience.

5. Initially, the focus was on men, not women. Because men were often traveling with women, Goldstein made a place for women at Har Tzion. Initially there were only two yeshivot for women in Israel—Har Tzion and Neve Yerushalayim. (Danzger, 1989).

6.   Of this same group, more than 92 percent (65) eventually found their way to Hasidic communities.

7.   Some feminists, such as Letty Cottin Pogrebin (1982), have written about anti-Semitism in the feminist movement as well.

8.   Bellah refers to the religious and personal growth movements of the seventies as "successor" movements to those of the sixties. He writes of such movements, especially the religious ones, as "survival units . . . [which] provided a stable social setting and a coherent set of symbols for young people disoriented by the drug culture or disillusioned with radical politics" (1976, p. 342). I refer to all movements "counter" to the dominant cultural values of the time as countercultural.

9.   All three admit that their parents were so upset that (the women) voluntarily left the movement. They also believe that the experience made them more receptive to Jewish orthodoxy.

10.   Robbins, Anthony, and Richardson believe that the "new" religious movements seem to be the "most enduring of the novel social phenomena arising during the 1960s" (1978, p. 100).

11.   Eastern mysticism was the singularly most attractive alternative for the ba'alot teshuvah, whether they had identified with the counterculture of the sixties or not.

12.   The absence of a fixed set of moral codes is, according to Robbins, Anthony, and Richardson (1978), more characteristic of one-level monistic movements like est, Scientology, transcendental meditation, and Shoshu than two-level monistic movements like Hinduism or Buddhism. But even in the latter, argue the authors, the emphases are on "pragmatic maxims" or "rules of thumb", not exact codes (p. 106).

13.   Not only did all of them eventually turn to Jewish orthodoxy, but a majority turned to Hasidism, where they could find well-defined moral meanings and a well-structured system of moral rules in the context of an emotionally expressive religiosity.

14.   See especially Janet Aviad (1983) on similar points.

15.   Even some feminists have recanted on their earlier positions. Arguing that we have gone from the "body politic" to the "erotic" in contemporary feminist discourse, Germaine Greer (1984b) suggests that the sexual revolution never happened: "Permissiveness happened, and that's not better than repressiveness, because women are still being manipulated by men" (quoted in *The New York Times*, March 5, 1984, p. C-10).

16.   In contrast to Christian "born again" converts, those "returning"

to orthodoxy are not asked to believe or immediately acknowledge faith; they are simply asked to act.

17.   In a remark to a *Boston Globe* reporter, he explains more about his appellation: "My Hasidic movement had to be customized, tailored to Boston. . . . We had to provide our Boston Hasids with an American flavor. That was the job that my father started and I continued it after he passed away" (October 21, 1985, p. 17).

18.   Interestingly, the data about participants in the Jesus movement reveal that many had had bad experiences with drugs, some were having sexual identity problems, others had had unwanted pregnancies or children, or had contracted venereal diseases, or were unhappy in some other way because of sexual activity and/or drug use (Richardson, Stewart, and Simmonds, 1978, p. xxv).

19.   This is not surprising, since yeshivot for contemporary ba'alei teshuvah were first established in Israel.

20.   In the traditional yeshivot, women do not study the Talmud, the combined text of the Mishnah and the Gemara. The following are based on Wegner's (1982) definitions. The Mishnah is the earliest attempt to codify Jewish law (second century c.e.). It is classified into six divisions called *sedarim*, "orders." The third order is the Seder Nashim ("Order of Women"), which contains the rules of marriage and divorce and other rules relevant to the status of women. *Gemara* is an Aramaic word meaning "learning"; the Gemara consists of a commentary that expands, through discussions and explanations, the rules of the Mishnah. This commentary was redacted during the sixth century c.e. Except for those laws central to their practice of orthodoxy, the women do not study the Talmud (See Wegner, 1982, p. 1, for further explication).

21.   *Tanya* draws heavily on the *Zohar*, a classic work of Kabbalah. Kabbalah deals with the mystical reasons behind the laws of halakhah.

22.   Similarly, Carol McMillan writes that if "we become answerable only to ourselves for our actions and feelings without recourse to some public, and/or external authority, the whole notion of ethics collapses" (1982, p. 18).

23.   Robbins and Anthony (1979) recount several sociocultural sources for the revival of religious movements in the decade of the seventies. In a section subtitled "New Religions and the New Individualism," they review the literature that suggests that human potential, yoga, and meditation groups correspond well to "the cult of the 'individual' identified by Durkheim as the integrative mystique of a highly modernized society. Such groups venerate a power within individuals, immanent,

sacred, and independent of social commitments" (p. 79). It is this kind of individualism that the women under study seem to reject.

24.   There have been any number of analytical perspectives offered to explain the context for the emergence of cults and new religions and neo-Orthodox revivals. These include secularization, crisis of community, value crisis, and the need for holistic self-definitions in an increasingly differentiated society. Summarizing these different perspectives, Robbins, Anthony, and Richardson (1978) write that the secularization thesis asserts that exotic spiritual perspectives are distorted and eventually assimilated into a secular, materialistic, and individualistic culture. The quest-for-community thesis suggests that encounter groups and communes become substitutes for the extended family, homogeneous neighborhoods, and personalized work settings. Another thesis relates the emergence of innovative spiritual movements to a context of normative breakdown and value dissension.

Chapter Two. Four Portraits

1.   Identifying someone as Hasidic, strictly Orthodox, or Modern within orthodoxy illustrates the importance of sensitivity to gender differences. Knowing where a man prays regularly and the educational setting in which he studies readily helps to identify his stance in orthodoxy. Dress and appearance also provide easy clues about what community men identify with and how rigorously they do so. If they are clean-shaven or wear yarmulkas alone, they are most likely to be Modern. On the other hand, if one has a beard and earlocks and wears a black hat, he is very likely to be either strictly Orthodox or ultra-Orthodox (Hasidic men wear specific kinds of coats, trousers, and hats, according to their Hasidic identification and are the most easily identifiable).

But how could one identify a "black hatter" Orthodox woman? Do we simply assume she identifies in the same way that her husband does or the way in which the men of her community do? Orthodox women do not vary in dress or appearance in the same way as men. While all may abide by the Orthodox concept of modesty (covering arms, legs, heads), they do so in a variety of ways, to varying degrees, and often with a flair. Some have maintained the slightly "bohemian" look of the sixties, others have adopted a "Laura Ashley" look, and still others are smartly dressed as modestly understated professional "yuppies." Since they are not required to pray or study daily, and since they are not as distinguished from one another in dress as are the men, I relied on each woman's personal identification as the best estimate of her ideological stance in orthodoxy.

2.   Again, no claims are made that these ba'alot teshuvah are statistically representative of their communities. Therefore the differences reflect differences among the ba'alot teshuvah under study, not necessarily differences among ba'alot teshuvah, in general.

3.   I interpreted the use of Yiddish as a rejection of modern Jewish living, a way of capturing the traditional and past *shtetl* culture (small village living associated with Jews of Eastern Europe) from which Hasidic living emerged. For Hasidim, Yiddish is for everyday language and Hebrew is the language for prayer. In many Lubavitch homes, Yiddish is the first language. For instance, Sharot describes the three Lubavitch schools for boys in Crown Heights. The most prestigious school has a non-English studies program in which the teaching is entirely in Yiddish and the curriculum is completely Jewish in orientation. This is the preferred school for core Lubavitch and for some ba'alei teshuvah who wish to establish their "credentials" and "status" in the community (Sharot, 1982, p. 199).

4.   Confession is not a part of religious obligation or expectation in Judaism. The rebbe is considered a moral instructor and spiritual leader. Ba'alei teshuvah in particular, and Lubavitch specifically, rely heavily on the judgments of the rebbe, whom they consider a sage and holy man.

5.   Orthodox women abide by the custom of *tzniut* (modesty). While the customs may vary, for instance, in what kind of headcovering they will use and how much of their arms and legs they will cover, the Lubavitch women I interviewed did not wear pants or slacks at home or in public. Hasidim have a distinctive use of dress and language. Most Lubavitch men dress in a conservative manner. They usually wear narrow-brimmed hats and dark suits. Most do not grow earlocks but do have beards. Women cover their arms at least to the elbows, and their dresses and skirts must cover the greater part of their legs. Even in the summer, they often wear dark stockings.

6.   Only married women are required to cover their heads. However, many Orthodox women will cover their heads with a scarf, not a wig, when indoors. Although this usage will vary with the woman, many Orthodox women wear wigs only in public. While the women understand that the perception of wearing a wig insinuates male control and possession (only a husband is to see his wife's hair), almost to a woman they spoke of the headcovering as a sign of their distinction, difference,

and separation from the society at large: a sign, they claim, of their holiness and pride. For a nice discussion of the theme of separation and Orthodox practice, see Baskin (1985).

7.   In Bunim's study (1986) the ultra-Orthodox women were more likely than the other Orthodox women to have their husbands seek religious, authoritative answers to their personal and religious questions. Of those in my study who said they discussed personal decision making with Torah authorities, most were Hasidic. In general, because they were married to other newly Orthodox Jews, Hasidic women usually sought religious advice together with their husbands. Like the modern Orthodox women in Bunim's study, the non-Hasidic women in my study were more independent of religious authority and were more likely than Hasidic women to search for the information they were seeking on their own through their own reading and research.

8.   In a personal communication to me, Judith Baskin points out that women were never high priestesses in Judaism but could come from priestly families. Bernadette Brooten cites evidence dating from the first century B.C.E. to the sixth century C.E. that women were active in the public sphere of Jewish society. They held such titles as "head of the synagogue," "leader," "elder," "mother of the synagogue," and "priestess" (cited in Baskin, 1985, p. 10.)

9.   The reader will note that there is some variation in the spelling of Hebrew and/or Yiddish words. I have tried to capture the respondents' pronunciations and their use of generally newly learned languages. Given their own backgrounds and specific Orthodox communities, some will fuse Yiddish and Hebrew and others will intermix the two when they speak.

10.   Mintz (1979) writes that generally Hasidim are not concerned with pursuing a career but rather are primarily concerned with earning a living in a way which will not interfere with their religious duties.

11.   Interestingly, almost three-quarters of the women under study had some familiarity with *Tanya*, although only about half of the women are Hasidic. Some of the women under study began their returns to orthodoxy within a Hasidic context. In addition, most had so little familiarity with Hebrew that translated texts were important sources for their early studies.

12.   In Orthodox Judaism, women are exempt from most commandments which must be performed at specific times. For example, men must pray at set times during the day; women need not.

13.   Interestingly, at this point she did reflect momentarily on the

fact that, probably because of sex discrimination, she had not been admitted to medical school when she applied.

14. She wears a comb, rather than either a tichel or a wig, as her sign of modesty. In Bunim's study, Agudah or strictly Orthodox women, like Alisa, were less likely than ultra-Orthodox women, but much more likely than Modern Orthodox women, to cover their heads. In my study, about as many strictly Orthodox women as the Modern Orthodox covered their heads—only about half in each group did so. Virtually all Hasidic women wore wigs or other headcoverings.

15. In general, the ba'alot teshuvah who identified themselves as strictly Orthodox tended to be better educated than the rest.

16. Debra does not wear a wig, although she does wear a hat at all public functions. Her turban, I surmised, was more for style, and perhaps my benefit, than for Judaic custom.

17. Although not always the case, often the non-Hasidic women in this study availed themselves of the many adult education courses and lectures offered by the Lubavitch Hasidim. Lubavitch communities are often in close proximity to other Orthodox communities.

18. The study of texts about ethical and moral behavior and critical self-examination about one's motivations and ethical life are an accepted part of the curriculum in some yeshivot. The Musar movement, which developed in the mid-nineteenth century in Lithuania and Russia in Orthodox Jewish circles, was begun by Israel Lipkin (Salanter) as a way of strengthening the connection between learning and behavior.

19. Israel Meir Ha-Kohen Kagan (1838–1933), known as Hafez Hayyim, is considered one of the most saintly figures in modern Judaism. His first book, *Hafez Hayyim*, was devoted entirely to a discussion of the laws of slander, gossip, and talebearing. He was also one of the founders and spiritual leaders of Agudat Israel, a world movement for Orthodox Judaism.

20. In Bunim's study (1986), none of the ultra-Orthodox, virtually none of the Agudah, and almost all of the Modern Orthodox women engaged in mixed swimming. I did not ask this question of my respondents, but Debra did say she goes swimming in her local Jewish community center once a day. There is no separate swimming there. Interestingly, although among the Modern Orthodox there are no proscriptions against mixed seating in public secular functions, over the past decade it appears as if Modern Orthodox have become more sex-segregated at secular functions than they have been previously. There is a growing consensus among researchers that the contemporary American Orthodox popula-

tion appears to be more "Right"—theologically, legally, and religiously—than it has been in the past (Helmreich, 1982; Liebman, 1979).

21.   The Hebrew word *Kabbalah* means "tradition." It generally refers to a large body of collected mystical teachings and writings accumulated and transmitted over the past two millennia. Kabbalah is considered by its students as the revelation of the inner, hidden mysteries of God, the universe, and the Torah (Handelman, 1984). Susan Handelman (1984) notes that the most profound, intriguing, and inviting of all Jewish theologies is Kabbalah. She further notes that it is in Kabbalah that the most intriguing and systematic explanations of the nature and the role of the feminine are discussed.

22.   Moshe Meiselman, a writer whom many feminists consider to be one of the leading apologists for Orthodox Judaism, lends credence to these women's interpretations when he notes that some Torah authorities view women's exemption from various commandments as "evidence of the greater ease with which women achieve spiritual goals" (1978, p. 43). Citing a seventeenth-century scholar, Meiselman writes: "Man's aggression is a detriment to his spiritual aspirations and he therefore must work harder and be given extra religious tasks. Women . . . because of their greater potential for spiritual growth, require fewer mitzvot to achieve spiritual perfection . . ." (p. 44). See Berman's (1976) criticism of such apologia in the text.

23.   One of the leading scholars on Jewish mysticism, however, provides a different perspective from that of Handelman. Gershom Scholem writes about the general character of Kabbalism as distinct from "other, non-Jewish, forms of mysticism. Both historically and metaphysically it is a masculine doctrine, made for men and by men. The long history of Jewish mysticism shows no trace of feminine influence. There have been no women Kabbalists . . ." (1961, p. 37). He concludes that Jewish mysticism "lacks the elements of feminine emotion" (1961, p. 37). He suggests that this does represent a paradox in that the same philosophy symbolizes the Shekhinah, the "feminine element of God himself" (1961, p. 38). Bernard Martin (1974) argues that in the rabbinic tradition and in medieval Jewish philosophy, "womanhood is frequently portrayed in negative terms, as a prime source of evil and corruption. All this was altered in the world view of Kabbalah. Femininity came to be regarded as an integral aspect of the Godhead and the sexual act as the symbol of the unification of the masculine and feminine elements in God himself" (1974, p. 52).

24.   In kabbalistic literature the Shekhinah is variously described as

daughter, bride, moon, mother, sea, faith, wisdom, speed, and as a "myriad of other figures, usually, but not always feminine by fact or association. . . . [T]he Shekhina is the chief object of both the divine and human search for wholeness and perfection" (Green, 1983, p. 255). For my purposes, it is not how accurate or controversial such interpretations may be, but rather what these women choose to take from Hasidut and how they choose to relate it.

25. My own limitations in the study of halakhah have forced me to rely heavily on Biale's work in presenting Jewish law as it pertains to the issues raised by the newly Orthodox Jewish women under study. I have also relied heavily on Baskin (1985); Berman (1976); Feldman (1974); Greenberg (1981); Hauptman (1974); Nathanson (1987); Neusner (1979); and Wegner (1991).

26. These texts refer to the Mishnah, Tosefta, Talmud, and Midrash. Wegner defines each accordingly: "The Mishnah . . . covers a wide range of topics of Jewish law. The Tosefta, a supplemental collection of legal rulings . . . follows the arrangement of, and further elaborates the Mishnaic material. The Palestinian and Babylonian Talmuds are voluminous commentaries on the Mishnah, produced respectively in the land of Israel between 200 and 400 c.e. and in Babylonia between 200 and 600 c.e. . . . Midrash is the generic term for a large body of exegetical material compiled over several centuries, that interprets Scripture and contains some material in common with Mishnah or Talmud" (1991, pp. 101–102).

27. Many writers note that rabbinic Judaism emerged in a patriarchal society and, as Neusner (1979) notes, was produced by a group of sages who imagined a man's world with men at its center. "Rabbinic legislation," notes Baskin, "perceived by its authors as divinely ordained, therefore considers women only in her relationship to man and as she falls under his control and can contribute to his comfort" (1985, p. 5). She continues: "[R]abbinic literature is not lacking in words of praise for the supportive, resourceful and self-sacrificing wife, nor is there a lack of consideration for her physical and emotional needs and welfare. All good for the woman, however, is predicated on her remaining subordinate" (1985, p. 5).

28. One significant premise undergirds all halakhic law. Women are considered to be different from men in significant and immutable ways (Baskin, 1985). However, the meaning of that difference varies.

29. Baskin (1985), Swidler (1976), and Hauptmann (1974) provide many examples of the variety of both negative and positive rabbinic attitudes held about women.

30.   Baskin (1985) explains that rabbinic Judaism is a religious tradition which has its origins in postbiblical Judaism (450 B.C.E.–70 C.E.). It developed in the first six centuries and became, she claims, the "normative form of Jewish practice up to the modern era" (p. 14). She writes: "Its founders, careful readers and interpreters of the Hebrew Bible, were known in the post-Biblical period as Scribes and later, Pharisees. During the rabbinic period, the movement's leaders were called rabbis (teachers)" (p. 14).

31.   A woman's marital status was derived from the discussion of the laws pertaining to Israelite slaves. The minimal rights of a free married woman are derived from the biblical passage which allows that the female slave has three basic rights—food, clothing, and conjugal rights (Biale, 1984, p. 126).

32.   A levirate widow is one whose husband dies without producing a son. She is required to marry her husband's brother unless he agrees to release her.

33.   Although biblical law limited women's inheritance privileges, the possibility of giving legal testimony, and the right to initiate divorce, a woman was not considered the same as a man's other possessions. For instance, he could not sell or dispose of her at will nor could he force or sell his daughter into prostitution. Rape laws made it clear that women were victims and, in torts and damages, payments for pain and shame were made directly to her (Greenberg, 1981; Biale, 1984).

34.   Wegner notes that some scholars have misconstrued women's capacity to engage in commerce and private transactions as indicating participation in the public cultural domain of rabbinic culture. But, she writes,

> this overlooks the fact that from a juristic standpoint, such activities are merely transactions between individuals in the private domain. . . . The distinction is illustrated by the fact that while the Mishnah explicitly permits women to bring and defend lawsuits . . . it denies them the right to testify personally in the public courthouse . . . where they must rely on the testimony of men to plead their cause (1991, p. 124).

35.   See Greenberg (1981) for a similar historical account.

36.   While Biale agrees that there is considerable opposition to wifebeating in Jewish law, she also suggests that there are clear references to

punitive beatings "for a just cause" (1984, p. 96). Greenberg (1981) writes: "A man was forbidden to strike his wife; if he struck her, he had to pay reparations for damages, pain, and shame" (1981, p. 62).

37. Wegner notes that in the mishnaic period daughters could be betrothed in childhood without their consent, but that Babylonian rabbis insisted that fathers had to wait until their daughters were old enough to say "I want so-and-so" (1991, p. 131).

38. Feldman notes that the laws of onah are concerned with women's sexual pleasure, not procreation (Feldman, 1974).

39. Maimonides makes it clear that a wife is not a captive or a slave who can be forced to have sexual relations against her will (Biale, 1984).

40. For a more nuanced and detailed discussion of the way in which women's rights are extended in a religious patriarchal context, see especially Neusner (1979) and Wegner (1988).

41. While this may also be true for men, they, unlike women, have the option to study the development and extensions of the laws.

Chapter Three. Sex-segregated Living

1. Ginsburg writes that through the rituals of mikveh and niddah, male and female sexual behavior as well as the bond between husband and wife are subject to communal concern and judgment (1981, p. 18).

2. Sennett suggests that ritual is a "participation in expressive action, action whose immediate social life connects with timeless truths" (1974, p. 267).

3. In the ancient religious worldview governed by categories of pure and impure, defilements and impurities were generally associated with the loss of any of the life-giving juices which nurture body tissue. The laws of purity and impurity include other instances of contamination besides the case of the niddah. For instance, contact with a corpse, leprosy, seminal discharges, or contact with certain insects could place an individual in a state of impurity. Adler (1976) explains that the menstrual blood, which inside the womb was a potential nutrient, is a token of dying when shed.

4. Biale (1984) recognizes the striking contradiction between Leviticus 15 and Leviticus 18 and 20. In the latter, intercourse with a niddah is an offensive sexual transgression (1984, p. 155). Biale also notes that in two late books in the Bible, Ezekiel and Ezra, the term *niddah* appears as a metaphor for moral impurity and debasement (1984, p. 154).

5. Biale (1984) notes that a woman who has given birth is also con-

sidered a niddah. The period of her impurity depends on the sex of her child (Leviticus 12:1–8). If it is a son, the woman waits an additional thirty-three days after the first seven days of her niddah. If it is a daughter, the time of impurity is doubled. In keeping with her general interpretation that impurity is not a punitive condition and that the birth of a daughter is not more disappointing than that of a son, she conjectures that "underlying this legislation is the sense that the birth of a female, who will one day herself menstruate and give birth, is seen as 'double bloody' and doubly impure" (1984, p. 152).

6. Since the destruction of the Second Temple, women's recurring impurity is the only one which is explicitly recognized as such and which still requires a subsequent ritual of purification. The legal obligation for ritual immersion is confined to brides just before their weddings and to married women. Converts also immerse themselves as a sign of rebirth into the tradition. Also, new pots and dishes often are immersed in the mikveh before use, since all parts of daily life are to be sanctified.

7. In her insightful paper on ritual purity and Jewish women, Wechsler (1981) contends that the relationship between sanctity and defilement is a "dialectical one" (1981, p. 16). Blood, and particularly menstrual blood, she writes, is intimately bound with life and death. She explains: "[C]hildbirth is the culmination of the mystery of life, and menstruation bespeaks of life in death (and vice versa). . . . [W]omen's sexuality is thereby linked, ineluctably, to death as well as to life. It points to the fullness of life—birth, sexuality, death—and to its passage" (1981, p. 12). She suggests that the purity laws of the early stages of Semitic culture reflect this duality. For a broader overview, see especially Mary Douglas (1966).

8. In fact, Greenberg notes that after the destruction of the Second Temple, the categories of pure and impure become almost "irrelevant to daily life" (1981, p. 113). For instance, she notes that a man "who had a bodily discharge no longer had to abstain from sex until he underwent purification. The only person still subject to purification rites is the menstruous woman" (1981, p. 113). Adler agrees that most of the laws of tumah applying to men were no longer in force. She writes that niddah survived because the "Biblical prohibition against intercourse with a *niddah* applies whether the Temple stands or not" (1976, pp. 70–71).

9. The evidence for this shift is circumstantial. Biale writes:

Placing sexual relations with a *niddah* among the sexual transgressions in Leviticus 18 and 20 may possibly be a response to the destruction of the first Temple. Leviticus 18 and 20 enumerate the sexual prohibitions, the laws which guarantee "sexual order" and establish the structure of family and society. When the prohibition on sex with a *niddah* appears in this set of laws, the vital core of the laws of *niddah* is shifted from the sphere of the Temple to the orbit of the family. Thus the power of the laws of *niddah* is preserved despite the disappearance of the Temple (1984, p. 158).

10. Greenberg, a modern Orthodox feminist, suggests that according to the traditional interpretation, a society will destroy itself if sexual relationships are not based on an ethical set of principles (1981, p. 112).

11. There is ample evidence of the hostility and fear of the menstruant woman. See especially Biale (1984, ch. 6) and Greenberg (1981, pp. 115–117).

12. Ginsburg (1981) and Greenberg (1981) note that the removal of foreign substances and bathing before the woman goes to the mikveh make clear that the ritual is not an act of hygiene, but rather one of spiritual cleanliness.

13. Wechsler develops this idea when she writes: "Jewish marriage is the 'new' Holy Tabernacle. As a woman's status of pure or impure regulates conjugal relations—a symbol for access to the sanctuary—it is still a valid category" (1981, p. 18).

14. Most ba'alot teshuvah marry other ba'alei teshuvah. That is, had they been practicing orthodoxy, they most likely would not have been openly living together.

15. While all the women in this sample practiced the laws of niddah not all adhered scrupulously to the practice of *negiah*. In this practice, couples will not hand things directly to one another nor will they have any physical contact during the wife's menses. Only one-quarter of the women who fell under the modern Orthodox rubric kept negiah, while almost half of those who fell under the strictly Orthodox category (and virtually all of those within the Hasidic category) practiced negiah. There are mixed halakhic interpretations for this practice, some stressing purity or impurity, others the fear of sexual arousal. (For a more complete discussion see Greenberg, 1981, p. 116.) Bunim (1986) finds similar distinctions in the practice of the family purity laws in her study of Orthodox women. Among the women she studied, all the members of the Kollel adhere strictly to the laws. Agudah and Young Israel women were less fastidious about their observance. One woman in Bunim's study did not practice niddah and two did not practice mikveh regularly (all were

Modern Orthodox). In my study all the women observed niddah and mikveh, although the non-Hasidic women were less fastidious than the Hasidic women.

16. Ehrenreich, Hess, and Jacobs report something similar among New Right women, who, claim the authors, believe that they should get something for their sexual efforts, rather than simply submitting or sacrificing themselves to their husbands (1986).

17. Although most of the statements made by the women tend to have some legal and/or traditional basis in Judaism, this was the hardest for me to trace. Both Biale (1984) and Feldman (1974) suggest that female sexual pleasure is an important part of the Jewish sexual ethic. Biale suggests that the correct Hebrew reading of the biblical legislation that a man is to "cheer his wife" is the key to understanding that a man must put his wife's pleasure and satisfaction before his own when he makes love to her (1984, p. 135). She also notes that there are no laws prohibiting a wide range of sexual expression in Jewish orthodoxy (1984, p. 138).

18. Biale believes that, according to Orthodox interpretation, male sexuality is seen as a greater threat than women's to familial and social structure. Therefore, she claims, it must be restrained through controls of marriage, procreative duties, and men's numerous responsibilities toward their wives. She also notes that there are powerful taboos against male homosexuality and masturbation (1984, p. 122).

19. Biale (1984) and Feldman (1974) cite sources where men are given very specific instructions on how to please their wives. Biale (1984) notes that there is a tension in the literature regarding views about foreplay, talking during sex in order to increase arousal, and prolonging the sexual act (see especially ch. 5). Women's sexual needs are anchored in law to ensure their fulfillment, writes Biale.

20. The basis of the sexual ethic comes from differing views of female and male sexuality. Although women's passion is considered to be as great as men's, writes Biale (1984, p. 122), they are considered tempermentally unable to initiate sex. This is considered to be the second part of the "curse of Eve." From the passage "Yet your desire shall be for your husband, and he shall rule over you" (Genesis 3:16) comes the interpretation that the woman is unable to act to fulfill her sexual desire and that all overt sexual initiative will come from the male, not the female.

21. The focus on female sexuality (although with radically different conclusions) is of key importance to both ba'alot teshuvah and some woman-centered feminists. Catharine MacKinnon is quoted as saying "Sexuality is to feminism what work is to Marxism: that which is most

one's own, yet most taken away" (Bart and Budinger, 1984, p. 11). Some feminists gain control over their bodies and sexuality by following separatist policies; many of the ba'alot teshuvah do so by appealing to Orthodox Jewish laws.

22.   However, *control* is a relative term. For instance, Hasidic women depend upon their rebbes and recognized Torah authorities in their communities for answers to questions about Jewish law. Irrespective of the Orthodox orientation, all Torah authorities are men. Non-Hasidic women are less likely to ask questions of such men and more likely to seek answers on their own. In this way, they entertain a wider range of interpretations for their questions. Despite Hasidic women's greater dependence upon Torah authorities, many of them made it clear that one learns to ask the question according to the answer one wishes to receive (which means, of course, knowledge of the laws and possible interpretations). For instance, when women are coming out of niddah and dubious about a "clean" or "unclean" stain, they are expected to have a *posek* (Torah authority) decide. One Hasidic woman looked me straight in the eye and said, "Do you really think I'd send my underwear to a *rav* to look at under the light?" It appears that as ba'alot teshuvah become more secure in their orthodoxy, questions to be decided by rabbinic authority are fewer. Of the four women who acknowledged having asked for halakhic information about sexual matters, three confided that this had to do with fertility problems. One woman was trying to change her niddah cycle to match more closely her own period of ovulation. It is interesting that none of the women in this study were loath to obtain medical assistance for fertility problems. My discussions with rabbis and lay leaders made it clear that these kinds of questions are handled on a case-by-case basis.

23.   In *Sex and Destiny*, Germaine Greer argues that chastity has a double virtue in that it endows sexual activity with added importance by limiting its enjoyment to special persons and special times (1984a).

24.   There are several ways in which the ba'alot teshuvah interpret their status as returnees or those atoning. While there is some distrust of ba'alei teshuvah among those who are "born" Orthodox, the theological status of a returnee is unambivalent. The ba'alot teshuvah, while perhaps unsure in their practices of orthodoxy, are quite clear that they are in a special state of holiness since they have chosen to become Orthodox. All Jews, according to orthodoxy, are presumably "returning" or "atoning" from birth.

25.   See also Baskin (1985), who notes that all three of the commandments specifically directed at women have to do with separation. She

writes: "[A]ll three can symbolize the chasm between the sacred and the profane, the holy and the secular, the realm of men who obey commandments and that of women who suffer disabilities, and ultimately between the realms of life and death themselves" (1985, p. 8).

26. Behind the methodological approach used in this study is what Giddens (1984) refers to as the double hermeneutic, a process of analysis that demands that the analyst interpret both actors' self-understandings and the larger contexts of action simultaneously.

27. Again, the reader is reminded that this is not a study of orthodoxy, Orthodox communities, or institutions. My focus is on the way in which these formerly secular women come to understand and contribute to religious communal practices.

Chapter Four. Revaluing Domesticity

1. I have given short shrift in this book to the economic and political conditions that promote the ideology of individualism and consequently to an analysis of what had led to the normative breakdown so many analysts describe in the context of the rise of "new religions." It seems to me that another theme running throughout the literature is one which borrows from Max Weber, but changes the relationship somewhat: that is that the spirit of secularism, shaped by the economic and political forces associated with postindustrial, capitalist, and patriarchal living, poses a crisis in meaning, and, in this sense, has helped to give rise to religious revival (see also Berger, 1982). For instance, Ammerman (1987), Hunter (1983), and Neitz (1987) provide ethnographic data on fundamentalist, Evangelical, and charismatic Christian groups as both products of and alternatives for modern secular living. In summarizing Jurgen Habermas's economic arguments related to the cultural crisis, Robbins, Anthony, and Richardson (1978) note that "early capitalism [was] dependent upon rationales of self-denial on behalf of the common good" (p. 99). However, the affinity of the Protestant ethic with small entrepreneurial capitalism has been ruptured, argue the authors, by "managerial capitalism." They write: "The resulting lifting of the minimal restrictions on individual self-interest which had been imposed by that ethic have resulted in various critical tendencies for American society." For a broad overview and nuanced analysis of the nature and place of religion in modern society, see especially the work of Berger (1969, 1982) and Bellah (1976, 1985).

2. Sociological and historical analyses support the claims that the contemporary nuclear family model focuses on the individual. William Goode (1964) characterizes modern nuclear-familial living as being focused on the individual, personal fulfillment, self-discovery, and self-realization (especially through love and sexuality). Lasch (1979) believes the contemporary nuclear family promotes the cult of self.

3. Even the disciplines through which we study the family mirror the narrowing focus and function of the contemporary nuclear family. In the nineteenth century, the family was often analyzed through such disciplines as political economy and ethics; however, in the twentieth century it is frequently studied through the sciences of psychoanalysis and psychology. As Zaretsky notes:

Psychoanalysis arose at the point of capitalist development at which the family had ceased to be a unit of commodity production, and was increasingly being seen as a refuge from the "economy" and "society." Its subject matter is the internal life of the family and of personal relations abstracted from political economy. It comprehends the family as an autonomous institution subject to its own laws of functioning (1973b, p. 63).

4. Interestingly, despite her early and cutting critique of the patriarchal family and its oppression of women, the feminist Sheila Rowbotham concedes that it is still the only refuge contemporary society offers. She writes:

The family is the only place where human beings find whatever continuing love, security, and comfort they know. In an unloving, insecure, and comfortless society, not surprisingly people value . . . the family even if they rebel against the enclosing and twisting characteristics which are inherent in the intensity of the nuclear family unity (1973, p. 59).

5. In *Habits of the Heart*, Bellah, Madsen, Sullivan, Swidler, and Tipton (1985) argue that middle-class Americans have lost the vocabulary they need to make moral sense of their lives. They describe a generation that feels morally disinherited. Tipton (1983) argues that the freedom to choose a religious belief undermines its plausibility as a timeless truth. See also Berger (1969) for an analysis of the impact of cultural pluralism

and individualism on traditional religion. Others, such as Michael Harrington (1983), argue that reason has failed to provide foundational beliefs on which to build moral and political structures that will meet most individuals' needs. Still others, such as Régis Debray (1984), suggest that belief fills the gap between practice and theory—that theories may exist without actions, but that actions cannot occur without belief systems. Harry Stein (1986) writes that liberalism has lost its claim to moral certitude and public values. Peter Steinfels asks: "How can moral principles be grounded and ultimately social institutions be legitimated in the absence of a religiously based culture?" (1979, p. 12). My point here is to suggest that the locus of concern for many scholars, including many feminists, has been the purported "value neutrality" of reason as part of the contemporary liberal discourse.

6. Thomas Luckmann (1990) argues that religion has not disappeared from the modern world but rather changed its "location." He calls this new location the "privatization" of religion. His thought-provoking discussion rests on the analysis that modern social constructions of religious significance have shifted from otherworldly transcendences to, in part, "minimal transcendences of modern solipsism whose main themes ('self-realization', personal autonomy, and self-expression) tend to bestow a sacred status upon the individual" (1990, p. 127). My argument is that the way in which Luckmann characterizes the "privatization" of religion also characterizes the liberal tradition so many of these women appear to reject, not only in secular society but in other religious experiences as well.

7. I use the term *postindustrial* advisedly. Here I am using it in a very specific sense, as does Judith Stacey (1987), to mean that there has been a decline in real wages and in the percentage of well-paid and career-structured jobs available to individuals.

8. Jay Brodbar-Nemzer (1986) compared the divorce rates of Orthodox, Conservative, and Reform Jews and found support for his thesis that the level of Jewish commitment correlates with marital stability. In his analysis of the divorce data from a 1981 survey of New York City's Jewish population, Orthodox Jews had the lowest divorce rate of all the groups compared.

9. Twenty-five of all those interviewed who work, work full-time.

10. These ba'alot teshuvah are squarely within a middle-class socioeconomic category. The combined average income for this group was $41,000 a year.

11. Other researchers claim that adherents' professional status gives

them status in the community at large (Danzger, 1989; Mayer, 1977). Among these women, this did not appear to be the case. Many husbands, including some among the Modern Orthodox, gave up lucrative positions after becoming Orthodox. Bunim (1986) writes that women's high professional status brought status to the husbands among the ultra-Orthodox women she studied. Again, the women in my study often associated high-status jobs with the materialistic culture they were initially rejecting. Once more the reader is reminded that these patterns represent those of newly Orthodox Jews, not of Orthodox Jews in general.

12. Interestingly, while this frequently represented a downward mobility for men, changes in job arrangements rarely resulted in a downward mobility for women. Women rarely changed careers, as did men; rather, they were more likely to engage as part-time lawyers or part-time clinic practitioners. The result is that in contrast to most dual-career couples, the ba'alot teshuvah are more likely to be equal in work status to their husbands than might be expected for the community at large or for the population of dual-job families. See especially, Fox and Hesse-Biber (1984) for a discussion of dual-worker families.

13. Purim is a time for women to indicate not only their creativity but their life-styles. Some of them patronize interior decorators and/or experiment with kosher nouvelle cuisine as well (Sacks, 1986).

14. Perhaps because of the marginal place Jews have historically held within many countries, the institutional base for many religious rituals, including prayer and study, has been within the home and the insular community.

15. For those interested in this complex and subtle argumentation, see Biale (1984), chapter 8, and Feldman (1974), chapters 3–6.

16. The Talmud describes three types of women (a minor, a pregnant woman, and a nursing woman) who because of special circumstances may be in need of contraception. Biale writes:

These three women are described as using a *mokh* to prevent conception. *Mokh* is the term for very fine soft cotton, so what the Talmud most probably intends is pressed cotton inserted into the vagina, somewhat like a tampon, to block the cervix or absorb the semen and prevent pregnancy (1984, p. 203).

Apart from the complicated reasoning involved as to why these three types of women would be at risk, the legitimacy of using contraception revolves around two possible readings of the statement of fact (not legislative pronouncement) by Rabbi Meir: (1) "Three women *may* use the mokh" or (2) "Three women *must* use the mokh" (see Biale, 1984, p. 207). It is clear from my discussion with some Orthodox rabbinic authorities that decisions are made on a case-by-case basis. Feldman (1974) argues that just as the laws of onah are concerned with the "naturalness" of the heterosexual act, so, too, the concerns about contraception are less about procreation and more about activities that border on, or are, explicitly autoerotic.

17. It should be noted, however, that halakhah simply prescribes or proscribes. The interpretation and customary tradition has developed over hundreds of years through talmudic and posttalmudic literature. Therefore, while the women may not be commanded to procreate, there are some who believe that a woman may undertake that mitzvah if she chooses. For instance, upon the advice of an orthodox Torah authority in her community, one woman claimed she was told it was all right to use a diaphragm with a spermicide. Despite this, she did not tell her husband about the spermicide since she believes that if he knew, he would not approve. When I asked one Orthodox Torah authority about this particular situation, he pointed out to me that different communities have different sources of interpretation. Different circumstances, he explained, demand different kinds of decisions. My point is that there is variation on these decisions even within communities. Of interest here is that while all the women under study agree that birth control should be governed by Jewish law, not all will seek rabbinic advice on the topic. For instance, non-Hasidic women were less likely to seek information from a rabbinic authority than were Hasidic women.

18. This presents difficulties for those with infertility problems. The issue of "naturalness" and paternity pervade discussions of technological advances in fertility-related research (Biale, 1984; Feldman, 1974; Rosner, 1972). In one Hasidic community, a posek told me that artificial insemination would be impossible since the wife could be considered an adulteress. On the other hand, Fred Rosner (1972) writes that rabbinic opinion generally sanctions artificial insemination by the husband under circumstances that virtually exclude pregnancy in any other way. Key issues in this process surround how to obtain the semen without transgressing the prohibitions against improper emission of seed (masturbation) or emission of seed for nought. The least objectionable method, writes Rosner, is coitus interruptus or the use of a condom. This constitutes the least interruption of the "natural act" (Rosner, 1972,

pp. 103–105). In the case of in vitro fertilization other halakhic issues arise. The abiding concern is that anything that interferes with the "naturalness" of the sexual act creates religious legal problems.

19. Feldman (1974) provides a convincing argument that preservation of the marital relationship is key in halakhic interpretations (p. 42). Therefore, he argues, since abstinence is never commanded as a form of birth control, even "dubious methods" may be used when no other alternatives are available (p. 42). He argues that the concerns about contraception are less with procreation and more with fears about activities that are autoerotic.

20. Biale gives some legitimation to this position when she summarizes the most permissive position within the bounds of halakhic discussion:

[A]ny woman may use a contraceptive device inserted prior to intercourse. He [Solomon Luria] considers as reasonable grounds for practicing birth control not only danger or extreme pain to the mother, but also concern over the welfare of her children, both physical and moral (1984, p. 218).

21. One Hasidic woman told me that she had rabbinic approval to use contraception. She had been hospitalized for severe bouts of depression after the birth of each of her first two children. She and her husband were fearful about the birth of a third at this time in their lives. Since the authoritative rabbinic ruling varies from community to community, variations in contraceptive use should not be unexpected.

22. Biale (1984) notes that traditional Christian sources differ from the Jewish reading of the same biblical passage. This difference hinges on a translation which subsequently interprets misfortune to mean form, and applied it to the fetus rather than the mother. Therefore, the text was understood as making a distinction between a fetus that had form and one which did not. The church fathers ruled that the fetus is formless until the fortieth day and becomes formed thereafter. In later Christianity, because the soul was believed to enter the fetus at the moment of conception, aborting a fetus at any stage of development was not permitted. In traditional Judaism, the fetus is referred to as water until the fortieth day (see Greenberg, 1981).

23. Maimonides (Moses ben Maimon, 1140–1204), a physical, legal scholar, and philosopher, was a major Jewish figure of the Middle Ages.

His legal code, *Mishneh Torah*, continues to be a major source of rabbinic law.

24.   Maimonides implied that the fetus is a person, thereby complicating the earlier interpretations, which did not explicitly make this claim.

25.   See Feldman, 1974, p. 49, for further elaboration on this rather esoteric explanation.

26.   Almost all of the Hasidic women had had arranged marriages. Among other Orthodox communities, overt matchmaking is less explicit, but does go on. Women often function informally in the role of marriage broker.

27.   The concern about the survival of the Jewish people, after World War II and in the face of ever-increasing rates of intermarriage, have made reproduction a primary focus of many Jewish leaders. Silberman reports that a 1980 national survey of high-school students indicated that 37 percent of Jewish students, compared to 32 percent of nonminority whites, expected to have three or more children. He also reports that educated Jewish women average 2.5 children, compared to 2.2 for the population at large. McLaughlin et al. (1988) report that by 1982 the average number of children ever born to women with thirteen years or more of education was 1.61 (p. 135). See also Giele (1982) for cohort differences in reproduction.

28.   My interviews with counselors for Orthodox Jewish communities reveal that premarital pregnancies do occur, but are almost always quickly followed by marriage.

29.   For a summary of the research documenting that employed women still bear the primary responsibility for home and family and that they face resistance to a redefinition of husbands' and wives' roles, despite women's employment, see Fox and Hesse-Biber (1984).

30.   Setta (1983) refers to this rapidly growing movement, founded in 1967 during the nascent stages of the feminist movement as an interdenominational, charismatic Christian group whose members come from both Pentecostal and non-Pentecostal churches. In 1979, each month, twenty-five new local Women Aglow fellowships were added to the national organization for a total of over 1,600 groups. Setta notes: "While feminists were turning to goddess religion in an attempt to reclaim the power denied them by patriarchal Christianity, Aglow women were transforming patriarchal religion so that the really important work, in their view, the work that had power, was woman's work in the home" (1983, p. 3).

31. Since there is virtually no empirical data about how they actually live their lives, I have relied heavily on Klatch's discussion of right-wing women. Because most of her interviews were held in Massachusetts, Klatch's sample is disproportionately Catholic. In her study the social conservatives are either Catholic or fundamentalist Christian. The laissez-faire group is divided among Catholics, ecumenical Protestants, and a minority of Jews.

32. Sometimes the terms *Moral Majority*, *New Right*, and *Evangelical* are used indiscriminately. Carol Pohli writes: "Strictly speaking, the first signifies only the political action committee which claims to represent the views of most conservative, Christian voters. . . . The New Right obviously includes the Moral Majority, but signifies non-Christian as well as Christian conservatives and Roman Catholic as well as Protestant Christians. Finally, the term 'Evangelical' refers to those Christians, usually Protestant, who agree about certain religious doctrines although they may give themselves different denomination labels" (1983, p. 532). Moreover, I have not made distinctions between Fundamentalists and Evangelicals. Although they may share similar conservative values, Fundamentalists are usually more right-wing and more doctrinaire than Evangelicals.

33. This is supported by Pohli (1983) and other writers who argue that women's involvement in the New Right, not unexpectedly, centers around control of their children's lives and local community control as seen in their support of antibusing and antiabortion laws. Their concern about sex education in the schools has been interpreted by some as an attempt to bring back under their control a traditional source of power, the education of their children within a certain moral framework.

34. This may explain some of the findings Pohli reports (1983) in her provocative article about Evangelical women. She suggests that they may not be as conservative as the male spokesmen for the Christian New Right.

35. See Lenore Weitzman (1985) on no-fault divorce for some corroboration of the fears of these women of the New Right.

36. The Jewish Orthodox are reluctant to take active political stands outside of those which directly affect Jews. They are, after all, as one reader of my manuscript pointed out, the moral minority. Moreover, there are different positions within orthodoxy. For instance, see my earlier discussion about abortion to understand why Jewish Orthodox women have not been active, as an identified group, in the prolife debates.

37. See, for instance, the entire volume of *Feminist Studies* number 6 (Spring, 1980).

38. While subscribing to Douglas's (1977) view that family life of the nineteenth-century was framed by conflict between the sexes, and, further, that such conflicts helped to foster a women's culture among the middle class, Epstein (1981) disagrees with Douglas's characterization of these women as a coherent, unambivalent group.

39. There is a history of social activism, then, for Evangelical women of the religious Right. No such secular history exists for the insular and minority Orthodox Jewish community.

40. Hayden's important point is that the ministerial ideal transfered to the family many of the properties of the Puritan village of seventeenth-century New England. The home was then a "Christian Commonwealth," with the housewife as "Minister of Home." In many ways, the ba'alot teshuvah view their homes as miniature Orthodox communities.

41. During the years from 1890 to 1920, there were several movements involved in family issues. The social purity movement, for instance, attacked prostitution and the double standard of sexual morality for men. The social hygiene movement addressed the issues of venereal disease. The birth control movement campaigned for free access to contraceptive information and devices. However, as Epstein (1983) also notes, issues of family and sexuality seem to have faded from public attention for the next four decades. There has been a revival of these concerns, she suggests, beginning in the mid-1960s, with the New Left and youth culture's criticism of American middle-class life, then extended by the women's movement and more recently by a number of New Right groups.

42. Ellen Trimberger explores the "troubled side" of the sexual radicalism of the 1920s in her analysis of Greenwich Village men and women. She speaks of the inability of Village men to realize the new ideals of sexually liberated women (women you can talk to and kiss) and the difficulties of Village women in a situation that denied them the material and psychological resources to take full advantage of their theoretical freedom. She writes:

Ironically the ideal of modern love that these men and women forged in a spirit of revolutionary struggle evolved by the 1920s into a construction of heterosexuality, the companionate marriage— perhaps even more entrapping to women then the Victorian pattern of separate spheres against which the radicals had initially rebelled (1983, p. 131).

Chapter Five. Women's Culture in the Making

1. Joan Kelley (1979) alludes to this simultaneous existence by suggesting that woman's place is not a separate sphere, but a position within social existence generally. She claims that women are members of the general culture and of a woman's culture simultaneously. The assumption is that the general culture and men's culture are one and the same.

2. See Temma Kaplan for a historic example of Jewish women's claim to the preservation of human life (1980, p. 45).

3. I know that some feminists may well take exception to the use of the word *culture*. Gerda Lerner (1980) might suggest that *sphere* rather than *culture* is a more appropriate word. She argues, "[I]f we call what women do in a patriarchal world and the way they do it 'women's culture,' then there is no point in counterposing this concept to 'feminism'" (1980, p. 53). For her, a woman's culture represents the "ground upon which women stand in their resistance to patriarchal dominance and their assertion of their own creativity in shaping society" (1980, p. 53). I use the term *culture* in the anthropological sense, to encompass women's activities, goals, symbolic discourse, familial, friendship, and affective ties, as well as their religious rituals. My argument is that, in part, sex-segregated living reinforces these women's celebration of difference and their commitment to women-centered values and visions. It is difficult to know what term or, better yet what terms best describe "the type of world women form when forcibly segregated along gender lines" (Smith-Rosenberg, 1980, p. 61).

4. Gender hierarchy and the problems of empowerment are less focused for ba'alot teshuvah in such a sex-segregated environment. However, irrespective of shifts in the interpretation and practice of some rituals, all such changes are still within male-defined parameters.

5. Of course, while women of the religious Right might well be represented in many of the aforementioned groups, for the most part those who identify with the Moral Majority are from Protestant traditions (Pohli, 1983). These ba'alot teshuvah think of themselves as a part of a moral minority.

6. Perhaps because they are not as restricted as Hasidic women, non-Hasidic women were more likely to be involved in political issues

involving changes in orthodoxy. Fifteen women identified with GET (Getting Equitable Treatment), an organization designed to lobby for changes in halakhic interpretation of divorce laws.

7. Some Hasidic women, for instance, subscribe to the *Jewish Women's Outlook*, the *Jewish Press*, the *Jewish Observer*, and (for Lubavich women) the *Yiddishe Heim*. Non-Hasidic women will also include subscriptions to more secularly acknowledged Jewish magazines such as *Commentary* and *Tradition*.

8. As Danzger (1989) notes, the term *modern* has to be used advisedly and in relationship to the more extreme and/or traditional institutions within orthodoxy. For instance, all yeshivot are traditional. They teach ancient laws and customs, accept the Divine Revelation of Torah to Moses at Mount Sinai, and the authority of the Oral Law. In the most traditional view, the entire Oral Law was given to Moses at Mount Sinai and all religious authority derives from this revelation. The only changes allowed are those implicit in Torah or the Oral Law.

9. There were some notable political differences between the Hasidic and non-Hasidic women, with Hasidic women more right-wing in their Israeli politics than non-Hasidic women, especially on the issue of settlement of the West Bank.

10. Seven ba'alot teshuvah claim that at least one of their parents or in-laws has "converted" to orthodoxy.

11. Interestingly, of the Orthodox therapists I interviewed, most admitted that their clientele is mostly female—they claim few Orthodox Jewish males will come to an Orthodox female therapist.

12. See Meiselman (1978) for a statement about charity as a characteristic component of all Jewish ethics.

13. Meiselman confirms the notion that those characteristics of modesty associated with the female are meant for the religious community at large. "When anyone, male or female, serves God, he must concentrate on the inner dimensions of his personality. Tzniut is the inner-directed aspect of striving, the essence of the Jewish heroic act. . . . Tzniut is not restricted to women. The high points in the lives of the major male figures of the Bible occurred in private" (1978, pp. 13–14).

14. Frantz Fanon describes the use of the veil, upgraded modesty behavior, and segregation of women in the Algerian struggle for independence against France "as an attempt to affirm the cultural personality of the dominated people, as a means of negating the oppressor culture" (cite din Hegland, 1986, pp. 13–14).

15. "Most feminists," explains Estelle Freedman, "did not adopt the radical demands for equal status with men that originated at the Seneca Falls convention of 1848. Rather they preferred to retain membership in a separate female sphere, one which they did not believe to be inferior to men's sphere and one in which women could be free to create their own forms of personal, social, and political relationships" (1979, p. 514).

16. Discussing the place of women's communities in the past, Carroll Smith-Rosenberg poses a most intriguing question. While she acknowledges that sex-segregated women's communities do not automatically produce feminism, she asks the following question: "[C]an feminism develop outside a female world?" She writes that the most important questions about women's culture

> . . . center on its relation to the existence of a female world. The planning meeting for the Seneca Falls convention, as others have so aptly pointed out, was, in reality, a Quaker women's meeting, with the addition of one non-Quaker woman. The early women's movement, as Blanche Glassman Hersh so cogently argues in her study of the feminist movement, flourished because of the experiences women had gained from decades of work in single-sex voluntary associations and schools, fighting for issues they defined as women's issues. The greatest strength they gained from this experience, I would argue, was to define themselves first as women and second as reformers. This identification as women—what I would call the defining characteristic of a female community—continued to characterize female reform movements through the Progressive Era and the winning of suffrage (1980, p. 62).

17. The strength of American feminism prior to 1920, argues Freedman, was the separate female community that helped to sustain women's participation in both social reform and political activities. She writes:

> When women tried to assimilate into male-dominated institutions, without securing feminist social, economic, or political bases, they lost the momentum and the networks which had made the suffrage movement possible. Women gave up many of the strengths of the female sphere without gaining equally from the men's world they entered (1979, p. 524).

18.   However, while they may have found mechanisms to reinforce woman-centered values, they have not developed the requisite mechanisms to reject what is still oppressive to them (for example, divorce laws).

19.   Both Freedman (1979) and Rapp (1979) warn against uncritically accepting women's traditions. Both worry about romanticizing the sources of women's oppression. Freedman outrightly dismisses the possibility of right-wing women to develop anything but a reactionary politics despite their potential to engage in "female institution building" (1979, p. 513). Rapp concludes:

> As we excavate and legitimize women's history, social organization, and cultural forms, we must not allow our own need for models of strong female collectivities to blind us to the dialectic of tradition. It will be our intellectual as well as political task to separate these strands as we grow more confident about the existence and value of female experience in our society and culture (1979, p. 513).

Chapter Six. Paradoxes

1.   See especially Koltun (1976); Greenberg (1981); Beck (1982); Heschel (1983); Schneider (1984); Kaye/Kantrowitz and Klepfisz (1986); Adelman (1986). For a good review essay on recent literature on Jewish feminism and the creation of a feminist Judaism, see Ellen Umansky (1988).

2.   See Oakley (1981); Smith (1974, 1988); Reinharz (1984); Kasper (1986).

3.   Each has a separate rabbinical and political association. Danzger writes:

> The Rabbinical Council of America (RCA) draws members primarily from Yeshiva University, a modernist yeshiva. Rabbis of Young Israel synagogues are predominantly members of the RCA and are also Mizrachi (modernists) supporters. Members of the Igud Harabonim are drawn primarily from traditionalist yeshivot and are supporters of Agudah (Danzger, 1989, p. 46).

4.   It is interesting to note that the distinctions Danzger draws are generally acknowledged as givens in Jewish orthodoxy. However, the

women in my study represent newly Orthodox Jews who, for the most part, were consciously searching for community. Therefore, the modern Orthodox women in my study, although more likely to engage in secular activities than the more traditional women and more likely to make their own personal decisions, nonetheless were quite identified with and tied to the Orthodox community. Again, the reader is reminded that this is not a study of Jewish orthodoxy or Orthodox communities, but rather of ba'alot teshuvah.

5.   In contrast, Jewish and Christian feminists challenge any such assertions about "feminine" positivism as illusory. Adler states unequivocally that, as peripheral Jews, women are "barred from the acts and symbols which are the lifeblood of the believing community" (1983, p. 13). Hyman makes clear that "the rationales for family purity should exploit neither medical fantasy or sexual mythology" (1976, p. 111). However, perhaps Daly presents the most scathing criticism of women's relationship to patriarchal religion. She believes that strong sex-role segregation bestows "false identities upon women and men" and that patriarchal religion perpetuates the "dynamics of delusion" (1973, p. 3). She wishes to reject "not only the myths of patriarchy but their externalization in ritual" (1973, p. 142). See also Heschel (1983) and Christ and Plaskow (1979).

6.   Here I am using the term *discourse* as Scott (1988) defines Foucault's use of it. In this sense the religious discourse is not a language, but a historically social and institutionally specific structure of statements, terms, and categories developed in male-dominated organizations and institutions.

7.   See especially my Chapter Four, notes 18 and 19.

8.   It has come to my attention that Rebbe Schneerson has dictated a paper on the topic of in vitro fertilization which is negative. At the time of this writing I have been unable to verify this information or obtain any more information.

9.   Research on women involved in the antiabortion campaigns reveal more ideological and political diversity than might be expected among them. See, for instance, Luker (1984); Petchesky (1984); and, more recently, Ginsburg (1989). See also, Carol Joffee's (1985) perceptive review article of both Luker and Petchesky.

10.   Patrick McNamara (1985) has uncovered pastoral literature and cassettes that reveal a similar understanding of gender relationships. McNamara writes that in Tim and Beverly LaHaye's chapter, in *Spirit-Controlled Family Living*, on the roles of the husband there are some inter-

esting qualifications on the issue of "headship" in the family. While in practice the husband still has the obligation to assume the role of the leader in the home, he must also come to decision making only after hearing and evaluating the wife's viewpoint and after scrutinizing his own motivations. The LaHayes propose a negotiatory process in settling differences between spouses, recommending prayer as one source of resolution. The LaHayes make clear that husbands must practice what is preached, if they are to expect a stable and working marriage. In fact, the LaHayes' definition of the husband as unselfish, gracious, trusting, sincere, polite, generous, humble, kind, and patient resonates with values long associated with "femininity" and the female.

11. It is important to remember that "born again" and newly Orthodox Jewish women have not always been fundamentalists in their respective religious traditions. Therefore, for the most part, they bring with them a past filled with knowledge of the expectations of a liberal secular society.

12. Perhaps what makes social conservative women so interesting are the practices which belie their rhetoric. As Klatch notes, Phyllis Schlafly personifies the paradox of the social conservative woman. Schlafly, educated at Washington University in Saint Louis, a lawyer and author of nine books, and twice a candidate for Congress, hardly matches the traditional female role espoused by social conservative women. However, as Klatch notes, the social conservative woman is drawn into the political arena to "defend traditional values, to retain her sense of self-worth, and to protect against the total masculinization of the world" (Klatch, 1987, p. 206).

13. Tipton (1982a) suggests that American youth in movements in the seventies carried similar sentiments.

14. While Jaggar recognizes that feminism owes a great deal to liberalism (ideals of human dignity, autonomy, equality, and individual self-fulfillment), she also argues that liberalism is an impoverished theory resonating more with the life experiences of privileged males than of others—stressing the superior value of "mental" activity to the neglect of daily physical labor; ignoring human interdependence (especially the long dependence of human young); and containing a strong element of egoism (1983, p. 46).

15. Karen Offen (1988) and Nancy Cott (1986) review historical accounts of the ways in which difference and sameness arguments have been used throughout the course of feminist thought and politics. Depending on the mode of analysis, this has led to very different interpretations

of women's circumstances and needs. For instance, Offen (1988) reflects on the somewhat paradoxical doctrine of "equality in difference," or equity as distinct from equality (p. 139).

16.   Of all the feminist theorists, the radical feminists, writes Rothman, are the clearest on rejecting the "linearity, the mechanistic thinking of technological society, and replacing it with a sense of organic wholeness, roundness, interconnectedness" (1989, p. 253).

17.   See especially Eisenstein (1981); Judith Stacey (1983). (Parenthetically, unlike Schlafly, who had a career, Friedan was a homemaker when she became an activist.)

18.   Offen (1988) suggests that the Anglo-American individualist tradition of feminism is the model on which many historians still base their discussions of feminism. She writes that as recently as the early 1970s, "this notion of feminism seemed to be the only 'politically correct' form available to American women. Even as this situation has changed, and competitive individualism itself has come under attack, individualist feminism retains its grip on the mind of the American public" (pp. 137–138).

19.   See also Germaine Greer (1984), who fears a feminism so egoistic as to lose its concern for children.

20.   "In European history," writes Offen,

especially in the nineteenth century, the relational premise of feminism was rooted in sexual dimorphism and based on a vision of specified, complementary responsibilities within an organized society that could even (and often did) override claims for personal liberty that extended beyond moral equivalency; these were not only accepted by progressive women and men in that culture but provided, as well, the foundation for making the broadest of claims for women's empowerment and the most sweeping changes in the sexual balance of power (1988, pp. 141–142).

21.   See especially Cott (1977) and Ryan (1983), who argue that the establishment of separate sexual spheres had as one of its paradoxical consequences the development of feminist consciousness and activity.

22.   Offen (1988) claims that between 1890 and 1920 "the aims and goals of relational and individualist approaches appeared increasingly irreconcilable, as different groups of women began to articulate differing

claims" (p. 143). She writes that this was especially true in England and in the United States where

> individualist feminism gained momentum as increasing numbers of highly educated, single women intent on achieving personal autonomy became visible for the first time, the participation of married women in the industrial labor force became a political issue, and—most significantly—birthrates began to fall. Following the Russian Revolution of 1917 and the development of a strong anticommunist reaction in the United States during the 1920s, feminist intellectuals veered sharply in the direction of downplaying sex differences (Offen, 1988, p. 143).

23.   Gerda Lerner (1980) offers a strong argument for creating sharp and clean definitions of what we mean by "feminism" and "women's culture" before answering in which conceptual framework we can place a particular piece of women's history.

24.   I am relying heavily on Hester Eisenstein's (1983) summary of the history of ideas among contemporary feminist thinkers. My interest in using her insightful analyses is to build the context for comparisons among contemporary religious-Right women, moral-reform feminists of the last century, contemporary radical feminists, and the newly Orthodox Jewish women under study.

25.   Offen's history of French feminism makes it clear that up until the publication of Simone de Beauvoir's *The Second Sex* in 1949, "physiological difference and the sexual division of labor predicated on it was rarely identified by self-styled feminists as a primary instrument of women's oppression" (Offen, 1988, p. 148). Given France's "perilous demographic" position, writes Offen,

> French feminists have found it both strategically and tactically useful . . . to emphasize and celebrate the uniqueness of womanhood, especially women's role and rights as mothers. . . . The confusion that abounds today in France . . . is symptomatic of the extent to which today's French women's advocates ignore . . . the legacy of their own predecessors (1988, p. 148).

The confusion Offen refers to is the reemergence of the relational mode of argument among French feminists. She refers to the group known as Psych et Po (Psychoanalyse et Politique), a group that insists on the centrality of biological differences between the sexes. Drawing heavily on Lacanian psychoanalysis, they argue that women's sexuality has been represented by patriarchal culture. Writes Offen: "The 'feminine,' in their view has been totally repressed, and their objective is to challenge existing language and culture through exploration of 'women's language'" (1988, p. 148). Sexual difference is key to their analysis, although the focus has shifted from nineteenth-century and early twentieth-century French feminists' concerns with procreation and mothering to sexuality and separatism.

26.　Eisenstein (1983) writes that for most writers in this first stage of second-wave feminism, female difference was the key element of oppression. She summarizes the foci of oppression. She writes that for Elizabeth Janeway (1971), Sherry Ortner (1974), and Michele Rosaldo (1974), the crucial element for oppression of women was the "association of the female with the domestic sphere" and the "exclusion of women from public life"; for Shulamith Firestone (1970), it was childbearing, and for Susan Brownmiller (1975), it was the "phallic power" of men to penetrate women; for Juliette Mitchell (1973), it was the relationship of women as a group to both production and reproduction; and for Kate Millett (1970), sex-role differences delimited and constrained women (Eisenstein, 1983, p. 45).

27.　In academe, this focus legitimized a new field of inquiry—women's studies. Social scientists like Jessie Bernard (1971) and Pauline Bart (1971) used this woman-centered focus to dramatize the inadequacy of current theoretical thinking about marriage, family, aging, and socialization. Since most developmental and theoretical models in the social sciences were based on life-cycle experiences and processes "normal" to men, women who varied from the models were "abnormal," not different. Women's studies made it evident that in most scholarly fields men's studies had been the norm. Scores of dissertations emerged during the seventies in the areas of family, gender, and work, arguing for major revisions in methods and theories. For a summary of the impact of this movement on the achievement field, both in psychology and sociology, see Kaufman and Richardson (1982). For a more recent review of the literature in different disciplines, see Cynthia Epstein (1988).

28.　Jean Baker Miller (1976), for instance, argues that women's psychology, not men's, should be the basis for human behavior. Implicit in much of this argument is that idea that many traits and qualities attributed to women are superior to those of men. Earlier than that, Ann

Koedt (1973) and Mary Jane Sherfey (1972) had argued that female capacity for sexual enjoyment was greater than that of men.

29. Judith Lorber (1981) refers to this as the beginning of what might be called the "maximalist" period.

30. Eisenstein writes: "In calling themselves 'radical feminists,' the early theorists distinguished themselves from two other groups, namely, liberal feminists, and the men of the New Left" (1983, p. 126). The "radical" in radical feminism, states Eisenstein, referred to a more fundamentally revolutionary stance than that of the New Left. Eisenstein notes:

> In their declarations of independence from the New Left . . . the newly formed radical feminist groups rejected the New Left on both theoretical and practical grounds. They argued that the New Left was hypocritical: while claiming to be fighting for the elimination of oppression, its members nonetheless had neither analyzed nor acknowledged their own role as oppressors of the women who had been fighting at their side (1983, p. 126).

31. Jagger (1983) suggests that radical feminism, as it evolved through the late seventies and early eighties, has become less political.

32. See also Judith Lorber, 1981.

33. However, radical feminists do not celebrate femininity as it evolves in patriarchy, but as it evolves in women's self-contained communities. Therefore, in comparison to ba'alot teshuvah who develop women-defined goals within a male-defined context, radical feminists develop women-defined goals within a female-defined context. Rich (1976), for instance, distinguishes carefully between the celebration of motherhood and the institution of motherhood as patriarchally defined.

34. Jaggar notes that radical feminism is changing rapidly and that her characterization of its theory may soon be outdated (1983, p. 84).

35. Perhaps Jane Alpert best captures the radical feminist's thinking when she writes:

> It seems to me that the power of the new feminist culture, the powers which were attributed to the ancient matriarchies . . . and the inner power with which many women are beginning to feel in touch and which is the soul of feminist art, may all arise from the same source. That source is none other than female biology: the capacity to bear and nurture children. . . . Motherhood must be

understood here as a potential which is imprinted in the genes of every woman; as such it makes no difference to this analysis of femaleness whether a woman ever has borne, or ever will bear, a child (quoted in Jaggar, 1983, pp. 94–95)

Conclusion

1. In another context, Smith-Rosenberg reasons that the "most complex and suggestive questions we can ask about the female experience or women's location in the power structure do not necessarily revolve around an analysis of overt exploitation" (1980, p. 61). Also, in her discussion of the relationship between politics and culture in women's history, she writes:

We cannot understand the public acts of a few women without understanding the private world that produced them. Women's interaction with each other formed an intrinsic component of the female experience and of feminism. It constitutes, consequently, a legitimate and fruitful category within women's history (1980, p. 55).

2. For a fuller discussion of these issues and a critique of them, see Cook (1983); Stacey and Thorne (1985); Farganis (1986); Kasper (1986); Cook and Fonow (1986); Grant et al. (1987); Stacey (1988), Kaufman (1990).

3. As Schussler-Fiorenza (in Setta, 1984) notes, formal patriarchal law is generally more restrictive than actual interactions and relationships among men and women; and, even more important, such laws are basically projections of male reality.

4. This, of course, is not to be confused with power over their lives, but rather that they have developed some countervailing pressure within the context of patriarchal power. Gerda Lerner (1980) alludes to this kind of distinction in her discussion of domestic feminism, a woman's sphere, women's culture, and the issues of power.

5. Lerner (1980) argues that women live "a duality—as members of the general culture and as partakers of women's culture" (1980, p. 52). She writes:

It is important to understand that "woman's culture" is not and should not be seen as a subculture. It is hardly possible for the majority to live in a subculture. . . . Women live their social existence within the general culture and, whenever they are confined by patriarchal restraint or segregation into separateness (which always has subordination as its purpose), they transform this restraint into complimentarity (asserting the importance of woman's function, even its "superiority") and redefine it (1980, p. 52).

6. Interestingly, despite the negative reaction from key Orthodox leaders, Fishman notes that "women's prayer groups continue to flourish in many cities, and have become a popular locus for Orthodox Bat Mitzvahs, giving girls the opportunity to read from the Torah and recite the *haftorah*, (the reading from Prophets)" (1989, p. 48). Therefore, while still within the parameters of patriarchal religion, some Orthodox women, including some ba'alot teshuvah in this study, have taken collective action and have exhibited some cultural resistance to those who would deny them those rites (rights). For a more complex discussion of cultural resistance, see Christine Gailey (forthcoming) and Lynn Stephen (1989).

7. See Ehrenreich (1983).

8. This is not unlike Gilligan's (1982) formulation of the concept of empathy.

9. See Miller (1976) and Rich (1976).

10. See, for instance, the entire volume of *Feminist Studies*, vol. 6 (Spring 1980); see also Rosenberg (1982).

11. See also Pohli (1983); Brusco (1986); and Ammerman (1987).

12. *Powers of the Weak* is the title of Elizabeth Janeway's (1980) book on the shaping and reshaping of power.

13. To use their newly found collective female identity in order to transform radically any of the ritual or law would undermine the authority, and therefore the certainty and appeal, of halakhic law. As noted earlier, these ba'alot teshuvahs' very attraction to Orthodox Judaism is that its moral certitude is embodied in the inviolability of halakhah.

14. See Kaplan (1982).

15. Writing on the possibility of Orthodox women rabbis, the Orthodox feminist Blu Greenberg notes: "More than any other, the Orthodox community has widely educated its women in Torah studies. Thus, though it rejects the formal entry of women into rabbinical studies, de facto, through the broad sweep of day school, yeshiva high school education, and beyond, it has ushered them, as a whole community, into the learning enterprise" (1984, pp. 23–33).

16.   Fishman (1989) notes that except for the ultra-Orthodox, adolescent daughters are increasingly receiving a bat mitzvah (limited, of course, to the all-female service).

17.   See, for instance, the article by Rabbi Susan Grossman and R. Susan Aranoff (1990) entitled "Women under Siege at the Western Wall" (*Women's League Outlook*, vol. 90, Spring, pp. 7–10).

18.   Although there are similarities, postmodernism presents major difficulties for feminists as well. Not the least of many critical questions it poses for feminists is whether the category of gender can survive a postmodern critique. Linda Nicholson asks: "[I]f postmodernism entails abandoning the use of cross-cultural categories, what then happens to the category of gender? [I]f postmodernism entails the abandonment of all generalizations, would not the end result be a nominalist ontology and an individualist politics?" (1990, p. 8).

19.   I am particularly indebted to the burgeoning literature on feminism and postmodernism; see, in particular, the challenging essays in Nicholson's book *Feminism/Postmodernism* (1990). In addition, as the coordinator of Northeastern's Boston Area Consortium on Feminist Theory for the past few years, I have had the privilege of helping to bring onto campus some of the leading figures in this debate. The lively discussions over the years have often dealt with the problem of rooting our politics in our gender identity. Even if we were able to locate a nonessentialist "gender," "sex," "woman" identity that included disparate time, culture, and sociopolitical contexts, many of us have come to realize that gender identity (like woman's sphere, culture, et cetera) can be the point of liberation or oppression and sometimes simultaneously both. A good deal of my thinking in this chapter has been influenced by these discussions.

20.   For instance, Rosaldo suggests that we frame our questions carefully to avoid answers that explain phenomena in universals or primary causes. Using male dominance as an example, she writes:

Male dominance does not inhere in any isolated and measurable set of omnipresent facts. Rather, it seems to be an aspect of the organization of collective life, a patterning of expectations and beliefs which gives rise to imbalance in the ways people interpret, evaluate and respond to particular forms of male and female action. We see it not in physical constraints in things, that men or women can or cannot do but, rather, in the ways they think about their lives, the kinds of opportunities they enjoy, and in their ways of making claims (1980), p. 349).

21. To predict whether the daughters will exhibit reactionary or radical stances would undermine the idea that an interpretive-feminist analysis begins from the standpoint of the subject, not that of the researcher.

22. This historical point, I believe, has made its way into academic feminist scholarship.

23. Bordo asks: "Could we now speak of the differences that inflect gender if gender had not first been shown to make a difference?" (1990, p. 141).

24. I am paraphrasing Sandra Harding's conclusions about feminist epistemologies (1990).

References

Adelman, P. 1986 *Miriam's Well: Rituals for Jewish Women Around the Year*. Fresh Meadows, N.Y.: Biblio.

Adler, R. 1976 "Tumah and Taharah: Ends and Beginnings." Pp. 63–71 in E. Koltrun (ed.), *The Jewish Woman: New Perspectives*. New York: Schocken.

———— 1983 "The Jew Who Wasn't There: Halakah and the Jewish Woman." Pp. 12–18 in S. Heschel (ed.), *On Being a Jewish Feminist*. New York: Schocken.

American Jewish Committee 1982 *New Pockets of Jewish Energy*. The Jewish Communal Affairs Department, The American Jewish Committee, 165 East 56th St. New York, N.Y.

———— 1983 "Jewish Divorce And American Law." *The William Petschek National Jewish Family Center Newsletter*, 3(4):1–3.

————1986 "Divorce." *The William Petschek National Jewish Family Center Newsletter*, 5(4):1–4.

Ammerman, N. 1987 *Bible Believers*. New Brunswick, N.J.: Rutgers University Press.

Anthony, D., and T. Robbins 1982 "Spiritual Innovation and the Crisis of American Civil Religion." Pp. 229–248 in Mary Douglas and Steven Tipton (eds.), *Religion and America*, Boston: Beacon Press.

Arendell, T. 1986 *Mothers and Divorce: Legal, Economic, and Social Dilemmas*. Berkeley and Los Angeles: University of California Press.

Aviad, J. 1983 *Return to Judaism: Religious Renewal in Israel*. Chicago: University of Chicago Press.

Banks, O. 1981 *Faces of Feminism*. New York: St. Martin's.

Bardwick, J. 1971 *Psychology of Women: A Study of Bio-Cultural Conflicts*. New York: Harper & Row.

215

Bart, P. 1971 "Middle Aged Women and Depression." Pp. 163–186 in V. Gornik and B. Moran (eds.), *Women in Sexist Society*. New York: Mentor.

Bart, P., and J. Budinger 1984 "Feminist Theories." Unpublished manuscript, University of Illinois at Chicago.

Baskin, J. 1985 "The Separation of Women in Rabbinic Judaism." Pp. 3–18 in Y. Y. Haddad and E. B. Findly (eds.), *Women, Religion and Social Change*. Albany, NY: SUNY Press.

Beck, E. 1982 *Nice Jewish Girls: A Lesbian Anthology*. Trumansburg, N.Y.: Crossing Press.

Bellah, R. 1976 "New Religious Consciousness and the Crisis in Modernity." Pp. 333–352 in C. Glock and R. Bellah (eds.), *The New Religious Consciousness*. Berkeley: University of California Press.

Bellah, R., R. Madsen, W. Sullivan, A. Swidler, and S. Tipton 1985 *Habits of the Heart*. Berkeley: University of California Press.

Berger, P. 1969 *The Sacred Canopy: Elements of a Sociological Theory of Religion*. Garden City, N.Y.: Doubleday.

—— 1982 "Secular Branches, Religious Roots." *Society* 20 (1):64–66.

Berger, P., and B. Berger 1983 *The War over the Family*. Garden City, N.Y.: Anchor/Doubleday.

Berheide, C. 1984 "Women's Work in the Home: Seems like Old Times." *Marriage and Family Review* 7:37–55.

Berman, S. 1976 "The Status of Women in Halakhic Judaism." Pp. 114–128 in E. Koltrun (ed.), *The Jewish Woman: New Perspectives*. New York: Schocken.

Bernard, J. 1971 "The Paradox of the Happy Marriage." Pp. 145–162 in V. Gornick and B. Moran (eds.), *Women in Sexist Society*. New York: Mentor.

—— 1973 "My Four Revolutions: An Autobiographical History of the ASA." Pp. 11–29 in J. Huber (ed.), *Changing Women in a Changing Society*. Chicago: University of Chicago Press.

Biale, R. 1984 *Women and Jewish Law*. New York: Schocken.

Blumer, H. 1969 *Symbolic Interactionism: Perspective and Method*. Englewood Cliffs, N.J.: Prentice-Hall.

Bordin, R. 1986 *Frances Willard: A Biography*. Chapel Hill: University of North Carolina Press.

Bordo, S. 1990 "Feminism, Post-Modernism and Gender-Skepticism." Pp. 133–156 in Nicholson, L., *Feminism/Post-Modernism*. New York: Routledge, Chapman and Hall.

Bosk, C. 1979 "The Routinization of Charisma: The Case of the Zaddick." *Sociological Inquiry* 49(2,3):150–167.

Breines, W. 1982 *Community and Organization in the New Left: 1962–1968*. New York: Praeger.

Brodbar-Nemzer, J. 1986 "Divorce and Group Commitment: the Case of the Jews." *Journal of Marriage and the Family* 48:329–340.

Brownmiller, S. 1975 *Against Our Will: Men, Women and Rape*. New York: Simon & Schuster.

Brusco, E. 1986 "Columbian Evangelicalism as a Strategic Form of Women's Collective Action." *Feminist Issues* 6(2):3–13.

Buhle, J. 1980 "Politics and Culture in Women's History: A Symposium." *Feminist Studies* 6(1):38–42.

Bunim, S. 1986 "Religious and Secular Factors of Role Strain in Orthodox Jewish Mothers." Ph.D. dissertation, Wurzweiler School of Social Work, Yeshiva University.

Cherlin, A., and C. Celebuski 1982 "Are Jewish Families Different?" in *Newsletter*, American Jewish Committee, New York. 2(3):5.

Christ, C., and J. Plaskow 1979 *Womanspirit Rising*. New York: Harper and Row.

Cohen, S. 1983 *American Modernity and Jewish Identity*. New York: Tavistock.

Coleman, J. 1971 *The Adolescent Society*. Glencoe, Ill.: The Free Press.

Conover, P., and V. Gray 1983 *Feminism and the New Right*. New York: Praeger.

Cook, J. 1983 "An Interdisciplinary Look at Feminist Methodology: Ideas and Practice in Sociology, History, and Anthropology." *Humboldt Journal of Social Relations* 10:127–152.

Cook, J., and M. Fonow 1986 "Knowledge and Women's Interests: Issues of Epistemology and Methodology in Feminist Sociological Research." *Sociological Inquiry* 56(1):2–29.

Cott, N. 1977 *The Bonds of Womanhood: "Woman's Sphere" in New England, 1780–1835*. New Haven: Yale University Press.

——— 1986 "Feminist Theory and Feminist Movements: The Past Before Us." Pp. 49–62 in J. Mitchell and A. Oakley (eds.) *What is Feminism?* Oxford: Blackwell.

Cowan, P. 1980 "A Renaissance in Venice." *Jewish Living*, March/April, pp. 52–57.

Cox, H. 1977 *Turning East: The Promise and the Peril of the New Orientalism*. New York: Simon & Schuster.

Culpepper, E. 1974 "Menstruation Mantra: Red, Crimson, Siena, Scarlet." Ph.D. dissertation, Harvard University.

Daly, M. 1973 *Beyond God the Father: Toward a Philosophy of Women's Liberation.* Boston: Beacon Press.

——— 1978 *Gyn/Ecology: The Metaethics of Radical Feminism.* Boston: Beacon Press.

Daniels, A. 1975 "Feminist Perspectives in Sociological Research." Pp. 340–380 in M. Mellman and R. Kanter (eds.), *Another Voice.* Garden City, N.Y.: Doubleday/Anchor.

Danzger, M. H. 1987 "Toward a Redefinition of 'Sect' and 'Cult': Orthodox Judaism in the United States and Israel." *Comparative Social Research* 10:113–123.

——— 1989 *Returning to Tradition: The Contemporary Revival of Orthodox Judaism.* New Haven: Yale University Press.

Davidman, L. 1986 *Strength of Tradition in a Chaotic World: Women Turn to Orthodox Judaism.* Ann Arbor: University of Michigan Microfilms International.

Debray, R. 1984 *Critique of Political Reason.* Trans. David Macey. New York: Verso/Schocken.

Delaney, J., N. J. Lupton, and E. Toth 1976 *The Curse: A Cultural History of Menstruation.* New York: Dutton.

Delmar, R. 1986 "What Is Feminism?" Pp. 8–33 in Mitchell, J. and A. Oakley (eds.), *What is Feminism?* New York: Pantheon Books.

Dinnerstein, D. 1976 *The Mermaid and the Minotaur: Sexual Arrangements and the Human Malaise.* New York: Harper & Row.

Douglas, A. 1977 *The Feminization of American Culture.* New York: Knopf.

Douglas, M. 1966 *Purity and Danger: An Analysis of Concepts of Pollution and Taboo.* London: Routledge and Kegan Paul.

DuBois, B. 1983 "Passionate Scholarship: Notes on Values, Knowledge and Method in Feminist Social Science." Pp. 105–116 in C. Bowles, and R. D. Kleine (eds.), *Theories of Women Studies.* London: Routledge and Kegan Paul.

DuBois, E. 1980 "Politics and Culture in Women's History: A Symposium." *Feminist Studies* 6(1):28–37.

Dworkin, A. 1983 *Right-Wing Women.* New York: Wideview/Perigee.

Ehrenreich, B. 1983 *The Hearts of Men: American Dreams and the Flight from Commitment.* New York: Doubleday/Anchor

Ehrenreich, B., E. Hess, and G. Jacobs 1986 *Re-making Love.* Garden City, N.Y.: Doubleday/Anchor.

Eisenstein, H. 1983 *Contemporary Feminist Thought*. Boston: G. K. Hall.

Eisenstein, H., and A. Jardine 1980 *The Future of Difference*. Boston: G. K. Hall.

Eisenstein, Z. 1981 *The Radical Future of Liberal Feminism*. Boston: Northeastern University Press.

—— 1982 "The Sexual Politics of the New Right: Understanding the 'Crises of Liberalism' for the 1980's" Pp. 77–98 in N. Keohane, M. Rosaldo, and B. Gelpi (eds), *Feminist Theory*. Chicago: University of Chicago Press.

Eister, A. 1972 "An Outline of Structural Theory of Cults." *Journal for the Scientific Study of Religion* 11:319–333.

Elshtain, J. 1984 "Symmetry and Soporifics: A Critique of Feminist Theories of Gender Development." Unpublished manuscript, University of Massachusetts, Amherst.

Epstein, B. 1981 *The Politics of Domesticity: Women, Evangelism and Temperance in 19th Century America*. Middletown, Conn.: Wesleyan University Press.

—— 1983 "Family Sexual Morality and Popular Movements in Turn-of-the Century America." Pp. 117–130 in A. Snitow, C. Stansell, and S. Thompson (eds.), *Powers of Desire*. New York: Monthly Review Press.

Epstein, C. 1988 *Deceptive Distinctions*. New Haven: Yale University Press; New York: Russell Sage Foundation.

Farber, B. 1984 "The Anatomy of Nurturance: A Structural Analysis of the Contemporary American Jewish Family." Paper presented to the National Council of Family Relations, San Francisco.

Farganis, S. 1986 "Social Theory and Feminist Theory: The Need for a Dialogue." *Sociological Inquiry* 56(1):50–68.

Feldman, D. 1974 *Marital Relations, Birth Control and Abortion in Jewish Law*. New York: Schocken.

Feldman, E. 1977 *Biblical and Post-Biblical Defilement and Mourning*. New York: Yeshiva University Press.

Firestone, S. 1970 *The Dialectic of Sex: The Case for Feminist Revolution*. New York: Bantam Books.

Fishman, S. 1989 "The Impact of Feminism on American Jewish Life." Pp. 3–61 in D. Singer and R. Seldin (eds.), *American Jewish Year Book*, vol. 89. New York: American Jewish Committee.

Foucault, M. 1976 *The History of Sexuality*. Vol. 1: *An Introduction*. New York: Random Books.

—— 1979 *Discipline and Punishment: The Birth of the Prison*. Trans. Alan Sheridan. New York: Vintage Books.

Fox, M., and S. Hesse-Biber 1984 *Women at Work*. Palo Alto, Cal.: Mayfield.

Freedman, E. 1979 "Separation as Strategy: Female Institution Building and American Feminism, 1870–1930." *Feminist Studies* 5:512–529.

Friedan, B. 1963 *The Feminine Mystique*. New York: Dell.

———— 1979 "Feminism Takes a New Turn." *New York Times Magazine* November 19:40,92–102,102–106.

———— 1981 *The Second Stage*. New York: Summit.

Gailey, C. 1991 "Overseas Migration and the Changing Family in the Tongan Islands." In A. Ong and C. Szanton (eds.), *The Predicaments of Family*. Berkeley: University of California Press.

Giddens, A. 1984 *The Constitution of Society: An Outline of the Theory of Structuration*. Berkeley: University of California Press.

Giele, J. 1982 *The Future of Women*. New York: Free Press.

Gilligan, C. 1983 *In a Different Voice: Psychological Theory and Women's Development*. Cambridge: Mass.: Harvard University Press.

Ginsburg, F. 1981 "Power, Purity & Pollution: The Revival of Menstrual Rituals in a Jewish Community." Unpublished manuscript, City University of New York.

———— 1989 *Contested Lives*. Berkeley and Los Angeles: University of California Press.

Glanz, D., and M. Harrison 1978 "Varieties of Identity Transformation: The Case of Newly Orthodox Jews." *Jewish Journal of Sociology* 20:129–141.

Glazer, N. 1970 *Renumbering the Answers: Essays in the American Student Revolt*. New York: Basic Books.

Glock, C. 1976 "Consciousness among Contemporary Youth: An Interpretation." Pp. 353–366 in Glock and Bellah, 1976.

Glock, C., and R. Bellah 1976 *The New Religious Consciousness*. Berkeley: University of California Press.

Goldscheider, C., and S. Goldstein 1985 *Jewish Americans: Three Generations in a Jewish Community*. Lanham, Md.: University Press of America.

Goode, W. 1964 *The Family*. Englewood Cliffs, N.J.: Prentice-Hall.

Gordon, L. 1977 *Woman's Body, Woman's Right: A Social History of Birth Control in America*. Harmondsworth: Penguin.

Grant, L., K. Ward, and X. Rong 1987 "Is There an Association Between Gender and Methods in Sociological Research?" *American Sociological Review* 52 (December): 856–862.

Green, A. 1983 "Bride, Spouse, Daughter: Image of the Feminine in Classical Jewish Services." Pp. 248–260 in S. Heschel (ed.), *On Being a Jewish Feminist*. New York: Schocken.

Greenberg, B. 1981 *On Women and Judaism: A View from Tradition*. Philadelphia: Jewish Publication Society of America.

––––––– 1984 "Will There be Orthodox Women Rabbis?" *Judaism*, Winter, pp. 23–33.

Greer, G. 1984a *Sex and Destiny*. New York: Harper & Row.

––––––– 1984b *The New York Times*, March 5, p. C10.

Gross, R. 1983 "Steps Toward Feminine Imagery of Deity in Jewish Theology." Pp. 234–247 in S. Heschel (ed.), *On Being a Jewish Feminist*. New York: Schocken.

Gutwirth, J. 1978 "Fieldwork Method and the Sociology of Jews: Case Studies of Hassidic Communities." *Jewish Journal of Sociology* 20:49–58.

Haber, B. 1979 "Is Personal Life Still a Political Issue?" *Feminist Studies* 5(3):417–430.

Handelman, S. 1979 "The Jewish Woman . . . Three Steps Behind?: Judaism and Feminism." *Di Yiddishe Heim* 20(4):8–14.

––––––– 1984 "The Crown of Her Husband: The Image of the Feminine in Chassidic Philosophy." Unpublished manuscript, Department of English, University of Maryland, College Park.

Harding, S. 1990 "Feminism, Science, and the Anti-Enlightenment Critiques." Pp. 83–106 in L. Nicholson (ed.), *Feminism/Postmodernism*. New York and London: Routledge.

Hargrove, B. 1979 *The Sociology of Religion*. Arlington Heights, Ill.: A.H.M. Publishing Corporation.

Harrington, M. 1983 *The Politics at God's Funeral*. New York: Holt, Rinehart and Winston.

Hauptman, J. 1982 "Images of Women in the Talmud." Pp. 184–212 in R. Reuther (ed.), *Religion and Sexism: Images of Women in the Jewish and Christian Traditions*. New York: Simon & Schuster.

Hayden, D. 1981 *The Grand Domestic Revolution*. Cambridge, Mass.: MIT Press.

Hegland, M. 1986 "Islamic Revival or Political & Cultural Revolution?: An Iranian Case Study." Unpublished manuscript, Department of Anthropology, Western Michigan University, Kalamazoo.

Heilman, S. 1977 "Inner and Outer Identities: Sociological Ambivalence among Orthodox Jews." *Jewish Social Studies* 39:227–240.

References

———— 1978 "Constructing Orthodoxy." *Society* 15(3):32–40.

———— 1982 "The Sociology of American Jewry: The Last Ten Years." *Annual Review of Sociology* 8:135–160.

Helmreich, W. 1982 *The World of the Yeshiva*. New York: The Free Press.

Herberg, W. *Protestant, Catholic, Jew*. New York: Doubleday.

Heschel, S. 1983 *On Being a Jewish Feminist*. New York: Schocken.

Hochschild, A., with A. Machung 1986 *The Second Shift: Working Parents and the Revolution at Home*. New York: Viking.

Hoff, L. 1984 "Violence Against Women: A Social Cultural Network Analysis." Ph.D dissertation, Boston University.

Horner, M. 1968 "Sex Differences in Achievement Motivation and Performance in Competitive and Non-Competitive Situations." Ph.D. dissertation, University of Michigan.

Hunter, J. 1983 *American Evangelicalism*. New Brunswick, N.J.: Rutgers University Press.

Hyman, P. 1976 "The Other Half: Women in the Jewish Tradition." Pp. 105–113 in E. Koltun (ed.), *The Jewish Woman: New Perspectives*. New York: Schocken.

Jaggar, A. 1983 *Feminist Politics and Human Nature*. Totowa, N.J.: Rowman and Allanheld.

Janeway, E. 1971 *Man's World, Woman's Place: A Study in Social Methodology*. New York: Dell.

Joffee, C. 1985 "The Meaning of the Abortion Conflict." *Contemporary Sociology* 14(1):26–29.

Kaplan, T. 1980 "Politics and Culture in Women's History: A Symposium." *Feminist Studies*, 6(1):43–48.

Kasper, A. 1986 "Consciousness Reevaluated: Interpretive Theory and Feminist Scholarship." *Sociological Inquiry* 56:29–49.

Katz, P., and F. E. Katz 1977 "Symbols as Characters of Culture Change: The Jewish Case." *Anthropos* 72(3,4):486–496.

Kaufman, D. 1985a "Feminism Reconstructed: Feminist Theories and Women Who Return to Orthodox Judaism." *Midwest Sociologists for Women in Society* 5:45–55.

———— 1985b "Women Who Return to Orthodox Judaism: A Feminist Analysis." *Journal of Marriage and the Family* 47(3):543–555.

———— 1987 "Coming Home to Jewish Orthodoxy: Reactionary or Radical Women?" *Tikkun* (July–August), pp. 60–63.

———— 1989 "Patriarchal Women: A Case Study of Newly Orthodox Jewish Women." *Symbolic Interaction* 12(2):299–314.

———— 1990 "Engendering Family Theory: Toward a Feminist-

Interpretive Framework." Pp. 68–106 in J. Sprey (ed.), *Fashioning Family Theory*. Newbury Park, Cal.: Sage.

Kaufman, D., and B. Richardson 1982 *Achievement and Women*. New York: The Free Press.

Kaye/Kantrowitz, M., and I. Klepfisz 1986 *The Tribe of Dina: A Jewish Women's Anthology*. Montpelier, Vt.: Sinister Wisdom Books.

Kelley, J. 1979 "The Doubled Vision of Feminist Theory: A Postscript to the 'Woman and Power' Conference." *Feminist Studies* 5(1):216–227.

Klatch, R. 1987 *Women of the New Right*. Philadelphia: Temple University press.

—— 1988 "Coalition and Conflict among Women of the New Right." *Signs* 13(4):671–697.

Koedt, A. 1973 "The Myth of the Vaginal Orgasm." Pp. 198–207 in A. Koedt, E. Levine, and A. Rapone (eds.), *Radical Feminism*. New York: Quadrangle.

Koltun, E. 1976 *The Jewish Woman: New Perspectives*. New York: Schocken.

Komarovsky, M. 1946 "Cultural Contradictions and Sex Roles." *American Journal of Sociology* 52(3):184–189.

Koskoff, E. 1986 "The Sound of a Woman's Voice: Women and Music in an American Hassidic Community." Paper presented to the American Anthropology Association, Philadelphia.

Kranzler, G. 1961 *Williamsburg*. New York: Feldheim.

—— 1978 "The Changing Orthodox Jewish Family," *Jewish Life* (Summer/Fall), pp. 23–36.

Lasch, C. 1979 *The Culture of Narcissism*. New York: Norton.

—— 1989 "Progress: The Last Superstition." *Tikkun* (4)3:27–30.

Leacock, E. 1977 "The Changing Family and Lévi-Strauss, or Whatever Happened to Fathers." *Sociological Research* 44:235–289.

Lerner, G. 1980 "Politics and Culture in Women's History: A Symposium." *Feminist Studies* 6(1):49–54.

Levy, S. 1975 "Shifting Patterns of Ethnic Identification among Hassidim." Pp. 25–50 in J. W. Bennett (ed.), *The New Ethnicity: Perspective from Ethnology*. St. Paul: West Publishing Co.

Liebman, C. 1964 "A Sociological Analysis of Contemporary Orthodoxy." *Judaism* 13:285–304.

—— 1974 *Aspects of Religious Behavior in American Jews*. New York: Ktav Publishing House.

—— 1979 "Orthodox Judaism Today." *Midstream* 25(7):19–26.

—— 1983 "Religion and the Chaos of Modernity." Pp. 147–164 in J.

Neusner (ed.), *Take Judaism, for Example: Studies Toward the Comparison of Religions*. Chicago: University of Chicago Press.

Lipman-Blumen, J. 1984 *Gender Roles and Power*. Englewood, Cliffs, N.J.: Prentice-Hall.

Lopata, H. Z. 1973 *Widowhood in an American City*. Cambridge, Mass.: Schenkman.

Lorber, J. 1981 "Minimalist and Maximalist Feminism." *Quarterly Journal of Ideology* 5(3):61–66.

Luckmann, T. 1990 "Shrinking Transcendence, Expanding Religion?" *Sociological Analysis* 50(2):127–138.

Luker, K. 1984 *Abortion and the Politics of Motherhood*. Berkeley: University California Press.

Martin, B. 1974 *A History of Judaism*. Vol. 2. New York: Basic Books.

Mayer, E. 1973 "Jewish Orthodoxy in America: Towards the Sociology of a Residual Category." *Jewish Journal of Sociology* 15(2):151–165.

―――― 1977 "Gaps Between Generations of Orthodox Jews in Boro Park, Brooklyn, New York." *Jewish Sociological Studies* 39(1–2):93–104.

―――― 1979 *From Suburb to Shtetl*. Philadelphia: Temple University Press.

Mayer, E., and C. Waxman 1977 "Modern Jewish Orthodoxy in America: Toward the Year 2000." *Tradition* Spring 16:98–117.

McLaughlin. S., B. Melber, J. Billy, D. Zimmerle, L. Winges, and T. Johnson 1988 *The Changing Lives of American Woman*. Chapel Hill, N.C.: University of North Carolina Press.

McMillan, C. 1982 *Women, Reason and Nature*. Princeton: Princeton University Press.

McNall, S., and J. Johnson 1975 "The New Conservatives: Ethnomethodologists, Phenomenologists and Symbolic Interactionists." *Insurgent Sociologist* 5:49–65.

McNamara, P. 1985 "The New Christian Right's View of the Family and Its Social Science Critics: A Study in Differing Presuppositions." *Journal of Marriage and the Family* 47(2):449–458.

Medved, M. 1984 "Second Glance on the Venice Ocean Front." *The Journal of the Pacific Jewish Center* Venice/Santa Monica, California: 4(1):1,10.

Meiselman, M. 1978 *Jewish Woman in Jewish Law*. New York: Ktav Publishing House.

Melton, J. G. 1983 "New Directions on the Cult Scene." *Christianity Today* August, pp. 27–37.

224

Melton, J. G., and R. L. Moore 1982 *The Cult Experience: Responding to the New Religious Pluralism*. New York: Pilgrim Press.

Miller, J. B. 1976 *Toward a New Psychology of Women*. Boston: Beacon Press.

Millett, K. 1970 *Sexual Politics*. New York: Doubleday.

Mintz, J. 1979 "Ethnic Activism: The Hassidic Example." *Judaism* 28:449–464.

Mitchell, D., and L. Plotnicov 1975 "The Lubavitcher Movement: A Study in Contexts." *Urban Anthropology* 4(4):303–315.

Mitchell, J. 1966 "Women, the Longest Revolution." *The New Left Review* November/December, pp. 1–27.

———— 1973 *Woman's Estate*. New York: Vintage.

Mitchell, J., and A. Oakley *What is Feminism?* Oxford, England: Blackwell.

Nathanson, B. 1987 "Reflections on the Silent Woman of Ancient Judaism and Her Pagan Roman Counterpart." *Journal for the Study of the Old Testament*, suppl. ser. 58:259–280.

Neitz, M. 1987 *Charisma and Community: A Study of Religious Commitment Within the Charismatic Renewal*. New Brunswick, N.J.: Transaction.

Nelson, C. 1974 "Public and Private Politics: Women in the Middle Eastern World." *American Ethnologist* 2:551–564.

Neusner, J. 1978 "From Scripture to Mishnah: The Origins of the Mishnaic Tractate Niddah." *Journal of Jewish Studies*, 29:135–148.

———— 1979 *Method and Meaning in Ancient Judaism*. Missoula, Mont.: Scholars Press.

———— 1983 *Take Judaism, for Example: Studies Toward the Comparison of Religions*. Chicago: University of Chicago Press.

Nicholson, L. 1990 *Feminism/Postmodernism*. New York: Routledge, Chapman and Hall.

Oakley, A. 1981 "Interviewing Women: A Contradiction in Terms." Pp. xx in H. Roberts (ed.), *Doing Feminist Research*. London: Routledge and Kegan Paul.

Offen, K. 1988 "Defining Feminism: A Comparative Historical Approach." *Signs* 14:119–157.

Parsons, A. 1985 "Redemptory Intimacy: The Social Construction of Family Bonds in the Unification Church." Paper Delivered to Eastern Sociological Society, Philadelphia.

Petchesky, R. 1984 *Abortion and Woman's Choice: The State, Sexuality and Reproductive Freedom* Boston: Northeastern University Press.

Pinsker, S. 1975 "Piety as Community: The Hassidic View." *Social Research* 42:23–46.

Pleck, J. 1977 "The Work–Family Role System." *Social Problems* 24:417–24.

——— 1981 *Changing Patterns of Work and Family Roles.* Wellesley, Mass.: Wellesley College, Center for Research on Women.

——— 1982 *Husbands' and Wives' Family Work, Paid Work, and Adjustment* Wellesley, Mass.: Wellesley College, Center for Research on Women.

Pogrebin, L. C. 1982 "Anti-Semitism in the Women's Movement: A Jewish Feminist's Disturbing Account." *Ms.*, June: 145–149.

Pohli, C. 1983 "Church Closets and Back Doors: A Feminist View of Moral Majority Women." *Feminist Studies* 6(1):529–558.

Poll, S. 1962 *The Hasidic Community of Williamsburg.* New York: Schocken.

Rackman, H. 1988 "Getting a Get." *Moment* 13(3):34–42.

Rapp, R. 1979 "Review Essay: Anthropology." *Signs* 4(3): 497–513.

Reinharz, S. 1984 *On Becoming a Social Scientist.* New Brunswick, N.J.: Transaction Publications.

Reisman, B. 1977 *The Havurah: A Contemporary Jewish Experience.* New York: UAHC.

Rich, A. 1976 *Of Woman Born.* New York: Norton.

Richardson, J., M. Stewart, and R. Simmonds 1978 *Organized Miracles.* New Brunswick, N.J.: Transaction Books.

Robbins, T., and D. Anthony 1972 "Getting Straight with Meher Baba: A Study of Mysticism, Drug Rehabilitation and Postadolescent Role Conflict." *Journal for the Scientific Study of Religion* 11(2):122–140.

——— 1979 "The Sociology of Contemporary Religious Movements." *Annual Review of Sociology* 5:75–89.

Robbins, T., D. Anthony, and J. Richardson 1978 "Theory and Research on Today's 'New Religions'." *Sociological Analysis* 39(2):95–122.

Rosaldo, M. 1974 "Women, Culture and Society: A Theoretical Overview." Pp. 17–42 in M. Rosaldo and L. Lamphere (eds.), *Women, Culture and Society.* Stanford, Cal.: California University Press.

——— 1980 "The Use and Abuse of Anthropology: Reflections On Feminism and Cross-cultural Understanding." *Signs* 5(3):389–417.

Rosenberg, R. 1982 *Beyond Separate Spheres.* New Haven: Yale University Press.

Rosenfelt, D., and J. Stacey 1987 "Second Thoughts on the Second Wave." *Feminist Studies* 13(2):341–361.

Rosner, F. 1972 *Modern Medicine and Jewish Law*. Brooklyn, N.Y.: Balshon Printing and Offset.

Roszak, T. 1968 *The Making of a Counter Culture*. New York: Doubleday.

Rothman, B. 1989 *Recreating Motherhood*. New York: Norton.

Rowbotham, S. 1973 *Woman's Consciousness, Man's World*. Harmondsworth: Penguin.

Rubin, I. 1972 *Satmar: An Island in the City*. Chicago: Quadrangle.

Russell, D. 1982 *Rape in Marriage*. New York: Collier.

——— 1986 *The Secret Trauma: Incest in the Lives of Girls and Women*. New York: Basic Books.

Ryan, M. 1983 *Womanhood in America*. New York: Franklin Watts.

Sacks, M. 1986 "Mishloach Manos: Community Building in the Suburbs." Paper Presented to the American Anthropology Association Meetings.

Safilios-Rothschild, C. 1970 "The Study of Family Power Structure: A Review 1960–1969." *Journal of Marriage and the Family* 32:534–552.

Sanday, P. 1981 *Female Power and Male Dominance on the Origins of Sexual Inequality*. New York: Cambridge University Press.

Schneider, S. 1984 *Jewish and Female: Choices and Changes in Our Lives Today*. New York: Simon & Schuster.

Scholem, G. 1961 *Modern Trends in Jewish Mysticism*. New York: Schocken.

Schwartz, P., and P. Blumstein 1983 *American Couples*. New York: Morrow.

Scott, J. 1988 "Deconstructing Equality-Versus-Difference: Or, the Uses of Poststructuralist Theory for Feminism." *Feminist Studies* 14(1):33–50.

Selengut, C. 1985 "Cults and Jewish Identity." *Midstream*, January 12–15.

Sennett, R. 1974 *The Fall of Public Man*. New York: Random House.

Setta, S. 1983 "This-Worldly Powerlessness, Other-Worldly Power: The Women's Aglow Fellowship." Unpublished paper, Northeastern University, Philosophy and Religion Department.

——— 1984 "In Memory of Her." *Anima* 10(12):96–97.

Shaffir, W. 1974 *Life in a Religious Community*. Toronto: Holt, Rinehart and Winston.

Shalev, C. 1983 *The Right to Procreate and Control of Reproductive Technology*. New Haven: Yale University Law School Reprint.

Sharot, S. 1982 *Messianism, Mysticism and Magic*. Chapel Hill: University of North Carolina Press.

Sherfey, M. J. 1972 *The Nature and Evolution of Female Sexuality*. New York, New York: Random House.

——— 1973 *The Nature of Evolution of Female Sexuality*. New York: Vintage Books.

Siegal, P. 1975 "Elements of Male Chauvinism in Classical Halakhah." *Judaism* 24:226–244.

Silberman, C. 1985 *A Certain People: American Jews and Their Lives Today*. New York: Summit Books.

Singer, M. 1978 "Chassidic Recruitment and the Local Context." *Urban Anthropology* 7:373–383.

Smith, D. 1974 "Women's Perspective as a Radical Critique of Sociology." *Sociological Inquiry* 44:7–13.

——— 1979 "A Sociology for Women." Pp. 135–187 in J. Sherman and E. Beck (eds.), *The Prism of Sex: Essays in the Sociology of Knowledge*. Madison: University of Wisconsin Press.

——— 1987 "Ethnographic Methods of Investigating Relations of Ruling: Studying the Making of a Dacum." Unpublished paper, Department of Sociology in Education Ontario Institute for Studies in Education.

Smith-Rosenberg, C. 1980 "Politics and Culture in Women's History: A Symposium." *Feminist Studies* 6 (1):55–64.

Stacey, J. 1983 "The New Conservative Feminism." *Feminist Studies* 10(4):559–583.

——— 1987 "Sexism by a Subtler Name?" *Socialist Review* November/December: 8–28.

——— 1988 "Can There be a Feminist Ethnography?" *Women's Studies International Forum*, 11(1):21–27.

Stacey, J., and S. Gerard 1988 "We Are Not Doormats: Post-Feminist Evangelicalism in the U.S." Unpublished manuscript, Davis, California, University of California.

Stacey, J., and B. Thorne 1985 "The Missing Feminist Revolution in Sociology." *Social Problems* 32:301–316.

Stein, H. 1986 "Liberals: Their Own Worst Enemies." *New York Times Magazine*, March 9, pp. 36,38,40–41,44.

Steinfels, P. 1979 *The Neoconservatives*. New York: Simon & Schuster.

Steinsaltz, A. 1982 *Teshuvah: A Guide for the Newly Observant Jew*. New York: The Free Press.

References

Stephen, L. 1989 "Anthropology and the Politics of Facts, Knowledge, and History." *Dialectical Anthropology* 14:259–269.

Straus, M., R. Gelles, and S. Steinmetz 1980 *Behind Closed Doors: Violence in the American Family*. New York: Anchor Books.

Swidler, L. 1976 *Women in Judaism: The Status of Women in Formative Judaism*. Metuchen, N.J.: The Scarecrow Press.

Taylor, S. J., and R. Bogdan 1984 *Introduction to Qualitative Research Methods*, 2nd ed. New York: Wiley.

Tipton, S. 1982 *Getting Saved from the Sixties*. Berkeley: University of California Press.

——— 1983 "The Moral Logic of Alternative Religions." Pp. 79–107 in M. Douglas and S. Tipton (eds.), *Religion and America*. Boston: Beacon Press.

Tobin, G. A., and A. Chenkin 1985. "Recent Jewish Community Population Studies: A Roundup." Pp. 154–178 in M. Himmelfarb and D. Singer (eds.), *American Jewish Yearbook*. New York: The American Jewish Committee and the Jewish Publication Society.

Trask, H.-K. 1986 *Eros and Power: The Promise of Feminist Theory*. Philadelphia: University of Pennsylvania Press.

Trimberger, E. 1983 "Feminism, Men, and Modern Love: Greenwich Village, 1900–25." Pp. 131–152 in A. Snitow, C. Stansell, and S. Thompson (eds.), *Power of Desire*. New York: Monthly Review Press.

Umansky, E. 1988 "Females, Feminists, and Feminism: A Review of Recent Literature on Jewish Feminism and the Creation of a Feminist Judaism." *Feminist Studies* 14(2):349–361.

U.S. Bureau of Labor 1977 *Statistics*. Pp. 344–345. Washington, D.C.: U.S. Government Printing Office.

Wallach, M. 1977 "The Chasidim of Stamford Hill." *Jewish Chronicle Magazine*, May 27, pp. 11–19,68.

Warner, S. 1988 *New Wine in Old Wine Skins: Evangelicals and Liberals in a Small Town Church*. Berkeley. University of California Press.

Washbourn, P. 1979 "Becoming Woman: Menstruation as a Spiritual Experience." In C. Christ and J. Plaskow (eds.), *Womanspirit Rising*. New York: Harper & Row.

Waxman, C. 1980 "The Impact of Feminism on American Jewish Communal Institutions." *Journal of Jewish Communal Service* 57(1):73–79.

——— 1983 *America's Jews in Transition*. Philadelphia: Temple University Press.

Weber, M. 1964 *The Theory of Social and Economic Organization*. Trans.

A. M. Henderson and T. Parsons (1947, Oxford University Press). Reprint. New York: The Free Press.

Wechsler, M. 1981 "Ritual, Purity and Jewish Women." Unpublished paper, Harvard University.

Wegner, J. 1982 "The Status of Women in Jewish and Islamic Marriage and Divorce Law." *Harvard Women's Law Journal* 5:1–33.

—— 1988 *Chattel or Person? The Status of Women in the Mishnah*. Oxford: Oxford University Press.

—— 1991 "The Image and Status of Women in Classical Rabbinic Judaism." Pp. 101–143 in J. Baskin (ed.), *Jewish Women in Historical Perspective*. Detroit: Wayne State University Press.

Weideger, P. 1977 *Menstruation and Menopause*. New York: Knopf, distributed by Random House.

Weidman-Schneider, S. 1984 *Jewish and Female: Choices and Changes in Our Lives Today*. New York: Simon & Schuster.

Weitzman, L. 1985 *The Divorce Revolution*. New York: The Free Press.

Wilson, B. 1969 *Religion in a Secular Society*. Baltimore: Penguin.

——. 1975 *The Noble Savage: The Primitive Origins of Charisma*. Berkeley: University of California Press.

——. 1976 *Contemporary Transformation of Religion*. Oxford: Oxford University Press.

——. 1979 "The Return of The Sacred." *Journal for the Scientific Study of Religion* 18(3):268–280.

Women's Economic Agenda Working Group. 1985 "Toward Economic Justice for Women: A National Agenda for Change." Washington, D.C.: Institute for Policy Studies.

Wuthnow, R. 1976 *The Consciousness Reformation*. Berkeley and Los Angeles: University of California Press.

Yinger, M. 1982 *Countercultures: The Promised Peril of a World Turned Upside Down*. New York: Free Press.

Zaretsky, E. 1973a "Capitalism, the Family and Personal Life: Part 1." *Socialist Revolution* 3(1,2):69–125.

—— 1973b "Capitalism, the Family and Personal Life: Part 2: *Socialist Revolution* 3(3):19–70.

•

Index

231

206n18; Jewish, 131, 203n1; liberal, 142–149; limitations of, 142–149; macho, 106; "mystique" of, 145; paradoxes of, 164; vs. postfeminism, 11–13; radical, 149–154, 206n16; religious Right and, 11; second-wave contemporary, 149–154, 208n26; sexuality and, 189n21; shift in focus of, 145–146; social, 147; and sociology, 157–158, 160; women's culture and, 128–130, 201n15, 202nn16,17; vs. women's rights issues, 49. *See also* difference arguments; individualist modes of analysis; relational modes of analysis; sameness arguments

fertility problems, 101, 135, 190n22, 195n18

food: dietary laws, 5, 119–120; religious importance of, 93–94

forshpil, *123*

Freedman, Estelle, 129–130

Friedan, Betty, 144–145, 206n17

Friedman, Manis, 30, 57

friendship: within the community, 122–126; with the non-Orthodox, 121

frum life, *49*

fundamentalism, 2, 138, 170n5, 198n32, 205n11

Gemara, *178n20*

gender differences: ba'alot teshuvah on, 8–9, 54; celebration of, 113–114; and female solidarity, 69; and gender roles, 57–58; in halakhah, 184n28; re-

ligious Right on, 139. *See also* difference arguments

gender equality, 12–13

gender identity: of ba'alot teshuvah, 8, 159–160, 165; and feminism, 3, 202n16; as liberation or oppression, 212n19; sex-segregation and, 122–126; of social conservatives, 105

gender inequality, 12, 58, 160

gender roles, 8–9, 12, 22–24, 57–58, 121, 204n5

Gershom, Rabbenu, 63

get, *134. See also* divorce

Getting Equitable Treatment (G.E.T.), 135, 200n6

gift giving, 94

Ginsburg, Faye, 83–84

Global Ministries of Love, 104, 138

God: closeness of women to, 45–46, 47, 53; individual relationship to, 67; indwelling of, 45–46, 53, 54, 56–57, 183nn23,24

Goldstein, Rabbi Mordechai, 16–17

gossip and slander, 51

Greenberg, Blu, 72–73, 188n10

Hafez Hayyim, 50–51, 162, 182n19

haftorah, *211n6*

hakhel, *65*

halakhah, *5*, 6, *171n12*; authority of, 133–134; challenges to, 161–163; development of, 59–61; inviolability of, 21, 22, 211n13; texts of, 59; women and formulation of, 29, 64, 68

Handelman, Susan, 55, 56

Index

Har Tzion, 16, 176n5
Hashem, *39*
Hasidism, *176n2*; characteristics
of, 36, 179n1; vs. non-Hasidic
orthodoxy, 36, 52–66, 172n16,
176n3; portraits of, 37–46; recruiting by, 24–26; schools, 27;
theology of, 52–66; Torah authority for, 133
Hasidut, *30*, 41, 47; feminine
principle in, *55–56*
Hauptman, J., 59
havurot, *5*
Hayden, Dolores, 141–142
headcovering, 38, 46, 49,
180nn5,6, 182nn14,16
Hebrew, use of, 180n3,
181nn9,11
Heschel, Susannah, 67–68
heterosexuality, 161
hippie movement, 15–21, 28
holidays: feasting on, 93–94; and
separation from family of origin, 119–120
homemaking, 92–93, 102–103,
105, 106–107, 141–142
home values, 106–112
Horowitz, Rabbi Levi Yitzhak,
17, 26, 178n17
household: decision making in, 40,
138–139, 204n10; division of labor in, 12, 92–93; help, 91–92
housework, 92–93, 102–103, 105,
106–107, 141–142

identity: false, 104n5; sense of,
21. *See also* gender identity
Igud Harbonim, 203n3
imagery, feminine, 53
impurity, 71–73, 186n3

incest, 135
income, 115
individualism: vs. family, 86–87,
88, 139; and feminism, 206n18;
vs. institutions, 133–136; and
moral ambiguity, 192n5; new
religions and, 178n23, 191n1;
of secular life, 8, 33–34, 175n30
individualist modes of analysis,
146–147, 206n22. *See also* relational modes of analysis
indwelling of God, 45–46, 53, 54,
56–57, 183nn23,24
infertility, 101, 135, 190n22,
195n18
influence, women's, 126–130
institutions: female, 126, 128,
203n19; and the individual,
133–136; separatist, 153
interconnectedness, 143–144
intimacy: of mikveh, 81; modesty
and, 82–83
intuitive knowledge, 152
in vitro fertilization, 135, 195n18
irresponsibility, of men, 105
Islamic revival, 170n5, 173n21
Israel: abortion in, 97–98; ba'al
teshuvah yeshivot in, 16–17,
28–29; and feminine ethos, 164;
year of religious study in, 163

Jaggar, A., 151–152
Jesus movement, 20, 178n18
Jewish Defense League (JDL),
117
Jewish Feminist Organization,
131
Jewish law, *see* halakhah
Jewish orthodoxy: and the femi-
nine, 55–57, 183n23; Hasidism

Index

women's movement, 18, 148–149.
  See also feminism
women's rights, 61–63,
  185nn33,34
women's sphere, 146, 200n3,
  206n21
women's studies, 208n27
work: attitude toward, 41–42,
  111, 181n10; and domestic
  workload, 105, 111; flexibility
  of, 114, 115; outside the home,
  39, 42, 46–47, 50, 91, 114–115;
  priority of family and religion
  over, 91, 92, 111, 193n11
workforce: inequalities in, 12;
  number of women in, 87–88

Yeshiva University, 118
yeshivishe velt, *133*
yeshivot, 6, 172n14; ba'al
  teshuvah, 16–17, 28–29; curriculum in, 182n18, 201n8
Yiddish, use of, 180n3, 181n9
Yiddishe Heim, 103
yom tovim, *119–120*
Young Israel, 49, 133, 172n16,
  203n3

Zalman, Schneur, 29–30,
  176n2
zeda, *120*
Zohar, 178n21